June

Please Enjoy

Caroline Linden

Star Food

Star Food

by Carole Andersen Travis

Line drawings by Kim E. Burroughs

Cartoons by Carole Andersen Travis

Teton Publishing House

Jackson, Wyoming

ISBN 0-9606622-0-0

I dedicate this book to my father,
Carl F. S. Andersen,
with love and affection for the years
of teaching so lovingly taught,
and to
Kenneth Hansen
for his friendship, generosity, and
the fine example he set in the field
of culinary expertise

THANKS

My deepest gratitude and love to my husband, Richard S. Travis, for his love and support, and to my mother, Caroline F. Andersen, for her love and assistance.

Special thanks must also go to my dear friend Phil Abramson, who got me Dick Duane as an agent, who got me Peggy Brooks as my editor, who got me Barbara Wood as my copy editor, who got me Patricia Smythe as my designer. *Mange Tak.*

CONTENTS

STARGAZING

*I*t started with a small boy climbing out of his third-story window late at night in Roskilde, Denmark, circa 1912. Clutching the rain spout, his telescope slung around his shoulder, the young boy would shinny up to the tiled roof of the family home. The stars shone above him in dazzling display, and as he scanned the heavens he dreamed of shooting lions in Africa.

The young boy's name was Carl Frederick Sigvard Andersen. Born in 1903, he was one of five children. His childhood was spent taking piano lessons, smoking cigars behind the seawall, studying ballet under Mr. Paul Hull of the Royal Danish Ballet, and taunting the town bullies. His sister Edith was his favorite sibling, and he loved helping his mother make puddings in the large, warm kitchen, where he would steal pocketfuls of sugar cubes to suck on while stargazing.

When Carl was twelve, the ballet lessons gave way to tumbling and hard study in Latin School. He was a fine tumbler, and years later, for sheer joy and daring, he would do running back flips over buffet tables he'd heaped with sumptuous platters of food. He admired Douglas Fairbanks, Sr., very much. Little did he know that one day he would cook for his acrobatic idol.

When it came time for Carl to begin an apprenticeship, his mother remembered his love of helping in the kitchen. Thus in 1919, at the age of sixteen, Carl was shipped off to Copenhagen to study at Den Kongelige Skydebane (translation: Royal Shooting Club). The Skydebane was situated across from the royal castle in Copenhagen and catered for the King and the leading dignitaries of the land. Its large, paneled hall was capable of seating and serving well over a hundred people.

There was one head chef at the Kongelige Skydebane. Under him there were one sous-chef and five cooks. Under the cooks were thirteen apprentices. The apprenticeship lasted four years and covered all aspects of culinary art. There were six categories of study, and the students spent three months on each:

1. SOUPS: hot, cold, quick, long-simmering, and stocks
2. FISH: hot, cold, aspics, in brine, and molded
3. COLD ENTRÉES: from a glazed poached fowl to a boned, stuffed, and rolled duck cut as a pâté

4. ROASTS: all methods of roasting and carving, plus the right vegetables to serve with each roast

5. BAKING: from breads to the most delicate of pastries

6. HORS D'OEUVRES: pâtés, aspics, and hundreds of other first courses and bite-sized delights

A student had to reproduce each recipe perfectly three times. If he failed any of the times, he had to continue making it until he'd created three consecutive triumphs. Only then could he move on to another recipe. When all categories had been completed, the process was started all over again. On the second round a seasoned apprentice was allowed to do more and had a tyro apprentice beneath him.

In the spring of 1921 the apprentice chefs paraded through the great hall of the Skydebane. Dressed in their starched whites and tall hats, they carried on their shoulders four large planks, each bearing a whole roasted venison, which King Christian X of Denmark had shot in the woods outside Copenhagen as part of the annual hunt and shooting match. Denmark's Parliament and dignitaries from far and near came each year to join in the shoot and enjoy the feast that followed.

King Christian X was an excellent shot, but in case he should miss one of the precision targets set up for the meet, the target was rigged so that it would fly away anyhow. It was obviously bad form for the King to be seen to miss a shot.

The King's venison was larded at one-inch intervals, then seasoned and roasted in massive ovens, where it was basted and watched over for hours. Then the head chef divided the meat, giving each apprentice a portion, which he took to the place assigned to him in the great hall. There the apprentices carved the succulent venison, which was then served by liveried waiters to the expectant guests.

When the serving was completed, the King sent champagne to his chefs and toasted the men who had prepared such a fine feast. The chefs raised their glasses and toasted the King in return. It was the first of many toasts Carl would receive for his culinary expertise—one he never forgot.

Throughout Carl's years of apprenticeship his dreams of lion shooting in Africa were gradually nudged aside by dreams of a place where a man could make his own way without the hindrance of regulations and tradition. The new dreams were of a place called America. So it was that upon his graduation from the Kongelige Skydebane, Carl picked up his inheritance from his father and traveled across the Atlantic to a land of which he knew little and whose language he didn't speak.

Ellis Island accepted Carl but would not release his money right away. Instead, he was given one quarter and a free ride to the island of Manhattan.

By pantomiming sweeping, cleaning, and sleeping to the managers of several small hotels, Carl earned a place to sleep—and a temporary job. The quarter bought a dozen cupcakes. After a harrowing, half-starved week, Ellis Island returned his inheritance.

Carl's secret ambition was to be an artist and cartoonist. He drew quite well and even sold a few items, but it wasn't much of a living. Cartooning seemed even less likely to be profitable, since he had so little command of the language, even though he had started to learn by going to the library and using a Danish-English dictionary along with a first-grade primer. Carl soon realized that most artists suffer from the same malady—poverty. He weighed the odds and decided to return to the profession for which he'd been so well trained.

His first job at the Hartford Club in Connecticut taught him that despite the rigors of the Skydebane he'd come to love the art of cooking. Then a multimillionaire hired him away, but Carl was still not content. His dreams took him west across America to a place called Hollywood, where movies were being made—he was still stargazing.

Carl arrived in Hollywood in 1925 and found fresh, clean air and a town growing in every direction. It was the land of his dreams. His first job in Hollywood was at Paulais, right next to the Egyptian Movie Theatre, which is still there. It had been built by Sid Grauman, who sold it and then put up Grauman's Chinese Theatre (now Mann's Chinese) right across the street. Sid ate in Paulais every day. Grauman's Chinese has remained a mecca for visitors with its sidewalks featuring the footprints, handprints, and signatures of Hollywood's most famous stars.

While working at Paulais, Carl realized that in southern California a car was a must, so he took a cab to the showroom of a Beverly Hills car dealer, went in, and picked one out. He didn't worry about the cost, since he still had most of his inheritance plus money he had saved from his employment in Connecticut. With European aplomb he instructed the salesman to drive him around Beverly Hills. As they drove, Carl watched what the man did, and when they returned to the agency he asked that the car be parked on a side street, facing the quiet residential area and away from Wilshire Boulevard.

Carl then paid for the car, took the keys, walked back to it, got in, put the key into the ignition, and drove for the first time in his life. Throughout the afternoon he bumped and lurched his way along lonely side streets until he'd mastered the technique of shifting gears and the process of parking. It was many years before he deemed it necessary to join the multitudes and get a driver's license.

While at Paulais, Carl's flirtation with Hollywood reached its peak.

Carl — Hollywood, 1927

Paulais often catered to the movie production crews that worked all over Hollywood—often through the night in those pre-union days. While taking large platters of food to a location at midnight one night, Carl finally saw his gymnastic movie idol in person—Douglas Fairbanks. It was about this time that he was sucked into a deal where "if he put up some of the money for a new motion picture, he'd be guaranteed a part in said same movie." It was the scam of the day, and many a hopeful newcomer to Hollywood fell for it. After all, couldn't Carl tumble almost as well as Fairbanks? And weren't people asking him for his autograph already? Some even mistook him for the new star, Clark Gable. Carl's ears didn't match "the King's," but the two men did resemble each other and had been born on the same day just two years apart.

Disgusted with being cheated, Carl moved farther west, to a relatively new area called Brentwood, and took a job in a restaurant named for its owner, Ben Hansen. Ben Hansen's was located on San Vicente Boulevard near Bundy Drive. Many stars lived in the area, and Carl was soon cooking for more movie people than he'd imagined existed—most notable among them George Raft, Leo Carrillo, Fanny Brice, Mae West (usually on the arm of George Raft), Myrna Loy, Victor McLaglen, and Edmund Lowe.

With all those celebrities about, you'd think Carl would have been doing some heavy stargazing, but at the time he had eyes only for the hostess-cashier. Her name was Caroline Faunce, and she had also attracted the attention of Leo Carrillo, who spent most of his time in Ben Hansen's talking to the lonely seventeen-year-old. Her dark hair and sparkling eyes, to say nothing of her figure, were enough to entice any artist, and soon Carl was sending "I love you" notes from the kitchen to the front desk. Since Carl was fifteen years older than Caroline, it took him more than a year to persuade her that marrying him was a good idea.

When Caroline married Carl, she moved into his Brentwood bungalow which he rented for $18 a month. The little house and its price were fine, but Caroline decided to remove the touches of early Hollywood bachelor—like the Chinese parasols covering the ceilings and the jumble of English riding boots, crops, and tennis racquets in the corners. Caroline also took down some of the nudes that Carl had sketched. (We've never been able to find out from him whether the sketches were made from live models or copied from some other artist's work.) Not long after she finished getting the house in order, I was born, and with a family on his hands Carl felt it was time to move on in the world.

The Janss Corporation was building a new community around the also new University of California at Los Angeles. Carl liked the area, with its broad boulevard divided by green lawns and swaying palm trees. Along one of the new avenues was a restaurant that had just opened, called the Chatam, owned by Walter and Irene Buechting. With three chefs working in the Chatam's tiny kitchen, the business was in the red. Carl made Walter an offer: "Fire your three chefs, give me free rein in the kitchen, and I promise I'll make this a profitable enterprise." Walter did—and Carl did.

That was in 1939. In 1949 Carl and Caroline bought the Chatam from Walter and Irene and renamed it Carl Andersen's Chatam. The Buechtings built a second restaurant two miles south which they also called the Chatam, as they had retained ownership of the name. But now, after years of confusion, Carl Andersen's Chatam is the only one left.

In the early forties Hollywood and the area around it still provided balmy days and smog-free air. The Chatam was in Westwood, on the borders of

Brentwood, Bel Air, and Beverly Hills, where the stars lived then as they do now. Carl was pretty well known by this time, and the famous and wealthy were soon calling on his services.

When Randolph Hearst wooed Marion Davies, in the house he'd built for her near the end of the incline on Santa Monica Beach, it was Carl who catered their private meals. For dinner for the two of them Carl was asked to prepare a roasted capon, a Chateaubriand, lamb chops, a vegetable, garnish, and fruit, and to serve it on a gilded platter. When the platter appeared, Marion would usually take a bite or two of capon while Randolph cut the heart out of the Chateaubriand. They hardly touched the rest. Less food could have been ordered, or the leftovers could have been saved for cold lunches or used to feed the servants. Instead, on very strict orders, the remains invariably went to the Great Danes, drooling anxiously in the courtyard, and any servant caught snitching part of the dogs' dinner was promptly dismissed.

During those years Carl also cooked for Sigmund Romberg, who was a constant party giver and loved Carl's Beef Stroganoff. Mrs. Henry Fonda rarely gave a party without Carl's assistance; she was especially fond of barbecues.

The Chatam restaurant itself has always been a safe haven for the stars. Since most of our customers are either in the movie industry or neighbors of those who are, there is no autograph seeking. Even the famous have to have a place to go where they can have a great meal without being harassed. Joe E. Brown, who loved children so; Johnny Mercer, with his gentle southern wit and humor; Edgar Bergen and his beautiful wife (no wonder Candice is so lovely!); the inimitable Groucho Marx; Rose Marie Guy, with the bow in her hair and her wonderful smile; Kathryn Grayson and her handsome husband; Leonard Nimoy and his pot-throwing wife (we used to save our large plastic mayonnaise containers for her to keep clay in); John Forsythe with his velvet vocal cords; and Robert Wagner are only some of those who have frequented the Chatam.

My first encounter with a movie star took place when I was fourteen and had just learned to take cash and make change. Cornel Wilde came in, and I was so flustered when he paid his $4.17 lunch check with a one-hundred-dollar bill that I gave him change for only a twenty. By the time I corrected my mistake, I was a wreck, though Mr. Wilde was laughing.

As the years passed, my knees stopped shaking, thanks to my best buddy in high school, Alan Ladd, Jr. Laddie took me home and showed me how the stars live. As teenagers we'd flop onto the large sofas in their family den, and Laddie would go into the projection booth and start pressing buttons. The west wall of the room disappeared and in its place rose a large viewing screen, and then the first Ladd movie came on. One night we watched four in a row.

Robert Wagner was fourteen years old when his family started dining with us. They called him R.J. His cigar-smoking father was wealthy, but he had known harder times and didn't want R.J. to grow up without understanding what a dollar really meant, so he got his sixteen-year-old son a job as a pot washer at the Chatam.

R.J. was a sharp kid who did as he was told, and he was soon great friends with my father. R.J. quickly picked up on Carl's accent and odd way of mumbling in the kitchen and gave him the nickname "Ma-nit-nit." Lord knows what Carl called R.J.

Many years later, in 1980, Carl and Caroline were sitting in the Bel Air Hotel having a nightcap when who should walk in but Robert Wagner, old R.J. himself. "Ma-nit-nit!" R.J. sang out, causing "Ma-nit-nit" to grin ear to ear.

I can still remember R.J. running upstairs in his dirty apron and coming back down in his snowy white tennis togs to wave a cheery farewell to one and all as he went out the front door to jump into his new convertible. The Chatam has never had such a pot washer since!

A good maître d' must know when to talk and when to shut up. One day I made the right decision.

About a year and a half before he passed away, Groucho Marx came in one afternoon with a female companion. When I saw that the great comedian was having difficulty deciding what to order, I walked over to his table holding a knife between my fingers as though it were a cigar. Leering at him while wiggling my eyebrows, I said, "Have the Danish Duck Sandwich and I'll give the secret word." Groucho loved it. He also loved the open-face duck sandwich I'd recommended. We do miss him.

My mother can remember when the other Marx brothers came to the restaurant, just as she remembers Gary Cooper, Eddie Cantor, Virginia Graham, and Buddy Rogers, all of whom I missed because I was in school at the time.

Sandy Duncan came often to the Chatam when she was an outpatient at the UCLA Medical Center, as did Ann-Margret while she was recovering from the facial reconstruction she had to have after her tragic fall in Las Vegas. I was working lunch one of the days when Ann-Margret came in. We seated her in a corner of the barroom upon request.

One of my mother's favorites is Doris Day, who loves animals. Miss Day likes to park out back so that her three-legged, pound-rescued dog won't get lonely. She shouldn't worry, as she usually has up to four other dogs in the car to keep him company.

Another favorite is Karl Malden, who with his family is a welcome regular.

Still others I've met during my many years of helping to manage the Chatam are Jeanne Crain, Shirley Jones and her family, Dick Anderson, Rory Calhoun, Peter Ustinov, Zubin Mehta and his wife Nancy, Rod Steiger, and Mrs. Jean Hersholt. When he lived close by, Jim Nabors would come in late at night. And back in the late fifties, though it was during a time when we didn't take reservations, I usually kept the little back table under the clock open for May Britt, who liked to dine there by herself.

Around 1970 my two young boys were earning bicycle money by busing dishes. Chris surpassed himself once by dropping twelve glasses of water into diners' laps. On another, better night he ran to me and loudly whispered, "Mom, that's Elizabeth Montgomery." Chris's brother, Brett, confirmed Christopher's discovery in the front side booth. Several of the staff thought them wrong, but the boys kept saying that they knew her voice and that she was too pretty to be anyone other than "their" Samantha. The boys were right, and Elizabeth was pleased to hear of the feud that had gone on over her identity.

I suppose the most touching reminiscence relating to stars is the memory of the night when Dom DeLuise and Jane Wyman arrived at the restaurant within moments of each other.

Dom had been coming in quite regularly, but it was the first visit that I knew of for Miss Wyman. She was with a lady friend, and both wore slacks and no makeup. As I escorted them to what we call a double-scoop, I apologized that I didn't have anything more private. Miss Wyman waved the apology aside and sat down. As I returned to the front desk, I was surprised to notice that no one else in the dining room had recognized this famous star.

Five minutes later Dom DeLuise came in with a young lady. After the usual greeting I started to steer Dom and his guest to the seat next to Miss Wyman.

"I can't sit there!" Dom whispered, as only Dom can whisper. "That's Jane Wyman at the next table!"

"I know," I soothed. "Who better to sit next to her than you?"

"But I'm a nothing compared to her. She's a great star."

Looking at Dom, I quietly told him that no one had yet recognized the great star, whereas everyone in the restaurant was looking his way and knew exactly who he was. Dom and his young lady took the table next to Miss Wyman's and hid their faces behind our large menus while she sat there smiling at his compliment. Soon all those who had known who Mr. DeLuise was soon realized who she was, too. As for Dom and Jane, she broke the ice and they talked for hours.

Crazy George Carlin (the boys' favorite), Bob Newhart, Ruth Buzzi, June Lockhart, Gower Champion, Eric Janrick, Barbara Bach, Michael Caine, Jack Lemmon, Stevie Wonder, Charo, Beth Howland, Susan Blakely, Elinor Donahue, Carol Burnett, Patrick Wayne, John Ritter, Matt Collins, Susan St. James, Christine Lund, Efrem Zimbalist, Jr., Natalie Wood, Charlton Heston, Fannie Flagg, Clifton Fadiman, Valerie Harper, Truman Capote, Rick Nelson, Art Carney, Yvette Mimieux, Jill Ireland, Ronnie Howard, Hal Linden, Bert Parks, and Tom Bosley are some of the others who have dined at the Chatam.

During the mini-skirt era Rod Steiger strolled in with a pretty young woman laced in mini-leather, and many years before the world recognized Charles Bronson as a sex symbol he used to sit at the old Chatam counter eating a late afternoon Chatam Special sandwich and drinking a cup of coffee. When the Chatam was remodeled, he took to bringing in the entire family for dinner.

Mrs. Yul Brynner, a customer for many years, started bringing in Rocky Brynner when he was very small. By the time Rocky was nearly through grammar school, he would have the chauffeur drop him by the Chatam so that he could sit and talk to my mother, Caroline, while she ate her late afternoon lunch and Rocky sipped a Coke. Rocky was caught up in her web of love, as so many other children have been through the years.

Years later Rocky went through a brief hippie stage (along with the rest of his generation), and whenever he entered the restaurant, his old friend Caroline would give him holy you-know-what. Usually he'd just smile at her, glad that she still cared.

Not all of the famous people who have enjoyed Carl's cuisine are connected with movies. Being close to UCLA, we have enjoyed a thirty-year friendship with the athletic department. All coaches, from Red Saunders through Johnny Wooden to Terry Donahue and Johnny Long, have been not only customers but friends. All football, basketball, track, swimming, and gymnast recruits are treated to lunch at the Chatam.

The great UCLA basketball coach Johnny Wooden inspired his teams with such faith and pride in doing well that year after year the team he coached was tops in the country. Red Saunders's football players loved him with a passion, and if he stayed too late at the Chatam on the night before a game, team members would come looking for him. More than once they found Red sitting on a barstool worrying over some play or players, and they always took him home to his wife, Ann, who loved Red as much as his teams did.

When the alumni gave Red a shiny new Cadillac convertible, he insisted I leave our busy dining room and go with him across Weyburn Avenue to the back of Westwood Drug, where his new car was parked. "Come on, Carole, get in!" he ordered. "Feel the deep carpet on the floor. Did you ever in your life see anything that beautiful? To think they wanted me to have this!"

I could see that Red Saunders was near tears. That was the other side of the hard-hitting man that so many wrote about.

When he is in the area, Tom Protho still comes in to give Caroline a squeeze and have his usual: turkey (all white meat) on white, mayonnaise, no lettuce.

Dick Vermeil always seemed too good-looking and much too kind to be a football coach, but his record with the Philadelphia Eagles proves otherwise.

O. J. Simpson may have gone to school at the other end of town, but he likes the Chatam, as does Gold Medal–winning decathlon champion Rafer Johnson.

Affable Coach Bob Horn, who looks after the UCLA swimming team, is a longtime favorite of everyone at the Chatam. One time, in the early seventies, he and a few members of his team happened to come upstairs to wash their hands just as I was feeding Rocky.

Rocky was an eight-ounce baby raccoon that fit neatly in one hand. While Rocky guzzled eagerly at his toy baby bottle, I watched the five strapping athletes turn to jelly. Soon the whole team was begging for turns at holding the "baby." From then on, until Rocky was old enough for us to leave him alone, the swim team trooped upstairs to help in the back-room nursery before having lunch.

Rocky was the star among all the animals we've owned. That's saying a mouthful, because we had had an armadillo as well as the usual dogs, birds, rats, mice, snakes, rabbits, and turtles. The armadillo had formerly belonged to the singer Patrice Munsel. She had had the animal living with her in her New York apartment, and it was house-trained to kitty litter and ate Gaines-burgers. She had named the armadillo Amanda, but when we turned "Amanda" over, we rechristened him Armando.

Rocky came to an untimely end when he ventured out onto our Bel Air patio one night during a heat wave and a coyote got him. We all went into mourning, including the entire UCLA swim team.

Whether a dish was destined for the table of a superstar or a salesperson from Woolworth's, Carl always put the same care and love into it. His advice to me as a child was "It doesn't matter what your line of work is, as long as you do it to the best of your ability and better than anyone else."

He taught me to cook as soon as I could balance on a stool by the stove. By the time I reached my teens we were having Sunday discussions about why soufflés rise and what makes a tender crêpe. By my early thirties I was helping to train pastry chefs.

As I grew and learned, I watched my talented father receive many awards and much praise, both from his patrons and from the press.

In the winter of 1976 Carl was asked to do a private dinner for eight for the visiting Queen Margrethe of Denmark. Fifty-five years earlier, when he had been an apprentice, Carl had been toasted by the Queen's father, King Christian X. Now he created a banquet that did justice to his mastery of the culinary art. Here is the menu:

Snow peas filled with gravlax and cream cheese
Watermelon rind in bacon
Laurent Perrier
Papaya filled with curried crab legs
Quails stuffed with baby mushrooms, foie gras
peeled grapes sauté, fresh cherries
Heitz Cellars Cabernet Sauvignon '72
Limestone lettuce and mushrooms vinaigrette
Cheesecake with strawberries

The work began many days before the party. Special foods had to be found and ordered, and wines had to be selected.

Carl created a replica of the Queen's crown out of thirty-two filigreed pieces of chocolate, sticking them together carefully with more chocolate. He planned to set the crown in the middle of his famous cheesecake. (Cheesecake is a rarity in Denmark, and visiting Danes are very partial to it. Many of them have left the United States with a cheesecake tucked beneath their arm.) The crown made, Carl turned his attention to the largest potato the produce man could find. Out of it Carl carved a lovely basket, complete with handle, into which went roses carved from a variety of vegetables.

When all was ready, the rose-filled basket was placed in the center of a large silver platter. Around the basket eight completely boned quails were set. Each quail was plumply stuffed with tiny mushrooms mixed with quail livers, bread crumbs, butter, and herbs. The quails nested on *foie gras* and were garnished with peeled grapes, which had been flown up from Chile, and fresh Bing cherries, which had been picked early in Beaumont, California.

The Queen, known to friends and family as Daisy, thoroughly enjoyed each and every course, but when it came to the Limestone lettuce and mushroom salad vinaigrette she was heard to say that she'd never eaten anything like it before and had two more servings.

The cheesecake was a royal success, as expected, as were the giant strawberries that ringed it, some dipped in chocolate, others in sugar.

This book is dedicated not only to my father, Carl Andersen, but to the memory of Kenneth Hansen, with whom Carl had much in common. Both men were born and reared in Denmark, and both trained at Den Kongelige Skydebane in Copenhagen. Kenneth served only part of his apprenticeship there; he went onto a French luxury liner to complete his culinary studies. Many years later the two men met again in Hollywood, and their friendship, like their restaurants, grew.

In 1946 Kenneth and his sister, Teddy, opened the now world-famous Scandia restaurant on the Sunset Strip. In 1958 Scandia moved across the street to 9040 Sunset Boulevard. The new restaurant is much larger, but it is as charming and exclusive as the old.

Few dignitaries from the northern countries of Europe have passed through the Los Angeles area without being wined and dined by Kenneth Hansen. He was a guest at the White House and served many crowned heads and statesmen from around the world. Movies galore have been set into motion by producers and directors while dining at the Scandia.

I was ten when I first met the Hansens and ate at their beautiful restaurant. Because of the long, close friendship between my parents and the Hansens, I also had the privilege over the years of eating Kenneth's wonderful food and receiving the many recipes which I have included here.

Kenneth went through chefs faster than any other restaurateur I know, but he was capable of using anger so that no chef ever left Scandia without more knowledge than he'd come with. Most of the chefs who had the honor of working with Kenneth now have their own restaurants or are in charge of celebrated kitchens.

Kenneth established the Vikings, a group of men who annually give of their blood, their time, and their money. Aside from donations to favored charities, the Vikings pack huge Christmas baskets for the needy. Each Viking has his own engraved glass sitting on a shelf in Scandia's bar.

Kenneth received the Royal Order of Danneborg from King Frederick IX of Denmark for his achievements as a restaurateur and culinary master.

On December 17, 1980, Kenneth Hansen died at the age of seventy-five. He was a living institution, and he will be remembered for his perfectionism,

Kenneth Hansen

his dedication to excellence, and his boundless energy for producing the best. I, for one, will miss hearing him sing. At special parties and functions he often sang "September Song" or "I Did It My Way." His voice was as full and robust as was his life. No one will replace him. He was a unique individual and a master in his field. He will be missed.

Both Kenneth and Carl should have written cookbooks of their own during their active culinary lives. Since they didn't, I have put down some of their favorite creations. It's with love and admiration for these two great chefs that I say: *Skoal!* and *Mange Tak!*

LEARNING TO COOK

Cooking is an art to be learned by study and practice. As with any other skill, the more you use it the better you become. To increase your skill you must keep adding new information. Here are a few tips that will increase your cooking knowledge:

• When you want to try out a new dish, look up recipes for it in every cookbook you have. Note first what basic ingredients are required in each. Next note what spices are needed and how much. In some cases only the amounts vary, whereas in others the spices themselves differ. Finally, check the procedures set forth in each book. By doing all this you should gain a better understanding of how to go about preparing the dish.

• Don't use a spice you don't like, even if you find that all the recipes in all the books call for it. With the exception of a few dishes that center around a certain spice, make the spice cupboard conform to your taste and palate.

• Watching and doing are the best ways to learn a new skill. If you love a cousin's homemade bread, go over and watch her make it. If you're kissing cousins, she'll allow you to make a batch right alongside her, and then you can learn all the little, seemingly insignificant things that go into a truly fine loaf of bread. Don't be shy about this. I'm sure your friendship will be closer and warmer if you get up the courage to ask Mrs. Smith down the street if you can come over and watch her make cookies this Christmas.

• When you read a recipe, follow the directions closely in your mind. If you come to a procedure that is not clear to you, go over it again, look up any culinary terms you don't completely understand, and mentally try again.

• Learn to improvise. If you follow the first rule of reading many recipes for the same dish, you'll soon become aware of the many different ways to cook the same food. Lasagna is a classic example. You can make it with one sauce, two sauces, or three sauces. You can make it with meat or without. You can make it with one kind of cheese or six different varieties. Learn the options, and you will learn to create.

• Don't be afraid to tamper with a recipe when you see it isn't working. If you can tell when you make macaroni and cheese that there isn't enough sauce for the amount of macaroni you've cooked, either extend the sauce with more milk, cheese, and seasonings, or put some of the macaroni aside for another use. If the Swiss steak you just looked at seems dry, add some stock or water; don't allow it to burn just because the recipe doesn't tell you to add more liquid during the cooking process.

• Don't always put the blame on the recipe when you have a flop. Don't give up, either. Altitude affects baking and cooking times. Fat and moisture contents affect the outcome of meat dishes, and the quality of products used affects everything. If you make a vinaigrette dressing with a sweet mayonnaise, the results will be disastrous. Old spices will produce a blah-tasting dinner. Oven temperatures and stove-top heat, plus the quality of your cookware, can all make or break a creation. If you don't understand the principle of folding in egg whites, go watch your cousin, your local TV cook, or read some more. The one good thing about mistakes is that you can learn from them.

• Exceptions; there are always exceptions. I've told you to use only those spices that you enjoy; however, such things as capers and anchovy paste have flavors you may dislike on their own, but when blended into a dressing or sauce they will please you, as they add a more delicious saltiness than regular salt does. Read the recipes for dressings and sauces that you've enjoyed in fine restaurants. If some of these contain anchovy paste, for example, you'll know you'll enjoy using it at home, too.

• *Please* buy the kind of wire whip or whisk the French use for sauce making, now widely available here. There is no sauce, custard, dressing, or gravy listed in any cookbook in the world that won't be smoother and easier to make with the aid of this most indispensable kitchen tool.

Homework

· Keep your kitchen *clean!* Ptomaine and botulism love dirt and poorly kept food. A clean kitchen ensures health.

· Wash your hands *and* nails before cooking. Good cooks are in constant contact with food.

· Scour wooden surfaces a minimum of once a week, and rinse with water containing bleach, followed by clear water.

· Many foods can be left out at room temperature for several hours as long as they are covered by toweling or waxed paper. Many food-spoiling spores are airborne; if the spores can't land on the food, the food is safe. Milk products and *uncooked* meat, fowl, and fish must be refrigerated until used. Once these products are cooked, they too can sit lightly covered until that night's dinner party. Reheating is then a very easy matter.

· Always cool stocks and stock-type soups as quickly as possible. Place the pot in a cool, airy place and prop up one corner of the pot with a knife so that air can flow underneath. If you live in a very hot climate, place the pot in a sinkful of cold water and then refrigerate it as soon as possible. Stocks and some soups spoil easily.

· It's an old wives' tale that you can't put hot food into a refrigerator. Grandma couldn't do it because the hot food melted the ice in her icebox, and thus her cooling system vanished. It is, however, a good idea to allow hot foods to cool at least to very warm before placing them in your refrigerator so that you don't overstrain the refrigeration system.

· *Never* put hot stuffing into a cold bird and allow the bird to sit. Bacteria loves a warm place. Stuff birds just prior to roasting them.

· Keep your knives sharp and in a separate drawer so that they don't get banged around and nicked.

· If a mayonnaise-based dressing or sauce that you've made and stored in a jar in the refrigerator is almost gone, *do not* add new dressing to the old. This is a major way of contracting food poisoning. Put the new dressing in a new vessel, and don't keep the old for more than three weeks.

· Always heat the frying pan in which you plan to fry and the oven in which you plan to roast or bake *before* placing food in either.

· When you wish a pot, pan, or platter to stay put on your work counter, place a damp, wrung-out cloth beneath it.

· Don't cook egg dishes or any food with acid in it in aluminum. Milk products should also be kept away from aluminum.

· Unlined copper cooking utensils can be dangerous to your health.

· Cooking in cast iron actually improves your health—doing so adds iron to your diet.

· Refrigerated foods should be kept in glass, plastic, or stainless steel *only*.

· Many recipes can be easily cut in half, and many can be doubled; but if you go past doubling you run the risk of failure.

· With *all* foods, smell for freshness and taste for seasonings.

Ingredients

Salt and Other Seasonings

· I have tried to put down the proper amount of salt needed in each recipe. Where I have said "to taste," the recipe contains ingredients that can vary in taste, so the amount of salt must vary from one time to the next. Even though I've done my best to give the correct amount of salt, you should *always* correct for seasoning. If you think a sauce is good but not perfect, take a spoonful out of the pot, sprinkle it with salt, and taste it again. If the spoonful of sauce comes alive, the dish needs salt, so add some until the whole pot comes alive. Many times a dull dish needs nothing more than another pinch of salt.

· It's sad when people ruin the taste of beautiful food with too much spice. Many a palate has been snuffed out by well-intentioned cooks who think that a lot is better than a bit. When you cook, know the spices you're dealing with or use them sparingly when you experiment with ones that are new to you. Many spices are very strong and it takes only a small amount to do the job.

Chicken Base

· You'll see "chicken base" listed in many of my recipes. Chicken base is a rich, chicken-tasting seasoning that is akin to the chicken bouillon cubes or granules that you buy in the supermarket. The big difference is in richness and taste. Chicken base is rendered chicken fat to which salt and seasonings have been added. It can be obtained through your butcher, and half a pound will last a long time. It costs more than any of its substitutes, but like many a real thing, it's worth the price. Chicken base will perk up almost any sauce, stew, or gravy, whether beef or chicken. When you use real chicken base, you can cut down on the amount of salt called for in a recipe. One teaspoonful is the most you'll need for a dish that feeds eight.

Butter, Oils, and Shortenings

• Clarified butter is simply butter that has been melted over very low heat and skimmed of the salt and fat solids that come to the surface. The melted butter is then poured off the sediment on the bottom of the pot. To get the largest amount of clarified butter, melt butter in a narrow, straight-sided pot or a glass jar set in simmering water. Skim the top when the butter is melted and hot through. Allow the butter to cool, and use it down to the sediment. With this method you don't pour the butter off the sediment; the narrowness of the vessel allows for good surface skimming.

• Clarified butter can tolerate much higher heat than unclarified butter; hence it is good for sautéing and light frying.

• Grease vegetable casseroles, soufflé dishes, and entrée baking dishes with butter for better taste—but not cake pans.

• Butter freezes beautifully. Buy a case when it's on sale, or go to your local dairy and get an even better price.

• Except in very hot climates, butter can be left out on a covered dish, thus providing you with soft, spreadable butter.

• To keep pâtés, stocks, and spreads fresher longer, pour a coating of clarified butter over the top and keep them refrigerated.

• Learn to know the dishes that demand butter. Nothing tastes or works just like it, regardless of what the ads say.

• Both butter and real vanilla extract should be used in any dish where their flavor will easily be detected.

• If you must use margarine in baking, use half butter and half margarine.

• Salted butter can be made into sweet butter by *washing* the salt out. This is done by kneading the butter in a bowl of ice water. It will become smooth and rather waxlike. A taste will confirm when it's sweet.

• If you're making a prodigious quantity of sandwiches, beat equal amounts of butter and low-cholesterol margarine together with an electric mixer until smooth and spreadable. Whipped butter can be spread to any thickness, and herbs can be added if you desire.

• A plain vegetable oil can be substituted in most bread recipes that call for butter. If you're on a polyunsaturated-fat diet, oil is a better substitute than most margarines.

• If you're a margarine user, be sure to buy low- or no-cholesterol margarine. Otherwise, you'll suffer both health- and taste-wise. Butter has vitamins, such as A, that most margarines don't.

• When you fry foods in oil, the temperature of the oil must always remain fairly high or the food will absorb the oil.

Flour

• The flour used in the recipes in this book should be all-purpose flour unless otherwise stated. Dip the cup into the flour and level it off with a knife blade. Sift flour only if a recipe tells you to. Almost all American flours are now presifted.

Cheese

• To measure grated cheese, lightly press it into the measure.

• When you top a dish with cheese, add cracker crumbs or bread crumbs to the grated cheese. This will help keep the cheese from clinging to itself, and portions will therefore be easier to serve.

• Dice cheese rather than grating it when adding it to a sauce for melting. Diced cheese doesn't become stringy.

Eggs

• Be sure there is no trace of oil on beaters or bowl when you whip egg whites. Any oily substance will cause the egg whites to fall and be unbeatable.

Wine

• Red or white wine should simmer in a sauce, stew, or gravy, but sherry and cordials should be added as a finishing touch during the last 5 minutes of cooking, as their flavor easily dissipates.

• Alcoholic beverages are added to cooked dishes for flavor, not for their alcohol content, which cooks away at the simmering point.

• When you cook with red wine, a sauce should turn a subtle shade of brown. If, however, the sauce attains a sickly purple or rose color, the wine you're using has soured. Discard the dish.

• It is best to add wine to a basic sauce after all other ingredients have simmered for a few minutes. Whisk the wine in with a wire whip, and continue to simmer the sauce until the wine's sharpness has subsided.

- Wine acts like vinegar in a marinade, helping to tenderize meat.

Garlic

- Garlic that's allowed to sauté in a mixture of half butter and half oil, or all oil, until it turns golden will be quieted down in odor but give off its true, slightly sweet taste.

- To peel a garlic clove, pull the single cloves away from the head of garlic. Place a clove on a work board and press it with the flat side of a large knife. When you hear a soft crackling sound, you'll know the skin surrounding the clove has popped. You can now peel the clove with ease.

Leftovers

First of all, if your family dislikes leftovers, learn to cook the proper amount for the number of people you're serving.

If there are only two of you and you feel like a nice chuck roast (fixed pot-roast style), buy a small chuck roast and cut it in half. Fix the nicer half as a pot roast for two. Cut the other half into stew meat and make the two of you a nice little Boeuf Bourguignon in two single-serving casseroles. This can be done for four people by simply starting off with a larger chuck roast.

If no one in your family likes the backs or wings of chicken, buy chicken parts rather than the whole chicken, or use all the parts your family doesn't like for a really good chicken stock. Use the stock for soup one night and make enough chicken salad for a lovely sandwich for Junior's lunch box with the stewed chicken meat; or clean the meat from the bones and make chicken noodle or cream of chicken soup. If you're a small family, sauté some mushrooms, add the chicken meat, stir in half a recipe of White Wine Sauce (see Index) and fold into it half a package of boiled noodles. Bake at 350° until hot and enjoy.

If you have any chicken noodle casserole left over, place it in a small flameproof dish, and top it with milk just to cover and your favorite cheese, grated. Heat in the oven or toaster oven until bubbly. I defy you to have a better lunch you didn't have to work for.

A lot of people who don't like leftovers feel the way they do because the food they're served the first time was overcooked to begin with. By the time the overcooked food is reheated, it's really dead.

Vegetables are a prime example. If you'll learn to cook your vegetables by the frying-pan method described in the vegetable chapter, you'll be able to reheat and use your vegetables or add them to a salad, soup, or stew.

Casserole dishes such as Lasagna should be heated in the oven *just* until piping hot and the cheese melted. By overbaking Lasagna, you ruin much of the flavor for the first serving and make a second heating impossible. Stop creating good dog food and start treating your food, palate, and wallet with respect.

Many times all a leftover needs is a new house. If you carefully put leftover Lasagna in a smaller, attractive casserole dish, and add a touch of water and some new cheese on top, you can serve it as a side dish with your baked chicken and everyone will rave.

Don't serve a leftover the next night; give your family time to forget. Wrap leftovers well so that their flavors don't deteriorate and *re-create* them a few nights later. When I have leftovers, I make a mental note as I wrap them for the refrigerator, often deciding or inventing what I'll do with them right then and there. This helps me plan and decide on menus for the week ahead.

In the summer at the ranch, there are rarely fewer than eight at the table. For lunch we always have ranch-style smorgasbord. I literally empty the refrigerator onto the table. Leftovers are carefully reheated or transformed into an omelette or salad or some such.

Another important thing to remember about leftovers is this—after the dinner party is over, don't kid yourself into thinking you'll eat the pâté within the next few days. Pack it nicely into a small jar and freeze it for the next time you have a few guests over or want a Swiss cheese and pâté sandwich on pumpernickel. I find that old cosmetic jars make wonderful containers for pâté and spreads. Simply soak off the labels, wash thoroughly, and boil them with 1 teaspoon baking soda for 5 minutes to ensure the release of all perfumes from the pores of the glass.

Naturally, stale bread is for bread crumbs (which can be frozen or kept in an airtight jar), or for meatballs, meat loaf, or french toast.

Make a game of saving and using food rather than throwing it away. Imagine yourself in a situation where the food in your house is all the food you'll possess over the next month. Wastefulness is truly a bad habit when inflation is running to the top of the charts. Becoming a better planner and learning to use all that's at your disposal will save you time, money, and a guilty conscience.

BREADS AND BATTERS

HOMEMADE GOODIES

RYE   WHEAT   OATS   BRAN

𝓑read: the staff of life, the palette for butter and jam, the housing of sandwiches, the scooper of egg yolks, the dipper of sauces, the provider of crumbs, croutons, and cubes.

Before the advent of refined white flour in the 1800s, bread was truly the staff of life. It was made with whole grains and unrefined wheat flour. People got a healthy intake of fiber, and such ailments as diverticulitis and cancer of the colon were unheard of.

Refined, bleached white flour changed our eating habits and our health. Nowadays people are learning the importance of roughage and fiber in their diets, and bakeries are producing more whole-grain loaves.

The white breads, which TV ads claim "children really love," are a disaster to your intestines and have almost no taste. As children, my friends and I would trim the crust from a piece of white bread and work it with our fingers until it was a small, gluey gray mass. This could be done easily in a matter of moments. Even then we knew there should be something more to the staff of life.

If you love to cook, the art of making bread should be in your repertoire of skills. The wonderful tastes and textures of homemade loaves are surpassed only by the magnificent aromas that will fill your kitchen. Whether white or whole-grain, there's nothing to match the goodness of homemade breads.

Some General Advice on Bread-Making

• Never dissolve yeast in *hot* water, which will kill the yeast spores. *Warm* water is what you need, about 105° to 110° F. (baby bottle temperature). I prefer dry yeast because of its shelf life, but cake yeast will work just as well in any recipe in this book.

• During cold weather, let bread rise in a gas oven with the pilot light on and the door slightly ajar, or in an electric oven with a pan of hot water on the bottom shelf. Bread loves to rise in moist, warm air.

• Always cover yeast dough with a clean towel while it is rising.

• When you put bread dough into bread pans for the final rising, punch the dough down into the pan to eliminate air bubbles.

• Beat bread dough with a wire whip before adding the last 2 or 3 cups of flour. In the bowl should be the warm liquid, yeast, salt, sweetening (if any), about half the flour called for, and eggs (if they are used). Beating with a wire whip at this stage will drastically cut down on the kneading time and result in a better dough.

• If a yeast dough is in the process of rising and you must leave it for some reason, punch it down, cover it tightly with plastic wrap and a damp towel, and place it in the refrigerator. The dough will be fine for up to 24 hours. When you remove the dough from the refrigerator, punch it down again and allow it to rise. Continue with the recipe as if you were in the last rising process.

• Since homemade bread contains no preservatives, it should be kept well wrapped and refrigerated for best results. If you can't use all the bread you have baked within three to four days, freeze some. Completely cooled bread freezes beautifully.

• Don't open the oven door during the first 15 minutes of baking a loaf of bread.

• If a yeast dough recipe calls for you to roll out the dough after its first proofing (see below), punch the dough down and allow it to rest, covered with a towel, for 5 minutes. After the short rest, the dough will roll out easily and smoothly.

• *Proofing* is the term used to describe the condition of a yeast dough when it has completely risen and doubled in bulk. To check whether the dough has proofed, poke your finger into it. If the fingerprint stays put, the dough has proofed and should be either punched down or baked, depending on the stage of bread-making you're in. If the fingerprint doesn't stay put, the dough has not finished rising—has not yet proofed.

• *Do not* allow the dough to overproof, as the yeast spores will die, the dough will fall, and the bread will be ruined.

• When baking bread in glass pans, lower the oven temperature by 25° F.

• When any bread, roll, or coffee cake made with yeast is ready for the oven, you can give it a glossy, richly colored glaze by brushing the surface with an egg beaten with 1 teaspoon water. You can also brush the loaves or rolls with milk or melted butter. Though you needn't brush with anything, the results are often superior and more eye-appealing.

• Bread bakes best in the lower half of the oven.

• Bread is done when it starts to leave the sides of the pan and sounds hollow when thumped on its bottom crust.

• Quick breads (breads without yeast) should never fill more than two-thirds of a pan before being baked. Spread the batter into the corners and make a slight trough in the center. This will prevent a broken and split crust.

• The secret of success with quick breads is to work them as little as possible. Stir the wet ingredients into the dry ingredients and whip with a wire whip *just* until all the ingredients are combined.

Honey Wheat Bread   *1 large or 2 medium loaves*

This bread is the best whole-grain bread I know, and it's good for your health and digestive system, too. A sandwich of tomato, cheese, dill pickle, lettuce, mayonnaise, and bean sprouts (if available) made on this bread is a total taste treat.

        2 cups warm water
        2 packages yeast
        ¼ cup (½ stick) butter *or* margarine
        2 teaspoons salt
        ¾ cup honey
        1 cup quick-cooking oats, such as Quick Quaker Oats
        1 cup white flour
      4½ cups whole-wheat flour
        ½ cup wheat germ
        1 cup bran

Put 1 cup warm water in a large bowl; add the yeast and allow it to dissolve. Heat the second cup of water in a small saucepan. Add the butter, salt, and honey. When the butter and honey are melted, add the oats. Cool the mixture to lukewarm. (If you're in a hurry, put the pan in a cold-water bath and stir until it reaches the desired temperature.)

Add the white flour to the yeast mixture; stir well with a wire whisk. Add the oatmeal mixture and 1 cup of the whole-wheat flour. Beat very well with the whisk. (The harder you beat at this point, the faster and easier the kneading will be.)

Add the wheat germ, bran, and almost all of the remaining whole-wheat flour. Flour a pastry cloth or board with whole-wheat flour and turn the dough out onto it. If the amount of flour you've added doesn't seem to want to stir into the dough, fear not—just dump the whole thing out onto the floured work surface and begin to knead by gathering the dough together and pressing it into a ball. Then begin to knead with the heel of your right hand by pushing hard on the center of the dough until you've almost pushed it into two parts. With the left hand fold the top half over the lower half and repeat over and over, turning the dough after every other push. Knead the dough until it begins to push back. The dough is kneaded enough when you poke it with a finger and the indentation immediately disappears.

Place the kneaded dough in a well-buttered bowl; turn to grease the dough on all sides. Cover it with a clean cloth and let it rise in a warm place for 1 hour, or until doubled in bulk. Punch the dough down and let it rest while you generously grease one large (12-by-4-inch) or two medium (9-by-4½-inch) bread pans. Form the dough into a loaf or loaves and place it in the pan(s). Let it rise 1 hour, or until doubled in bulk. Bake the bread in a 400° oven for 45 minutes to 1 hour, depending on pan size.

Life Bread   *2 round loaves*

You can now buy stone-ground whole-wheat flour, wheat germ, bran, and new wonder grains such as triticale in most markets. With these fiber-filled products you can produce a wonderful bread that is so healthful and nutritious that it'll put anything on your supermarket shelf to shame. This bread not only tastes delicious; it can be sliced very, very thin without crumbling, which makes it perfect for Danish open-face sandwiches.

Note that this recipe requires no fat, eggs, or refined sugar. It's totally healthful in addition to being tasty.

    1½ cups warm water
    1 package yeast

1 cup triticale flour, *or* gluten flour, *or* graham flour
2 cups whole-wheat flour
1 cup bran
1 cup wheat germ
1 cup rye flour (dark if available)
½ cup rolled oats
1 cup warm water
½ cup black molasses
4 teaspoons salt
  More whole-wheat flour if needed

Pour 1½ cups warm water into a bowl. Add the yeast and stir to dissolve. Add the triticale (or flour of your choice) and 1 cup of the whole-wheat flour. Beat with a wire whip until very smooth. Add the second cup of whole-wheat flour and stir well to combine. Push the dough to the sides of the bowl, making a large well in the center. Add all the other ingredients, including the additional cup of water. Stir to combine. Turn the dough out onto a board or cloth that has been well coated with whole-wheat flour. Knead the dough until it no longer sticks to the board and is smooth and springy, about 5 minutes.

Place the dough in a buttered bowl and turn to coat it on all sides. Cover the bowl with a clean towel and allow the dough to rise in a warm place until doubled in bulk, about 1½ hours, or until an indentation made with your finger remains in the dough.

Punch the dough down and shape it into two round loaves. Place them on a greased cookie sheet that you've sprinkled with cornmeal. Cover them with a towel and allow them to rise until doubled in bulk. You may mark the risen dough with a cross or parallel slashes just before popping the loaves into the oven. Bake them in a 375° oven for 45 minutes, or until the bottoms sound hollow when tapped. Cool on a rack.

White Bread   *2 loaves*

1 cup warm water	¼ cup (½ stick) butter
2 packages yeast	2 teaspoons salt
1 cup milk	6 cups flour
⅓ cup sugar	2 eggs

Put the warm water in a bowl and add the yeast. Heat the milk, sugar, butter, and salt in a small pan until the butter has melted. Cool to luke-warm. Add the lukewarm milk mixture to the yeast mixture along with 1 cup of the flour. Add the eggs. Beat with a wire whisk, add 2 more cups of the flour, and beat again. Stir in the remaining 3 cups of flour and turn the dough out on a floured pastry cloth or board. Knead until it is smooth and elastic. Put it in a greased bowl, turn to coat it, cover it with a towel, and allow it to rise in a warm place, usually 1 to 1½ hours. Punch the dough down and shape it into two loaves. Place the loaves in well-greased bread pans and turn them to coat. Again cover with a towel and allow the loaves to rise until doubled in bulk. Bake in a 400° oven for 35 minutes, or until the bottom of the loaves sounds hollow and the bread has come away from the sides of the pan.

Food Processor White Bread   *1 loaf*

2 packages yeast
1⅓ cups warm water
5 teaspoons sugar
1½ teaspoons salt
2¼ cups flour, plus ¼ cup in reserve
1 tablespoon butter, softened

Dissolve the yeast in the water; add the sugar and salt. Put 1½ cups flour in the work bowl of the food processor with the butter. Add the yeast mixture, turning the machine on and off for 10 to 15 seconds until the ingredients are blended. Add 1¾ cups more flour and process until a ball of dough forms on top of the blade. If the machine slows and a ball won't form, add the reserved ¼ cup flour and process until a ball forms. Turn the dough into a buttered bowl; turn to grease all the sides. Let the dough rise for approximately 1 hour. Stir it down and put it into a large buttered bread pan. Let it rise again for 45 minutes, or until it is proofed. Bake the bread in a 375° oven for 40 minutes, or until the bottom of the loaf sounds hollow.

Crescent Rolls   *36 rolls*

2 packages yeast
3 tablespoons warm water
1 cup water
½ cup (1 stick) butter *or* margarine, cut into pieces
1 teaspoon salt
½ cup sugar
3 eggs, beaten
5 cups flour
Melted butter

Dissolve the yeast in 3 tablespoons warm water. Put 1 cup water, the butter, salt, and sugar into a saucepan and heat until the butter is almost melted. Pour the mixture into a large bowl; cool to lukewarm. Add the beaten eggs, then the yeast mixture, then half the flour (2½ cups). Beat with a wire whip until very smooth. Stir in the remaining flour and turn the dough out onto a pastry board or cloth. The dough should be quite soft.

Knead the dough for at least 5 minutes; be sure it is smooth and elastic. Put the dough into a bowl well greased with butter and turn to coat it. Cover it with a clean cloth and allow it to rise in a warm place for 2 hours, or until doubled in bulk.

Punch the dough down, divide it into three equal parts, and allow it to rest for 5 minutes. Roll each third, one at a time, into a circle ¼ inch thick. Brush the circles with butter, cut them into pie-shaped wedges, and roll the wedges into crescents, starting at the widest part. Place the crescents on a buttered cookie sheet with the points underneath. Cover them and allow them to rise for 45 minutes to 1 hour. Bake them in a 400° oven for 15 to 20 minutes, or until they are golden brown.

Just Enough French Bread   *2 long loaves*

Do you like those narrow loaves of chewy french bread, the kind you pull apart, bite down on, and have to pull at to get a piece? If you do, this bread is for you. It's called Just Enough because it makes two cookie-sheet-long loaves, which a party of four to six can easily devour at one good spaghetti dinner.

> 1 package yeast
> 1 cup warm water
> 1 tablespoon sugar
> 1½ teaspoons salt
> 2½ cups flour

Dissolve the yeast in the water. Stir in the sugar, salt, and flour. The dough should be *very* stiff. Turn it out onto a floured board and knead it for 10 minutes. If the dough isn't stiff and hard to knead, add more flour until it is. Grease a bowl, add the dough, turn to grease the top, cover, and allow the dough to rise in a warm place until doubled in bulk, at least 1 hour.

When the dough has risen, punch it down and shape it into two long, narrow loaves the length of a cookie sheet. Grease a cookie sheet and sprinkle it with cornmeal; place the loaves on the cookie sheet, cover, and allow them to rise again. Heat the oven to 400°; slash the tops of the loaves diagonally, ¼ inch deep, every 2 inches. Brush the loaves with milk and bake them for 30 minutes, or until they are done.

Sourdough Starter
2½ cups

    1 large potato
    3 cups water
    1 teaspoon sugar
    ½ teaspoon salt
    1 package yeast
    2 cups flour

Boil the potato in water to cover until it is mushy; reserve the water. Put a quarter of the potato in a bowl and mash it well with a fork. Add 2 cups of the liquid in which it was boiled. Cool the potato mixture to lukewarm; add the sugar, salt, yeast, and flour. Beat the mixture until it is smooth, and set it in a warm place to "work" overnight. It's best to make the new starter one morning and not use it until the next day, giving it at least 24 hours to work. If the starter bubbles up to more than double its size, stir it down and let it work some more. After the starter has worked for 24 hours, cover it tightly and refrigerate it until you wish to use it.

To restart the starter: After making a recipe with your starter, take what's left and add ½ teaspoon sugar, 2 cups lukewarm water, and 2 cups flour. Beat until smooth and again allow it to "work" in a warm place for 24 hours; refrigerate.

Sourdough French Bread
1 large round loaf

    2 cups Sourdough Starter (preceding recipe)
    ½ package yeast
    ¼ cup warm water
    1 tablespoon sugar
    1½ teaspoons salt
    2 tablespoons vegetable oil
    3¼ cups flour

Put 2 cups of the starter in a bowl. Dissolve the yeast in the warm water, then add it to the starter, followed by all the other ingredients. Turn the mixture out onto a floured pastry cloth or board and knead it for at least 10 minutes. The dough should be stiff. Work it until the surface begins to break with each knead. Put the dough in an oiled bowl, turn it to coat, and cover it with a towel. Set it in a warm, draft-free place and allow it to rise until doubled, usually 1 to 1½ hours.

Punch the dough down and form it into a ball by folding the edges under and away from you with your fingertips. Put the ball of dough on a cookie sheet that you have greased and sprinkled liberally with cornmeal. Cover the dough and again allow it to double in bulk. Slash the top with a large, very sharp knife in any pattern you like. Brush the loaf with milk (I do this with my hands) and bake it in a 400° oven for 1 hour, or until the bottom sounds hollow and the top is crusty brown. If you make this bread with a new starter, it'll be delicious but not as sour as you might like it. The sourness will increase as the starter gets older.

Sourdough Rolls   *24 rolls*

Follow the preceding recipe for Sourdough French Bread, but instead of forming the dough into one large loaf, pinch off pieces of dough and shape them into rolls. Place the rolls on a greased cookie sheet sprinkled with cornmeal and allow them to rise (30 minutes is usually enough for rolls). You may slash the tops of the rolls. Brush them with milk and bake them in a 400° oven for 15 or 20 minutes, depending on their size.

Pumpernickel Bread with Sourdough Starter   *1 large round loaf*

1 package yeast
½ cup warm water
⅓ cup cornmeal
1 cup cold water
3 tablespoons molasses
1½ tablespoons caraway seeds
1 tablespoon butter
2 teaspoons salt
1 cup Sourdough Starter (see Index), made a day ahead
2 cups rye flour
2½ cups white flour

Dissolve the yeast in the warm water. Combine the cornmeal and cold water in a saucepan and whisk until smooth; bring the mixture to a boil over medium heat, stirring continuously. When the mixture is thick, remove it from the heat and stir in the molasses, caraway seeds, butter, and salt. When the cornmeal mixture has cooled to warm, add it to the yeast mixture along with the starter. Stir in the rye flour and beat until very smooth; stir in the white flour. Turn the dough out onto a lightly floured board or cloth and knead it until it is smooth and elastic. Form the dough into a ball; turn in a greased bowl to coat; cover it with a cloth. Allow it to rise in a warm place until doubled in bulk, usually 1½ hours. When it has risen, punch the dough down and form it into a round loaf. Place the loaf on a greased baking sheet that you have sprinkled with cornmeal. Again allow the dough to rise until doubled in bulk. With a sharp knife make a slash in the top of the loaf. Bake it in a 400° oven for 1 hour and 15 minutes, or until the bottom sounds hollow. Cool it on a rack.

This recipe can be doubled.

Sour Cream Coffee Cake   *12 to 16 servings*

For years Grandmom Faunce arose early each morning to make Sour Cream Coffee Cake. She continued even after her seven children had left home, since others of the family still lived in the houses clustered on what was known to us as the Faunce Reservation, and they liked to troop over to Grandmom's house for their daily ration of Sour Cream Coffee Cake.

But when in the late fifties the government, in its infinite wisdom, demolished all the old houses on the Reservation to prepare for urban renewal, in the hullabaloo of moving and rebuilding Grandmom Faunce lost her coffee cake recipe, and I've been looking for a replacement ever since. This version is adapted from one in a book titled *The Great Cook's Guide to Cakes*. I have changed it so that the result more closely resembles the coffee cake I remember.

    ½ cup (1 stick) butter
    ½ cup (1 stick) margarine
    1 cup granulated white sugar
    3 eggs
    3 cups *sifted* flour
    ½ teaspoon salt
    1 tablespoon baking powder
    1 teaspoon baking soda
    1 cup sour cream
    1 teaspoon vanilla
    ½ cup granulated white sugar
    ½ cup packed brown sugar
    ¾ cup chopped walnuts *or* pecans
    2 teaspoons cinnamon

Heat the oven to 350°. Grease a 10-inch tube pan or oblong baking dish. The tube pan must be *well* greased.

Cream the butter, margarine, and sugar until fluffy. Add the eggs one at a time, beating thoroughly after each addition. Sift the flour with the salt, baking powder, and baking soda. Add the flour mixture to the butter-sugar-egg batter and beat at low speed until well combined. Add the sour cream and vanilla and beat until smooth and blended.

Mix the white sugar, brown sugar, nuts, and cinnamon together in a small bowl. Pour or spoon half the cake batter into the pan. Sprinkle the batter with half the sugar-nut mixture. Spoon the second half of the batter into the pan and top it with the remaining sugar-nut mixture. Bake the tube pan for 50 minutes, the oblong pan for 35 to 40 minutes. Test the cake with a toothpick. When it tests done (the toothpick comes out clean), remove it from the oven and allow it to cool for 30 minutes before removing it from the pan.

This cake keeps well—if it's well hidden!

Raisin Bread   *2 loaves*

Plain or with cinnamon, this makes wonderful toast for a cold morning—or a sunny one.

> 2 packages yeast
> ⅓ cup warm water
> 1 cup milk
> ½ cup sugar
> ½ cup (1 stick) butter
> 1 teaspoon salt
> 4 eggs, beaten
> 1 15-ounce box raisins, golden preferred
> 6 to 6½ cups flour

Dissolve the yeast in the water. Heat the milk, sugar, butter, and salt until the butter is just melted. Cool to lukewarm. Add the lukewarm milk mixture to the yeast mixture, beat in the eggs, and add the raisins. Add half the flour and beat well with a wire whip. Stir in the remaining flour, turn the dough out onto a floured pastry board or cloth, and knead it until smooth and elastic. Put the dough in a buttered bowl, turn to grease all sides, cover it with a towel, and allow it to rise until doubled in bulk, at least 1½ hours.

Punch the dough down, shape it into two loaves, and put them into well-buttered bread pans. Again allow the dough to rise. Bake the loaves in a 400° oven for 50 minutes, or until the bottoms sound hollow. If the loaves seem to be getting too brown during baking, lay a piece of foil over them. Leave the foil flat—don't fold it over or around the loaves.

If you're partial to cinnamon in your raisin bread: after the dough has gone through its first rising, divide it and flatten each half into a rectangle as wide as your bread pans and twice as long. Sprinkle the dough liberally with cinnamon and then roll it up, starting with the narrow end. Place the seam of each loaf on the bottom of the pan. Bake as usual.

Stollen   *6 medium ovals*

      2 cups milk
      1 cup honey or sugar
      1 cup (2 sticks) butter *or* margarine
      2 teaspoons salt
      3 packages yeast
      1 cup warm water
     2½ cups flour
      1 cup currants *or* raisins
      1 pound candied cherries
      8 ounces candied citron
      8 ounces candied pineapple
      5 eggs
      1 teaspoon vanilla
      2 teaspoons brandy
      6 to 7 cups flour
      1 cup walnuts
      2 tablespoons grated lemon rind

Heat the milk, honey, butter, and salt until the butter is melted. Cool to lukewarm. Dissolve the yeast in the warm water in a very large bowl. When the milk mixture has cooled, add it to the yeast mixture and stir in the 2½ cups flour. Beat with a wire whisk until smooth; cover with a towel and set in a warm place until bubbles appear. This usually takes 30 minutes.

While the yeast mixture is working, put the currants (or raisins), cherries, citron, and pineapple in a colander and rinse well with very hot water. Drain. (If the currants are hard, soak them in hot water for 5 minutes and then rinse them along with the rest of the fruit.) This procedure cleans the fruit of preservatives.

When the yeast mixture starts to form bubbles, beat in the eggs, vanilla, and brandy. Beat in 2 cups flour and add the drained fruit, the walnuts, and the grated lemon rind. Add 4 more cups flour, or enough to make a soft dough. Turn the dough out onto a well-floured pastry cloth and knead it until smooth. (This is a large batch of dough. To knead it, pick up a side of the pastry cloth and fold the dough over with the aid of the cloth.)

Put the dough into a well-greased bowl and turn to coat it; cover it with a towel and let it rise in a warm place until doubled. This will take at least 1½ hours but, depending on the temperature, may take over 2 hours. Punch down the dough and divide it into six equal parts. Flatten and shape each part into an oval approximately 1 inch thick. Fold each oval over like a roll and pinch the edges together. Brush the loaves with melted butter and cover them to let them rise again. Bake for 5 minutes in a 400° oven, lower the heat to 350°, and continue baking until the loaves are lightly browned and the bottoms sound hollow, usually another 30 minutes. Cool on racks and coat well with powdered sugar.

You can make three large Stollen if you wish, but bake them a bit longer. The loaves freeze well and if made with honey keep well in a bread box or refrigerator as long as they are wrapped airtight.

To serve, slice the Stollen ¾ inch thick, put the slices on a cookie sheet, and put them under the broiler. They brown very quickly because of their sugar, butter, and fruit content, so watch them closely. Serve with butter and coffee. Or simply slice them as they are—and enjoy.

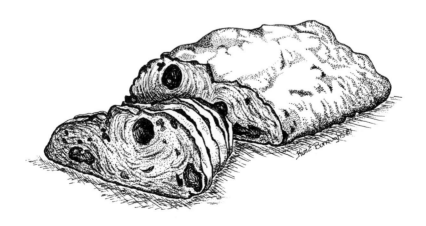

Whole-Grain Loaf

1 large loaf

This cake bread is both healthy and tasty—great in lunch boxes, spread with butter or cream cheese, or taken on a hike. I serve it to visiting skiers in the morning with a mug of hot coffee.

1¾ cups whole-wheat flour
⅓ cup bran
½ cup wheat germ
1 teaspoon salt
2 teaspoons baking soda
1 teaspoon cinnamon
¼ teaspoon cloves
⅔ cup chopped nuts of your choice
¼ cup shredded coconut (optional)
1 cup applesauce, *or* 2 ripe bananas, mashed
½ cup honey
2 eggs
⅔ cup buttermilk
⅓ cup vegetable oil, polyunsaturated preferred
1 cup raisins *or* currants, soaked for 5 minutes in *hot* water

Put all the dry ingredients in a bowl and mix well. Blend all the wet ingredients in a blender, food processor, or by hand with a wire whisk. Make a well in the dry ingredients; pour in the wet ingredients and stir until combined. Stir in the well-drained raisins or currants and pour the dough into a large, well-greased bread pan 12 inches long, 4½ inches wide, and 3 inches high. (If you don't have a pan that large, use two medium-sized pans. The batter should come halfway up the sides of the pan before baking. If the batter fills more than two-thirds the height of the pan, the bread will run over before it has baked enough to hold an edge.) Bake in a 350° oven for 45 minutes to 1 hour—the length of time depends on the altitude and the shape of the pan. The loaf should come away from the sides of the pan and a toothpick should come out clean. Cool the bread in the pan for 10 minutes, then turn it out onto a rack.

This bread freezes beautifully, and it will keep fresh in a drawer for a week or more if it is well wrapped.

Pumpkin Bread   *2 loaves*

3½ cups flour
½ teaspoon baking powder
2 teaspoons baking soda
½ teaspoon salt
2 teaspoons cinnamon
1 teaspoon ground cloves
1 teaspoon nutmeg
1½ cups white sugar
1½ cups brown sugar
1 cup vegetable oil
2 cups canned pumpkin
4 eggs
1 cup finely chopped or ground nuts, walnuts or pecans preferred

Sift together all the dry ingredients except the nuts. Put the sugars, oil, and pumpkin in a bowl and beat. Add the eggs one at a time and beat well after each addition. Add the dry ingredients by thirds and stir to combine well. Fold in the nuts. Grease and flour two bread pans. Pour in the batter so that it comes slightly more than halfway up the sides of the pans. Bake in a 350° oven for 50 minutes, or until done.

Popovers   *12 popovers*

Popovers are simply great. They're much less fattening than biscuits or muffins and, to my way of thinking, twice as delicious. This popover recipe is incredibly easy, and super if you've just run in from somewhere and need to have dinner ready in half an hour.

Since popovers are much like Yorkshire pudding, they're wonderful (and easier) to have with prime rib. They're also handy, as they come right out of the muffin tins and don't need to be cut.

If you have a window in your oven, watch the show—it beats watching the clothes drier.

1 cup flour
½ teaspoon salt
1 cup milk
2 eggs
Butter *or* margarine

Butter muffin tins *very* well. Put the flour and salt in a bowl; stir. Into a 2-cup measure pour 1 cup milk, break in the eggs, and stir with a fork until the eggs are broken up. Pour the milk-and-egg mixture into the flour mixture and beat well with a wire whip. It's very important that you beat this mixture thoroughly. Fill the muffin tins halfway. Put them in a *cold* oven, turn the heat to 450°, and *do not open the oven door for 30 minutes.* Always bake popovers in the center of the lower half of the oven, and preferably alone, for best results.

Gougère   *6 to 8 servings*

A gougère is a mouth-watering cheese ring created by the French. It is based on *pâte à chou*, from which we make such things as cream puffs, chocolate eclairs, Paris-Brest, and canapé puffs. A gougère is easy and fun to make and delightful to serve; it always elicits compliments.

> 1 cup water
> ½ cup (1 stick) butter
> ½ teaspoon salt
> 2 good dashes Tabasco
> 1 cup flour
> 4 eggs
> 1½ cups grated Swiss cheese (about 4 ounces)
> 2 tablespoons grated Parmesan, *or* more Swiss cheese

Place the water, butter, salt, and Tabasco in a medium-sized saucepan. Bring the mixture to a boil, or heat it until the butter is completely melted. Dump in the flour all at once. With a wooden spoon beat the mixture until it forms a doughy mass that comes cleanly away from the sides of the pan. Give it one more good whip of the wrist and remove it from the heat.

Allow the *pâte à chou* to cool in the pan for a few minutes, then break in the first egg and beat the dough until the egg is thoroughly incorporated. Use a wooden spoon and take care to *stir* in the egg first, *then* beat. If you don't, the mixture may very well slip out of the pan, which is great for a laugh but lousy for the gougère. When the first egg has been beaten well into the mixture, add the next and incorporate it as you did the first, and so on until all 4 eggs have been added.

Add the Swiss cheese and stir to blend. Heat the oven to 425°. Spread oil or shortening on a cookie sheet in the form of an oval about 14 inches in length and about 4 inches wide. Using a dessert or soup spoon, scoop up balls of gougère batter and arrange them in an oval on the oiled cookie sheet.

Leave about ¼ inch of space between the balls of batter. When the oval is complete, you should have about a quarter of the batter left over. Top each ball of batter with another teaspoonful of batter. Sprinkle the top of the gougère with the Parmesan cheese or more grated Swiss. Bake in the lower half of the oven at 425° for 35 minutes, or until it is well puffed and nicely browned.

Serve hot from the oven in place of bread or rolls, as an accompaniment to salads or soups, or as the main feature next to a bottle of wine set in front of a cozy fire. A gougère served with eggs and ham for breakfast or brunch is always a scene stealer. Don't cut the gougère; pull the balls of puffed-up dough apart with your fingers and enter heaven with your first bite.

Muffins   *16 to 24 muffins*

2 cups flour
3 teaspoons baking powder
1 tablespoon sugar
½ teaspoon salt
2 eggs
1 cup milk
4 tablespoons vegetable oil *or* melted butter

Mix all the dry ingredients together in a bowl. In another bowl beat together all the wet ingredients. Add the wet ingredients to the dry ingredients and stir until well combined. *Do not overbeat.* Fill *well*-greased muffin tins two-thirds full of batter. Bake in a 400° oven for 15 to 20 minutes, depending on the size of the muffin tins.

Bran Muffins   *18 to 24 muffins*

  2¼ cups buttermilk
   2 cups All-Bran cereal
   2 tablespoons bran flakes
   1 egg
  ⅓ cup vegetable oil
   1 teaspoon vanilla
   4 tablespoons honey
   1 cup plus 2 tablespoons whole-wheat flour
  ½ teaspoon salt
   2 teaspoons baking powder
   1 teaspoon baking soda
   2 tablespoons sugar
   1 cup raisins, soaked in hot water and drained

Pour the buttermilk over the All-Bran and bran flakes. In another bowl beat the eggs with the oil, vanilla, and honey. When the cereals have soaked for 5 minutes, add them to the egg mixture. Stir all the dry ingredients together and add them all at once to the egg-bran mixture. Stir only until combined. Add the well-drained raisins, combine, and fill paper baking cups, set in muffin tins, two-thirds full. Bake in a 350° oven for 20 minutes, or until a toothpick comes out clean.

Cornbread   *6 to 12 servings*

Cornbread is so easy to make and so good for you that you should throw it together often.

   1 cup cornmeal
   1 cup flour
   2 tablespoons sugar
   1 teaspoon salt
   4 teaspoons baking powder
   1 egg
   1 cup milk
   4 tablespoons vegetable oil

Stir the dry ingredients together. Beat the wet ingredients together, add them to the dry ingredients, and stir just until combined. Put the batter in a 9-by-9-inch greased pan. Bake at 400° for 30 minutes.

Sourdough Pancakes

½   teaspoon soda
2 tablespoons water
1 cup Sourdough Starter (see Index)
⅔ cup flour
1 tablespoon sugar
½ teaspoon salt
2 eggs

Dissolve the soda in the water; add to the Sourdough Starter along with all the other ingredients. Beat to blend well. Ladle the batter onto a lightly greased griddle, about 2 tablespoons per pancake. Bake until the tops are covered with bubbles. Turn and bake on the other side.

If you like thick pancakes, add only 1 egg. If you double the recipe, use 3 eggs instead of 4.

Whole-Grain Pancakes

1¼ cups whole-wheat flour
2 tablespoons bran flakes
2 tablespoons wheat germ
2 tablespoons sugar *or* honey
½ teaspoon salt
2 teaspoons baking powder
2 teaspoons baking soda
¼ cup vegetable oil, polyunsaturated preferred
2 eggs
1½ cups buttermilk

Combine all the dry ingredients in a bowl and mix well. In a smaller bowl combine the oil, eggs, and buttermilk. Pour the buttermilk mixture into the dry ingredients all at once and stir until the ingredients are well combined. Pour the batter onto a hot griddle and cook in the usual manner. Because of the whole grains, these pancakes take a little longer to bake than those made with white flour.

Spätzle (Dumpling-like noodles)   10 *servings*

2¼ cups flour
½ teaspoon salt
3 eggs
¾ cup milk
3 or more quarts boiling water
2 teaspoons salt (for boiling water)

By food processor:
Put the flour and salt in the work bowl. Start the machine and add the eggs
and milk all at once. Process 5 seconds; then turn the machine on and off
four times.

By hand:
Beat the eggs and milk together with a wire whip. Add the flour and salt and
beat for 1 full minute.

To cook:
The best home Spätzle maker is a colander with *large* holes, at least ⅓ inch
in diameter. The metal frying basket found in some deep fat fryers works
well too. If you don't have a large-hole colander, you can do what my great-
grandmother did: Pour the Spätzle batter out onto a wet dinner plate. Tip
the plate slightly toward the boiling water, and with a dinner knife cut the
batter into the water. Dip the knife into the water often to keep it from
collecting batter. Cut the batter into strips as thin as possible.

However you form the Spätzle, boil them in salted water for 8 minutes, or
until tender. When the Spätzle are done, drain them in a regular colander
and then toss them with butter and croutons. Or make my favorite Spätzle
by sautéing them in butter until lightly browned and then sprinkling them
with Parmesan cheese.

HORS D'OEUVRES

$\mathcal{T}$here are hors d'oeuvres that can be put out on a plate 5 minutes before the guests arrive, and there are hors d'oeuvres that take as much time to prepare as a main course. Some of the time-consuming hors d'oeuvres can be made ahead and frozen or kept in airtight containers ready for an occasion when you expect company.

If I'm serving a meal of three or four courses with two or more wines, I prefer to keep the hors d'oeuvres to a minimum, for no matter how good the food is, there is a limit to your guests' capacity. In such cases I usually serve a single cheese plate or an attractive arrangement of raw vegetables, plus olives and perhaps some tiny sweet gherkins. The idea is to tempt the palate but not let the guests overdo.

Hors d'oeuvres that begin a dinner party should complement the meal and not be so offbeat as to clash. If you're serving chicken- and avocado-stuffed crêpes with wine sauce as the main course, which is delicate in taste, you don't want to put out a pot of spicy bean dip as an hors d'oeuvre. With roast beef or barbecued chicken, the bean dip would be fine.

At a cocktail party where no actual meal is served, the sky is the limit and you can go wild creating pâtés, dips, meatballs, stuffed eggs, stuffed miniature cream puffs, vegetable platters, cheese platters, fresh fruit platters, barbecued chicken wings, homemade crackers, guacamole, veal turnovers, etc., etc.

A complete hors d'oeuvres table for a cocktail party should have a minimum of five selections and preferably ten or more, the number to be determined by the number of guests and the length of the party. If the party is a pretheater or predinner affair and the entire group will be moving on elsewhere, you can keep the amount modest; but if you're having one of those all-evening affairs, open up the dining-room table and fill it full.

Liver Pâté   *10 to 12 servings*

½ pound chicken livers, *or* any liver you have or like
1 small or ½ large onion, chopped
½ cup (1 stick) butter *or* margarine *or* chicken fat, duck fat, etc.
1 teaspoon salt
2 pinches cayenne
⅛ teaspoon garlic powder
¼ teaspoon nutmeg
1 teaspoon dry mustard
⅛ teaspoon cloves
1 tablespoon brandy (sherry may be used, but brandy is better)

Simmer the livers in water to cover for 20 minutes. Rinse them under cold water and set them aside to drain. Sauté the onion in 2 teaspoons butter or fat until transparent. When the livers and onions are cool, process them in a food processor or blender until smooth. Add all the other ingredients except the brandy and process again until smooth. Add the brandy and process just until blended. Turn the mixture into the mold or bowl from which you wish to serve it. Cover the pâté with waxed paper and refrigerate it until firm. If you're getting ready in advance for a party, put the pâté in the freezer until the day before the party.

If you don't have a food processor or a blender that can handle the job, chop the chicken livers and onions as fine as possible with a pastry blender, or put them through a food grinder. Put the chopped or ground liver and onions in a bowl, add all the other ingredients, and beat until totally combined. As you can tell, this is a versatile recipe that allows you to use your choice of liver (elk liver is great) and your choice of fat. I've made this with dozens of combinations—all of them good!

Party Pâté   *24 servings*

  ½ pound chicken livers *or* calves' liver
  ½ teaspoon dehydrated onion
  ¼ teaspoon minced garlic (fresh or dehydrated)
  ½ cup stock, boiling
1½ envelopes gelatin
  ¼ cup cold water
  2 tablespoons butter
  ½ teaspoon salt
  ¼ teaspoon pepper
  ¼ teaspoon nutmeg
  ⅛ teaspoon ground cloves
  ½ tablespoon dried parsley
  1 cup whipping cream, scalded and cooled

Simmer the livers over low heat in water to cover for 20 minutes. Refresh them under cold water and drain. Add the onion and garlic to the boiling stock; set aside. Sprinkle the gelatin over cold water and let it sit for 5 minutes. Add the gelatin to the stock mixture and reheat until the gelatin dissolves; cool. In a food processor, process the livers along with the butter, salt, pepper, nutmeg, cloves, and parsley. Add the gelatin mixture and process until smooth. Turn the mixture out into a bowl. Add the whipping cream, blend with a wire whip, and turn the pâté into a lightly buttered mold. Cover the top with lightly buttered waxed paper and refrigerate until set.

To unmold, run a thin, sharp knife around the edge of the pâté; lower the mold into hot water for about 5 seconds and turn the pâté out onto a serving dish.

This is a great stretcher, as it makes four times the volume of pâté you would normally get if you made a conventional pâté with ½ pound chicken livers.

You might like to increase the volume even more by not scalding the whipped cream, but whipping it instead and folding it into the pâté mixture when it is *cold* but *not* set.

Mushroom Pâté   *24 servings*

Awhile ago a friend asked me to create a fresh mushroom pâté. I served it at a luncheon, and the reactions were so good the recipe was requested—but when I looked I couldn't find it anywhere.

It turned up recently. It had been scribbled on the back of some notes on watercress. I recognized it by the ingredients and by a tiny notation in my shorthand that means it's a goodie. I hope you agree.

1 small onion, minced
1 large shallot, minced (optional but nice)
1 pound mushrooms (fresh! their bottoms closed! their flesh firm!)
2 tablespoons butter (*must* be the real thing)
¼ cup white wine *or* chicken consommé
1 teaspoon lemon juice
¼ teaspoon salt
⅛ teaspoon pepper
Pinch each garlic powder and nutmeg
¼ teaspoon dry mustard
4 drops Tabasco, *or* a good pinch cayenne
6 tablespoons butter *or* chicken fat

Peel and mince the onion and shallot. Wash the mushrooms, dry them on a towel, and slice them thin. Melt 2 tablespoons butter in a *large* frying pan. Add the onion, shallot, and mushrooms. Sauté over high heat, stirring constantly, until the mushrooms give off their liquid and all is reduced in volume. Add the wine and lemon juice. Continue to stir and cook over high heat until all the liquid has evaporated. Remove from the heat and allow to cool.

When the mushroom mixture is cool, place it in a food processor or blender. Add all the other ingredients. Run the machine until the pâté is very smooth, stopping a few times to push the mixture down from the sides.

Pack the pâté in a small crock, bowl, or pan. Make it attractive, as this pâté is best served from a container, although it may be unmolded.

To store, cover with plastic wrap and refrigerate. It's even better the next day and will keep for a week. Serve with dry toast, Finn Crisps, or any other bread or cracker you enjoy.

Toast Rounds

Toast rounds are the greatest thing to serve with your pâtés, meat spreads, or cheese spreads, and they are a good way to use up stale bread. Simply cut circles with a biscuit cutter from any thinly sliced bread of your choice. Try to cut as many circles (or any other shape you prefer) from each slice of bread as possible, but don't cut the crust (you can use stale crusts in stuffings). Bake the toast rounds on a buttered cookie sheet in a 375° oven for 10 to 15 minutes, or until the bread is just toasted to a light and lovely brown. Since different breads brown at different rates, you must check them often to ensure getting the right color. When the tops have browned, turn them over, and if the undersides are not lightly browned, return them to the oven for a few more minutes.

If you plan to pipe some turkey spread, salmon paste, or other spread onto the toast rounds, brush them with melted butter before baking. If you like herbs, add them to the butter, but make sure that the ones you use will go with the topping you are planning.

Foldovers   *48 pieces*

1 recipe Infallible Pie Crust I, II, *or* III (see Index)
1 cup sliced mushrooms
2 tablespoons butter
2 teaspoons lemon juice
½ cup chopped parsley
½ cup chopped scallions
½ cup grated Jack cheese
2 tablespoons sesame seeds
4 tablespoons grated Parmesan cheese

Make the pie dough and set it in the refrigerator. Sautè the mushrooms in 2 tablespoons butter; when half done, sprinkle the lemon juice over the mushrooms and continue cooking over high heat until done. Set the mushrooms aside while you chop the scallions and parsley and grate the cheese. Mince the mushrooms and combine them with the parsley, scallions, and cheese.

Remove the pie dough from the refrigerator and roll it out on a board strewn with the sesame seeds and the Parmesan cheese. Turn the dough over as you roll, being sure that it incorporates the seeds and cheese. Roll the dough thin and cut as many 3-inch rounds from it as possible. Put a teaspoonful of the mushroom mixture on each round, wet the edges of the dough, fold it over, and pinch the half-circle closed with your fingers. Prick the Foldovers with a toothpick and bake them in a 400° oven for 8 minutes, or until they're lightly browned.

These are delicious hot or cold. They may be reheated in a microwave or low oven on a heat-resistant oven-to-table plate as your guests are walking in the door.

Veal Turnovers   *48 to 56 turnovers*

2 medium onions, chopped fine
2 tablespoons butter
1 pound ground veal (ground beef can be used, but the flavor won't be as delicate)
3 tablespoons butter
1 tablespoon flour
¾ cup water *or* stock
2 hard-boiled eggs, chopped fine
2 tablespoons chopped parsley
1 teaspoon salt
¼ teaspoon pepper
½ teaspoon rosemary
1 recipe Grandmom's Pie Crust (see Index) *or* pie crust of your choice
1 egg yolk
1 teaspoon water

Sauté the onions in 2 tablespoons butter; when they are transparent, add the veal and cook until it is done. Remove the mixture from the pan with a slotted spoon. Add 3 tablespoons butter to the pan and melt it; add the flour and blend. Add the water or stock and simmer for 3 or 4 minutes, until the sauce is thick and smooth. Combine this sauce with the meat and all the other ingredients, stirring to combine them completely.

Roll out the pastry and cut 3-inch circles. Put a teaspoonful of the veal mixture on each circle, moisten the edges, fold the circles over, and seal them. Prick the turnovers with a toothpick so that steam can escape, and brush them with a wash made from the egg yolk and water. Bake in a 400° oven for 20 to 25 minutes, or until the turnovers are beautifully browned.

These can be made up to the point of baking, frozen, and then baked the day of your party. Freeze on a cookie sheet. When thoroughly frozen, put them into plastic bags to store.

🐝🐝🐝🐝🐝🐝🐝🐝🐝🐝🐝🐝🐝🐝🐝🐝🐝🐝🐝🐝🐝🐝🐝

50,000 MEATBALLS

During World War II meat was rationed and chefs used all their ingenuity to produce healthful meat dishes that didn't require a side of beef. The great demand for meat was my father's (Carl Andersen's) incentive to create soufflé-type meatballs that made customers line up clear around the corner of Weyburn and Westwood Boulevard during the war. His new meatballs consisted of about 55 percent meat, lots of eggs, onion, and lovely seasonings. The ingredients, and the beating they took, produced a light, delicious meatball that held together, froze beautifully, and could take prolonged heating. The recipe has changed very little over the years. The meatballs were so well received that the Chatam began to sell them to customers for parties at home. Fred Hayman, then manager of the Beverly Hilton (he's now the owner of the glamorous clothing store Giorgio's of Beverly Hills), was one customer who was impressed with the meatballs. He began ordering them by the hundreds, and then the thousands, for the many parties and functions at the Hilton.

Fred Hayman's friendship with my parents, Carl and Caroline, grew, along with his orders, until one day in late June he called and said he needed 50,000 meatballs. That would have been a large order at any time of year, but that day was the day before vacation. (Each year the Chatam closes for the first two weeks of July.) Caroline felt that she had to say yes, but she hardly knew how she would manage.

All the help that could be mustered, including a visiting Danish cousin who'd just flown into town, was pressed into service, and somehow 50,000 meatballs were delivered to the Beverly Hilton.

🐝🐝🐝🐝🐝🐝🐝🐝🐝🐝🐝🐝🐝🐝🐝🐝🐝🐝🐝🐝🐝🐝🐝

Chatam Meatballs

100 meatballs

If you smile at your butcher, he'll grind all three meats together for you—twice!

½ pound ground beef
½ pound ground pork
½ pound ground veal
1 medium onion, cut into eighths
2 tablespoons butter
8 eggs
1 teaspoon salt
¼ teaspoon pepper
1 tablespoon chopped parsley
½ cup bread crumbs
2 tablespoons flour
1 teaspoon chicken base
½ teaspoon ground allspice
¼ teaspoon thyme
½ teaspoon curry powder
1 teaspoon Lea & Perrins Worcestershire sauce
1 teaspoon A-1 sauce

In the work bowl of a food processor, combine all the ingredients and process for 1 or 2 minutes, until the mixture is elastic and will not drop from a spoon. The entire secret of these meatballs is getting the texture right. (A friend of mine says the consistency is like "mushy Silly Putty.")

Now for the hard part. Put on a big pot of water and bring it to a boil. The pot should be wide-mouthed and have at least a 4-quart capacity. Add 1 teaspoon salt to the water and reduce the heat so that the water is barely simmering.

Because of the gooey, elastic nature of the meatball mixture, you cannot roll them in the palms of your hands as with most meatballs. Scoop out a rounded teaspoonful of meat mixture, and with the thumb of the left hand firmly scoop the mixture off the spoon so that the ball rests on the back of the left hand between the first joint of the thumb and the knuckle of the index finger. Now take the empty spoon that's still in your right hand, and with the back of it scrape the meatball into the simmering water. Perhaps I can put it another way. Put your left hand out in front of you; close all the fingers, but keep them out straight. Now bend the fingers slightly toward the palm. Lay your thumb alongside so that the knuckle of your index finger is right next to the first joint of your thumb. Right there is where each meatball should be scooped off.

Once all the meat mixture has been scooped into the water, let the meat-balls simmer for 15 minutes. Pour the meatballs into a colander and drain them. In the largest skillet you have, put 2 tablespoons vegetable oil and 1 tablespoon butter. When the fat is hot, add the meatballs and brown them over high heat, turning them with a spatula every few minutes until they're toasty brown on all sides.

You now have at least 100 wonderful meatballs that you may freeze in plastic-lined bags or plastic containers. If you're going to serve them soon, simply keep them covered in the refrigerator.

When you're ready to serve the meatballs, put 2 tablespoons butter and 2 tablespoons water in a large frying pan and heat the meatballs until they are good and hot. This can be done in a chafing dish, or you may put the meatballs in a covered casserole, add the butter and water, and heat in a 350° oven for 30 minutes, or until piping hot.

To serve them as hors d'oeuvres, all you need are toothpicks. For a main course, add the meatballs to spaghetti sauce, gravy, or a casserole.

Chatam Meatballs freeze wonderfully and always hold together, because of the large number of eggs in them and because they contain no liquid. Though they require the use of a food processor, they are relatively inexpensive, and once you get the knack of forming the balls, they are easy and fun to prepare. My food processor just manages to hold the entire contents of this recipe. With some brands of food processors you might have to run it through in two batches after you have mixed all the ingredients together in a bowl to the best of your ability.

Scandia Meatballs   *about 72 meatballs*

In any profession there are stars. In the field of bartending, Scandia has always possessed some of the brightest. François Mouvet, with his handsome good looks, sparkling eyes, and ready stories (always embellished with his delightful French accent), has been pleasing Scandia customers since the restaurant first operated on the north side of Sunset Boulevard. Ludwig Vigle's charm and warm smile accompany every drink and tidbit. Among the most toothsome tidbits that are offered at the large copper-and-brass bar are Kenneth Hansen's meatballs.

Carl calls Kenneth's meatballs "rich man meatballs" because Kenneth used all the steak ends and trimmings from the marvelous steaks that Scandia serves. Most restaurant kitchens grind their scraps for meatballs, hamburgers, and so on, and the smart cook will do the same. If you trim a roast, or trim the ends off some nice New York strippers, save them. Freeze them in a bag until you have a pound of scraps, and then go to town making your own meatballs. A good cook wastes nothing.

To Kenneth's wonderful recipe and the men who've served them to so many over so many years, I say *Skoal!* and *Mange Tak!*

½ pound ground beef *or* veal
½ pound ground pork
1 egg
½ cup fresh bread crumbs, soaked in ½ cup warm milk
½ cup chopped onion, lightly sautéed in butter
1 teaspoon salt
¼ teaspoon pepper
    Pinch ground allspice
2 tablespoons vegetable oil
2 tablespoons clarified butter
1 tablespoon flour
1 cup broth *or* consommé *or* milk (your choice)

Have the butcher grind the meat twice. Sauté the onion until it is transparent and soak the bread crumbs in milk. Mix all the ingredients in a bowl. Beat with a wooden spoon or an electric mixer until the mixture is smooth and very well combined. Place it in the refrigerator, covered with plastic wrap, for 2 hours.

Shape the meat mixture into balls of the desired size and fry them in the oil and butter until browned on all sides. Drain off all the fat and discard it. Sprinkle the meatballs with flour, shake the pan well, and add the broth. Shake the pan again and simmer the meatballs in the gravy for 3 to 4 minutes. Serve.

If you want to make large meatballs, as opposed to cocktail size, cover the pan and cook the meatballs in their gravy for 10 minutes.

By food processor:
With a food processor you needn't have the butcher grind the meat twice; the machine will do it for you. Sauté the onion and soak the bread crumbs. Put all the ingredients in the bowl of the food processor and turn the machine on and off until the mixture is smooth and of good consistency. Proceed as above.

Note: The best meatballs are made with a combination of meats, but you can use all beef or all pork and still obtain fine results.

Clam Puffs
about 100 puffs

Puffs

> 1 cup clam broth (from the canned minced clams used in the filling)
> ½ cup (1 stick) butter, cut into chunks
> 1 cup flour
> 4 eggs
> 1 egg
> 1 teaspoon water

Heat the clam broth and butter over moderate heat until the butter melts. Add the flour all at once, and stir with a wooden spoon until the mixture clings to itself and comes away from the sides of the pan. Add the 4 eggs one at a time, beating thoroughly after each addition. Drop the dough by the level teaspoonful onto greased cookie sheets. Be sure to keep the puffs small, as they increase greatly while baking. Beat the remaining egg with 1 teaspoon water and brush the puffs with the mixture. Bake in a 400° oven for 15 minutes, lower the heat to 300°, and bake another 15 minutes without opening the door. Cool the puffs and cut them horizontally to insert the filling.

Filling

3 cans minced clams	⅛ teaspoon sugar
6 3-ounce packages chive cream cheese	⅛ teaspoon celery salt
	Pinch paprika
6 dashes Tabasco	2 pinches turmeric
½ teaspoon salt	½ teaspoon chervil

Drain the clams and mix all the ingredients together in a food processor or an electric mixer bowl. Refrigerate until chilled. Fill the puffs and heat them on a cookie sheet in a 350° oven for 15 minutes. Serve.

These puffs can be frozen on a cookie sheet; when they are firm, put them in plastic bags and store for future use. To serve, heat the oven to 400° and place as many puffs as you need on a cookie sheet, directly from the freezer. Put the sheet in the oven and heat for 20 minutes. Allow the puffs to sit for a few moments, then serve.

Hors d'Oeuvre Puffs   *about 100 puffs*

1 cup water
½ cup (1 stick) butter, cut into chunks
1 teaspoon chicken base, *or* 1 bouillon cube
2 teaspoons dehydrated onion (optional)
1 cup flour
4 eggs

Place the water, butter, chicken base, and onion in a saucepan. Heat over moderate heat until the butter has melted. Add the flour all at once and stir with a wooden spoon until the mixture clings to itself and comes away from the sides of the pan. Remove from the heat. Add the eggs one at a time, beating well after each addition. The dough will break into scallops. Continue beating until it goes back together into a stiff, batterlike dough. When all the eggs have been incorporated, spoon the dough onto a lightly greased cookie sheet, about ½ teaspoon for each puff. Be sure to make them small; they puff up to three or four times their uncooked size. They should be large-bite-size when done. Bake the puffs in a 400° oven for 15 minutes, lower the oven temperature to 325°, and bake another 15 minutes, or until they are well puffed and lightly browned. Open the oven door, allow the puffs to sit for 5 minutes, and then remove them from the cookie sheet. Cool and cut horizontally.

Fillings

TURKEY: Process in a food processor until smooth: ½ pound cooked turkey, ¼ pound (1 stick) butter, and 2 tablespoons mayonnaise. And salt and pepper to taste.

HAM: Process in a food processor until smooth: ½ pound cooked ham, ¼ pound (1 stick) butter, 2 tablespoons mayonnaise, ½ teaspoon dry mustard, and ½ teaspoon dill seed (optional).

SHRIMP: Mix in a bowl or food processor: ½ pound cooked small bay shrimp, ¼ cup mayonnaise, 1 teaspoon chopped chives, 2 teaspoons finely minced scallion, 1 tablespoon finely chopped celery, and 1 teaspoon lemon juice. Season to taste with salt and pepper.

OTHER OPTIONS: Make any of the following salads, cutting all ingredients into very fine dice: chicken salad, tuna salad, crab salad, egg salad. A liver pâté also goes well in Hors d'Oeuvre Puffs.

It is a good idea to bake the puffs and slit them for filling ahead of time, but try to fill them as close to serving time as possible.

Bacon and Pickled Watermelon Rind   *about 36 pieces*

1 pound bacon, sliced
1 jar pickled watermelon rind

If the pieces of pickled watermelon rind are larger than 1 inch square, cut them in half. Cut the bacon in half so that the strips are not longer than 5 inches. Wrap a piece of bacon around each piece of pickled watermelon rind and secure with a toothpick through the center; place on a cookie sheet that has a lip. Cook the bacon and watermelon rind in a 350° oven until the bacon is three-quarters done, but not brown and crisp. Pour off all the excess grease, and with a slotted spatula remove the pieces to a smaller baking pan until shortly before serving time.

When ready to serve, heat the bacon and watermelon rind in a 350° oven until heated through and the bacon is done.

These are so easy and so good that they'll disappear before your eyes. Even if you're having a small party, use a whole package of bacon, as these freeze beautifully. Cook them to the three-quarters point, transfer them to a foil package, and pop them into the freezer. When company comes, pop them out of the freezer and into the oven.

Rumaki and other hors d'oeuvres made with bacon are all cooked as described above. Following is a list of some all-time favorite combinations:

LIVER AND BACON: Use a quarter of a chicken liver for each piece of bacon.

WATER CHESTNUTS AND BACON: If large, cut the water chestnuts in half.

BABY GHERKINS AND BACON: Use a ½-inch piece of pickle.

SHRIMP AND BACON: Use 35-count shrimp, cleaned, shelled, and raw.

ONIONS AND BACON: Use cocktail or pearl onions.

GREEN OLIVES AND BACON: Use green olives stuffed with pimiento.

Remember to use half a strip of bacon for each hors d'oeuvre. All of these, *except* the shrimp, onion, and olive, freeze well.

Carl's Cheese Crisps   *100 pieces*

These tempting morsels of cheesy goodness were created and produced in large quantity by my father, Carl Andersen, at the family restaurant for sale as hors d'oeuvres. They freeze beautifully, but Carl finally stopped making them because they are so fragile. We would ask people to be very careful in transporting them home, but invariably someone who didn't understand would pick up the cheese crisps for a party that night and toss them into the backseat of the car. An hour later the irate recipient would be on the phone complaining that we'd sold him a box of broken cheese crisps.

In your own home, if you do break a few when removing them from the cookie sheet, save them. You can crush them completely with a rolling pin and sprinkle them on top of your next cheese-topped dish. Remember, a good cook wastes nothing.

1 pound Cheddar cheese (the sharper the better), shredded
½ pound (2 sticks) butter, softened
⅛ teaspoon cayenne pepper, or less, to taste
2 cups sifted flour

Grate the cheese and allow it to come to room temperature. Have the butter at room temperature as well. Sift the flour and cayenne together. Mix the cheese and butter, add the flour, and work together until well blended.

Form the dough into rolls ¾ inch in diameter. Wrap in waxed paper or foil and freeze.

When you are ready to bake them, remove as many rolls as you need from the freezer and allow them to sit for 15 to 20 minutes. Heat the oven to 400°. Grease cookie sheets lightly. Slice the dough ⅛ inch thick and place the slices on the cookie sheets. Bake 8 to 10 minutes, or until a very delicate shade of brown begins to appear. *Do not overbake.* If the cheese crisps get brown, they will be bitter. It's better to have no tan on them at all than to have them brown.

Carl's Cheese Crisps will stay fresh and lovely for a couple of weeks if stored in a tightly closed tin. They also freeze well and need be taken out of the freezer only moments before serving.

Note: If your cheese crisps tend to fall apart, it's because you didn't blend the ingredients thoroughly enough. Get in there with your hands and make sure the dough is well mixed. It is also imperative that all ingredients be at room temperature.

Sesame Cheese Sticks   *about 150 pieces*

  1½ cups *unsifted* flour
  ½ teaspoon salt
  3 tablespoons sesame seeds
  ½ cup Cheddar cheese (about 3 ounces)
  ½ cup Swiss cheese (about 3½ ounces)
  ½ cup (1 stick) butter
  2 tablespoons water
  6 drops Tabasco
  ½ cup sesame seeds
  ⅓ cup grated Parmesan cheese

By food processor:

In the work bowl fitted with the steel blade, put the flour, salt, and sesame seeds; turn the machine on and off. On top of the flour mixture place the cheeses and butter, cut into 1-inch cubes. Process until the mixture resembles coarse meal. Mix the water and Tabasco together. Start the machine; add the water through the tube and process until the mixture forms a ball. Roll half the dough out on a pastry cloth strewn with sesame seeds. Sprinkle the Parmesan cheese on top of the dough as you roll it out ¼ inch thick. Repeat with the other half of the dough. Cut the dough into long, ½- to ¾-inch strips; cut the strips into 2-inch segments. Bake in a 400° oven on a lightly greased cookie sheet for 8 minutes. *Do not allow them to brown;* a light tan is preferable.

By hand:

Combine the flour, salt, and sesame seeds in a bowl. Cut the butter into the flour mixture with a pastry blender or two knives. Grate the cheeses and add them to the flour mixture. Toss well with two forks. Combine the water and Tabasco. Sprinkle over the dough and work the mixture into a ball with your hands. Follow the rolling and cutting procedures as for the food processor method.

Bean Dip

8 to 12 servings

1 8-ounce package cream cheese, softened
1 can Frito bean dip
20 drops Tabasco
1 8-ounce container sour cream
½ package Laura Scutter taco mix
1 cup chopped scallions
½ cup grated Jack cheese
½ cup grated Cheddar cheese

Mix all the ingredients until well blended. Put the dip in a baking dish or bowl suitable for serving and bake in a 350° oven for 20 minutes, or until the mixture is bubbly. Serve hot with tortilla chips.

This is a truly great bean dip. It's doubtful that you'll have any left over; but if you do, add it to enchiladas, or heat it and spoon it into taco shells before putting in the meat mixture. It's also excellent when added to a can of refried beans. If you're a tostada freak, it's the best bean concoction you've ever spread on a tortilla. *Olé!*

Guacamole

8 to 12 servings

3 avocados, peeled, stones removed
Juice of ½ lemon
2 tablespoons mayonnaise (homemade, Best Foods, or Hellmann's)
8 drops Tabasco
⅛ teaspoon cumin
⅛ teaspoon garlic powder
1 small tomato, peeled, seeded, and chopped
2 tablespoons minced onion
Salt and pepper to taste
1 tablespoon Salsa Verde (optional, see Index)

Put all the ingredients in a blender or food processor and blend until smooth. Serve with tortilla chips, or use in tacos, tostadas, or enchiladas.

Note: It's easier to peel half an avocado than a whole one. It also causes less damage to the fruit. To de-stone an avocado the way the pros do takes a bit of skill but is very simple. Cut the avocado in half lengthwise. Pry the halves apart with the blade of the knife. Holding the half with the stone in your left hand, whack the blade of a large butcher knife into the stone and then flick it out with a twist of the wrist.

SOUPS

Chicken Stock   1½ quarts

Chicken stock is the most versatile ingredient a good cook can have on hand.
Canned broth is available, but fresh is much better. Chicken stock recipes
usually call for one 5-pound chicken, but what you really need is 5 pounds of
chicken. The 5 pounds can be made up of necks, backs, wings, tails, fat,
giblets, extra skin, or the entire skin from a chicken that has been skinned for
another recipe. If you save the unused parts from every chicken you cook,
your freezer will soon contain the 5 pounds you need for that wonderful pot
of stock. If your collection adds up to only 4 pounds, don't panic—4 pounds
will do.

Just as the exact amount and kind of chicken can be varied in the stockpot, so can the vegetables. If you make a salad using celery, cut those lovely
leaves from the top of the stalks and put them in a plastic bag. When you
make your stock a few days later, add the celery tops rather than two good
whole stalks, which can be used to better advantage in dishes that call for
looks and taste. If you sliced onions for homemade hamburgers the other
night and you have some left, add those to the stockpot rather than a whole
new onion. A good stockpot loves all those things you so often discard. A
good stock not only gives you better food and finer sauces, but it helps the
food budget as well.

1 4- or 5-pound chicken, *or* 4 to 5 pounds chicken parts,
  such as necks, backs, wings
2 large carrots, sliced
1 large onion, cut into quarters
6 cracked peppercorns
1½ teaspoons salt
½ teaspoon celery salt
5 sprigs parsley
3½ quarts cold water

Put all the ingredients in a large pot. Bring to a slow boil, and simmer over low heat for 3 hours with the lid slightly ajar. If you are using a whole chicken rather than parts, remove the chicken from the stock after 2½ hours of simmering, but continue to simmer the stock until the 3 hours are up. Strain the stock through a sieve lined with cheesecloth. Pour it into 1-cup containers or ice-cube trays. Either way, cool and freeze. If you make cubes, figure that 1 cube equals 1 tablespoon of stock. Store the cubes in plastic bags. Stock is really very important if you wish your soups, sauces, and stews to be truly excellent in quality and flavor. Use the chicken in Chicken à la King (see Index), chicken salad, or chicken salad vinaigrette. If you wish, you may add one or more of the following to the stockpot: 1 bay leaf, 4 whole cloves, 1 clove garlic, ½ teaspoon leaf thyme, 2 ribs celery (leaves included), or 1 veal knuckle. I keep my stock fairly simple, as I use it in a very wide variety of dishes and I like to add different spices to each.

CRCRCRCRCRCRCRCRCRCRCRCRCRCRCRCR

THE AVOCADO TREE

On my grandmother's homestead there was an enormous avocado tree, which had grown to a height of forty feet or more. A picking device could reach the fruit up to twenty feet, but the most luscious, enormous pears hung some thirty feet off the ground.

My Great-Uncle Charlie came by on a day when a good many of the family were trying to figure a way to get those top prime avocados. He was my grandmother's brother, and we children were scared to death of him because of his raging voice and alcoholic gusto.

"No trouble at all," bellowed Charlie as he started to climb the tree.

Grandmom tried to talk her brother out of such insanity, as did the others, but up he went. Finally, with the grace of a trapeze artist, he reached the last strong branch which jutted out from the main trunk some twenty-five feet above the ground.

"Be careful!" "Don't do it, Charlie!" "Don't go out there, Charlie—there's nothing to hang onto!"

Everyone watched bug-eyed as Uncle Charlie casually balanced himself on the limb and tried to pick a big, beautiful avocado. But it was higher than he thought. He teetered and swayed—and then, to the accompaniment of female screams, fell off, sailing through the air with arms and legs outstretched as though he were lying on a bed.

Even before we heard the horrid thud of his landing, my grandmother had fainted. My mother or one of my aunts clapped a hand over my eyes and whisked me to the house, for they, like my grandmother, were sure that Uncle Charlie was dead.

(He wasn't.) Uncle Charlie survived and Grandmother revived. But we never did get those top avocados.

You needn't climb out on a limb in order to get great avocados. Supermarkets all over the United States carry them for a price.

P.S. If you have an abundance of avocados, mash the flesh, add 1 teaspoon lemon juice per avocado, pack into glass or plastic containers along with a stone from one of the avocados, and freeze— great for guacamole, avocado soup, or salad dressings.

CRCRCRCRCRCRCRCRCRCRCRCRCRCRCRCR

Avocado Soup   6 servings

3 tomatoes
2 tablespoons butter
1 medium onion, chopped
½ teaspoon salt
¼ teaspoon pepper
¼ teaspoon cumin
1 tablespoon flour
2½ cups chicken stock
1 tablespoon chopped parsley
2 large or 4 small avocados
⅔ cup half-and-half *or* light cream

Pour boiling water over the tomatoes; let them sit for 2 minutes, then peel, seed, and chop them. Melt the butter in a skillet and sauté the onion until transparent. Add the chopped tomatoes and simmer for 5 minutes. While the tomato-onion mixture is simmering, add the salt, pepper, and cumin. Sprinkle the flour over the mixture and blend it in well. Then slowly add the chicken stock, stirring until smooth. Add the parsley and simmer for 5 minutes. (If you wish, all this can be done ahead of time.) Allow the soup base to simmer while you peel and mash the avocados with the half-and-half. (A blender or food processor works the two into a wonderfully smooth concoction.) Add the avocado mixture to the simmering soup stock and heat it just to the boiling point. Serve in hot bowls and top with crumbled tortilla chips if you wish. I like the chunkiness of the onion and tomatoes; but if you wish a totally smooth consistency, run the soup stock through a food processor or blender and then add the avocados. Either way, this is a truly delicious soup.

As a main course, this recipe serves 2.

Oyster Stew   1 serving

Oyster stew is heartwarming and soul-satisfying. It requires two main ingredients: first, a love of oysters; and second, low heat. Since oyster stew is not something you make for a party (since you have to know your customers' tastes), I'm giving you the recipe for just one order—you may double it or triple it.

Oyster stew is often concocted by an oyster lover just for himself; he hovers over the pot, watching for the exact moment when the oysters begin to curl at the edges. The minute he sees those edges begin to curl, in go the milk and cream; and then, with the care of a master brewer, he adds the seasonings—tasting for salt and sprinkling in just the right amount of cayenne.

If the oysters are very large, you might like to remove them from the stew after the addition of milk and cream and cut them into bite-sized pieces. Return them immediately to the pot and continue the slow cooking process.

Some people like a dash of Worcestershire sauce in their oyster stew; others like finely minced onions or leeks, which they permit to sauté gently in butter before adding the oysters.

Oyster stew is a special dish, and as an oyster lover you owe it to yourself to fix it to your personal satisfaction. Get out the oyster crackers, put your steaming oyster stew into a hot soup bowl, and enter heaven.

If you use canned oysters or oysters out of a jar, check the liquid—if it's clear, you're OK; if the liquid is cloudy or murky, *don't use it.*

> 2 tablespoons butter
> 3 to 7 oysters and their liquid, depending on size (Pacific oysters are very large)
> ½ cup milk
> ½ cup light cream
> 1 good twist of the pepper mill
> Salt to taste
> Pinch celery salt
> Pinch cayenne (a good pinch, please)
> 1 teaspoon chopped parsley (optional)
> 1 tablespoon sherry (optional)

Over very low heat, melt the butter in a saucepan. Add the oysters and their liquid and gently turn them in the butter, watching closely. When the edges of the oysters begin to curl and get ruffled, add the milk and cream. Gently stir, and add all the other ingredients as the stew slowly heats to the boiling point. *Do not let it boil,* however; the oysters don't like it!

New England Clam Chowder   6 *servings*

The first recipe below is the one I like best for New England clam chowder. It is not thickened, and its consistency is that of an oyster stew. The second is thickened in the traditional manner. I have written these recipes for those who do not live by the sea. I find it very disconcerting to look into a fine cookbook only to be told that I'll need "12 fresh chowder clams or quahogs"! The recipes here are for landlubbers who do not have access to fresh clams.

Both versions will serve 3 or 4 as a main course, 6 as a starter.

Chowder I

3 tablespoons butter
1 onion, not over ½ pound
2 potatoes, not over 1 pound
½ teaspoon salt
¼ teaspoon coarsely ground pepper
1 8-ounce bottle clam juice
½ cup water, or enough to cover vegetables
1 8-ounce can minced clams, plus liquid
1 cup half-and-half
1 teaspoon finely chopped parsley (fresh or dried)
Tiny pinch each leaf thyme and leaf oregano
Dash celery salt

Melt the butter over low heat in a soup pot or large saucepan. Chop the onion and peel and dice the potatoes. Add the vegetables to the pot along with the salt and pepper. Cover and simmer over low heat for 5 minutes. Do not allow the vegetables to take on color. Add the clam juice (don't forget to shake the bottle) and enough water to cover the vegetables thoroughly. Cover and simmer for 15 minutes, or until the potatoes test done. Add all the other ingredients and heat for 4 to 5 minutes, but do not allow the chowder to boil. Test for salt, correct if necessary, and serve in warm soup bowls.

As with most soups, this is even better the second day. If you have a large family, or simply love chowder, you may double this recipe, but do not double the amount of potatoes; instead use 3 potatoes, not to exceed 1½ pounds.

Chowder II

3 tablespoons butter
1 onion, not over ½ pound
2 potatoes, not over 1 pound
¼ teaspoon coarsely ground pepper
1 8-ounce bottle clam broth
½ cup water, or enough to cover vegetables
2 tablespoons butter
3 tablespoons flour
1 cup half-and-half

1 8-ounce can minced clams, plus liquid
1 teaspoon finely chopped parsley
   Pinch each leaf thyme and leaf oregano
¼ teaspoon celery salt
   Salt to taste

Melt the butter in a soup pot or large saucepan. Chop the onion and peel and dice the potatoes. Add the vegetables to the pot along with the pepper. Cover and simmer over low heat for 5 minutes. The vegetables should not brown. Add the clam juice and water to cover. Cover and simmer 15 minutes, or until the potatoes test done. While the vegetables simmer, make a *roux* in a small saucepan by melting the 2 tablespoons butter, then adding the 3 tablespoons flour. Stir the *roux* with a wire whip over a moderate flame for 2 minutes. Slowly add the light cream and whisk until the mixture is thick and smooth. (If you don't have a wire whip, heat the cream to just below the boiling point and then stir it into the *roux*.) Cook the sauce for 3 minutes, then add the clams, their broth, and the seasonings. Add the thickened sauce to the onion-potato mixture and stir until well combined. Taste for salt and correct if necessary. Heat to the boiling point and serve.

If you finish the preparation of the soup and find it too thick, add more cream, water, or clam broth and correct the seasonings accordingly.

Many times a professional chef has told me, "Oh, just add a pinch of this or a pinch of that," when they really meant ½ teaspoon. In these recipes I *do* mean a pinch. You should not be able to distinguish either the thyme or the oregano. All the ingredients should blend into one lovely flavor that bespeaks clam.

Don't forget the crackers!

Potato and Leek Soup
12 servings

3 medium leeks, white part only
1 medium onion
2 pounds (about 4 large) potatoes
8 cups stock *or* water mixed with 2 teaspoons chicken base
1 teaspoon salt
¼ teaspoon pepper
¼ teaspoon celery salt
3 tablespoons butter *or* animal fat
1 cup light cream

Wash, pare, and slice all the vegetables. Melt the butter in a soup pot. Add the leeks and onion. Simmer over low heat until the onion is transparent. Add all the other ingredients and simmer until the vegetables are very soft.

Put the soup through a strainer or puree it in a blender. (I prefer the blender method; it's easier and you get more soup.) Add the cream and taste for seasoning. Add salt and pepper as needed. Heat almost to the boiling point, but do not allow it to boil. Serve in hot soup bowls, plain or topped with chopped chives, parsley, or watercress or a combination of all three.

Vichyssoise   *12 servings*

Use the same ingredients as for Potato and Leek Soup, but delete the butter. Simply put the vegetables, seasonings, and stock in a pot and cook till very soft. Put the soup in a blender, process, and strain. The Vichyssoise should be very smooth. Correct for seasonings and add light cream. Chill thoroughly. Serve topped with chopped chives or watercress in chilled bowls.

Fresh Mushroom Soup   *10 to 12 servings*

1 pound mushrooms *or* mushroom stems
3 tablespoons butter
2 teaspoons lemon juice
⅓ cup white wine
3 tablespoons butter
1 small onion, chopped fine
3 tablespoons flour
1 quart chicken stock, *or* 1 quart water mixed with 2 teaspoons chicken base
1 cup milk
¼ teaspoon pepper
1 tablespoon chopped parsley
2 good pinches cayenne
Salt to taste
2 tablespoons brandy *or* sherry

Wash the mushrooms or stems and slice them thin. If you are using large mushrooms, cut them in half; put the cut sides down and slice them thin. Melt the butter in large frying pan, add the mushrooms, turn the heat to high, and add the lemon juice. Stir the mushrooms over high heat until they just begin to take on color. Add the wine and cook over high heat for 5 minutes. Set aside. Melt 3 tablespoons butter in a large saucepan. Add the onion and cook over medium heat for 3 minutes, or until the onion is transparent. Do not let it brown. Stir in the flour and cook another 2 minutes. Slowly add the stock or water, and stir with each addition until smooth. Add the milk, pepper, parsley, cayenne, and salt (if needed). Simmer the soup stock over low heat for 15 minutes. Put the mushrooms and all their liquid in the soup pot in which you plan to finish the soup. Strain the hot soup stock into the mushroom mixture. Discard the onion and parsley left in the sieve. When you are ready to serve the soup, heat to a simmer; add the brandy and simmer for 5 minutes.

The Chatam restaurant makes a thicker mushroom soup than I do. They use sherry, which is delicious but pronounced in flavor. I prefer brandy, which disperses into the soup, leaving nothing but a hint of richness behind. So if you like a thicker soup, use 4 or 5 tablespoons flour instead of 3; and if you love sherry, substitute it for the brandy. Either way, it's good as a first course with a glass of Dry Sack or your own favorite dry sherry.

Cream of Spinach Soup   *4 to 6 servings*

½ to 1 cup chopped cooked spinach
2½ cups spinach liquid
3 tablespoons butter
2½ tablespoons flour
Salt, if needed
½ teaspoon chicken base
¾ cup light cream *or* milk
Water, if needed

Chop the freshly cooked or leftover spinach. Measure the liquid and heat. Melt the butter, add the flour, and stir over medium heat for 2 minutes. Add the broth and stir with a wire whip until very smooth. Add the spinach, chicken base, and salt if needed. Simmer for 3 to 4 minutes, lower the heat, add the cream, and stir to combine. Taste again for seasoning. If the soup tastes strong, add ½ cup water, heat, and taste again. Do not allow the soup to boil once the cream has been added. Serve in hot soup bowls.

This recipe may easily be doubled and is delicious made with broccoli in place of the spinach. As a main course, these quantities will serve 2.

🐊🐊🐊🐊🐊🐊🐊🐊🐊🐊🐊🐊🐊🐊🐊🐊🐊🐊🐊🐊🐊🐊🐊

HEADS UP–TIPS DOWN

A large group of dignitaries were guests at a festive party given at the Kongelige Skydebane in Copenhagen, Denmark. The year was 1921. It was springtime, and asparagus was in season. The chefs of the royal kitchens cooked the lovely spears to perfection and piled them onto silver platters in pyramid fashion. Each pyramid contained forty or more spears.

A waiter approached a table with a fresh platter of asparagus, and the first guest he offered it to picked up his knife and cut the tips from every spear on the platter. Then, with a deft hand, he scooped the severed tips onto his plate.

The gentleman next to him protested, saying that other people were also fond of the tips. "Not as much as I," replied the uncouth guest. The poor waiter had to return with his headless stalks to a kitchen full of scolding chefs.

Should you ever have such a total clod at your table, don't weep in your wine, smile into your soup–Cream of Asparagus, of course.

🐊🐊🐊🐊🐊🐊🐊🐊🐊🐊🐊🐊🐊🐊🐊🐊🐊🐊🐊🐊🐊🐊🐊

Cream of Asparagus Soup
2 to 4 servings

4 tablespoons (½ stick) butter
6 tablespoons flour
5 cups asparagus broth (from dinner the night before)
¼ teaspoon pepper
⅛ teaspoon celery salt
⅛ teaspoon onion salt
1 teaspoon chicken base
1 cup (at least) leftover asparagus, cut into ½-inch pieces
1 cup half-and-half

Melt the butter in a small soup pot. Add the flour, and cook the *roux* over moderate heat for 2 minutes, stirring. Do not allow the *roux* to brown. In the meantime heat the asparagus broth. Slowly add the broth to the *roux*, whisking with a wire whip all the while. Add the seasonings and simmer the soup stock for 10 minutes. Lower the heat and add the asparagus and half-and-half. Blend well and taste for seasonings. Add salt if needed. Heat well, but do not boil. Serve in hot soup plates.

During some lean days of the past, we made a delicious meal out of nothing but this soup served with a hot loaf of homemade bread. It's soul-satisfying.

Note: If your asparagus broth doesn't come to 5 cups, make up the difference with chicken broth and use less chicken base.

Split-Pea Soup
8 to 12 servings

1 piece (about 3 or 4 ounces) salt pork
1 large onion
2 large carrots
2 tablespoons butter
2 cups dried split peas
1 teaspoon salt
¼ teaspoon cracked pepper
¼ teaspoon celery salt
2½ quarts cold water
4 sprigs parsley, chopped fine
½ bay leaf (optional)
¼ teaspoon thyme (optional)

Cut the salt pork into julienne strips. Peel the onion and chop it fine. Peel the carrots and set aside. Melt the butter in a large pot, add the salt pork, and cook over medium heat for 2 minutes. Add the onion and sauté the salt pork and onion for another 3 minutes, stirring often. Rinse the peas in a colander. Discard any that are discolored. Add the peas, carrots, and all the other ingredients to the pot and bring to a boil. Lower the heat and simmer for 2 to 3 hours, or until the peas are cooked through. Stir the soup as it cooks; split peas tend to stick to the bottom of the pot. When the peas are done, remove the carrots and slice them, then return them to the pot. Check for seasoning and serve in hot soup bowls.

If your Split-Pea Soup is going to be the main course, or if you like a good, hearty soup, add leftover ham, or franks that have been cut into thin slices. If you're not a pork eater, omit the salt pork and simply sauté the onion in butter. Later, add leftover corned beef or boiled tongue cut into julienne strips. Once Split-Pea Soup is done, it can continue to simmer until you have added all the goodies you wish. A large potato cut into small cubes helps to make this a hearty one-course meal. The potato should be added 30 minutes before the soup is done.

Garlic croutons go well on top of Split-Pea Soup. A little sherry added during the last few minutes of cooking gives this soup a continental flair, and a dollop of sour cream or yogurt added to each bowl is sheer heaven. Enjoy.

SALADS AND DRESSINGS

Caesar Salad Dressing   1 quart

Carl Andersen's Chatam restaurant serves Red Pepper Jam with their Danish open-face cold duck sandwich and their Danish open-face salmon sandwich. (Both are superb!) Many years ago Carl got the recipe for Red Pepper Jam from a friend whose family always made it for the holidays. When our produce man, Mr. Yamato, said that the man who grew them claimed it was impossible to make jam from red peppers, my father told Mr. Yamato to tell the farmer to stick to his farming and he would stick to his jamming.

My father's friend Kenneth Hansen, of Scandia restaurant, had a remarkable premixed Caesar Salad Dressing recipe, which he got about the time we got the Red Pepper Jam recipe. One evening after a delightful meal, the two men decided on a swap: Red Pepper Jam for Caesar Salad Dressing. The Red Pepper Jam comes to you exact (see Index); I've adapted the Caesar dressing since Carl changed it once he got hold of it, and since both the original and Carl's revision make well over a gallon!

If you have a blender or food processor, make Caesar Dressing I; if you don't, make Caesar Dressing II.

Caesar Dressing I

    2 eggs
    ⅓ cup red wine vinegar
    ⅓ cup lemon juice
    2 cups vegetable oil
    ¼ cup catsup, Heinz preferred
    1½ tablespoons A-1 sauce
    1½ tablespoons Lea & Perrins Worcestershire sauce
    ½ teaspoon Tabasco

½ teaspoon Accent
1 teaspoon cracked pepper
2 teaspoons salt
2½ teaspoons garlic powder
3 or 4 anchovy fillets, *or* 2 teaspoons anchovy paste

Put the eggs, vinegar, and lemon juice in a blender or food processor. Start the machine, and slowly add the oil in a thin stream. Add all the other ingredients; unless you have them right by the machine, turn the machine off while you add the spices. Blend until thoroughly combined and smooth. The dressing should have the consistency of thin mayonnaise or very thick cream. Allow the dressing to chill at least 2 hours.

Caesar Dressing II

2⅔ cups mayonnaise (homemade, Best Foods, or Hellmann's)
¼ cup lemon juice
⅓ cup red wine vinegar
¼ cup catsup, Heinz preferred
1½ tablespoons A-1 sauce
1½ tablespoons Lea & Perrins Worcestershire sauce
½ teaspoon Tabasco
½ teaspoon Accent
1 teaspoon cracked pepper
2 teaspoons salt
2½ teaspoons garlic powder
3 or 4 anchovy fillets, *or* 2 teaspoons anchovy paste

Put all the ingredients in a bowl and beat until thoroughly combined and smooth. Chill at least 2 hours before using.

Both dressings will keep up to two weeks in a glass container in the refrigerator.

Caesar Salad

4 servings as a side dish, 2 as a main course

2 or 3 quarts (1 large or 2 medium heads) romaine lettuce, washed, drained, and torn into large salad-size pieces

1 cup Caesar Salad Dressing I or II (preceding recipes)
½ cup (at least) grated Parmesan cheese
1 to 1½ cups croutons, your choice (following recipe)

Mix all the ingredients thoroughly and pile the salad on chilled plates. Be sure that the lettuce is very cold and fresh.

Croutons

½ cup (1 stick) butter
2 or 3 garlic cloves
Sourdough French Bread (see Index)

Mash the garlic cloves and mix with the butter to form a smooth paste. Spread the garlic butter on both sides of Sourdough French Bread slices. Stack the slices, trim the crusts, and cut the bread into cubes. Spread the cubes on a cookie sheet and bake in a 400° oven until brown. Stir and check the croutons every few minutes so as to brown all sides and assure distribution of the butter.

These croutons will keep, stored in an airtight container, for a month.

Right "On Salad" Dressing   *8 servings*

This is a very difficult recipe to put on paper, but quite an easy recipe to make. Creating a dressing directly on salad greens produces an exceptional salad with fewer calories and no leftover dressing to sit in the refrigerator. If you get up the courage to try this recipe once, you may never buy bottled dressing again. Please note how little oil is used for this very large salad.

The recipe can be cut in half. The hard part lies in the fact that except for the vinegar and oil, all the amounts for the seasonings are *approximate*. Each seasoning must be sprinkled over the greens in the same fashion and in the same amounts as you'd sprinkle salt. For a large bowl of salad greens the amounts are accurate, but you must learn to gauge as you sprinkle. But take heart: I've never known anyone to fail at this, and you can always add more seasonings after you've tossed the salad.

4 quarts lettuce (about 1 large head), washed, drained, and torn into pieces
2 tomatoes, peeled and diced
½ cup chopped scallions
1 tablespoon chopped parsley

1 or 2 avocados, diced
1 cup sliced celery
1 sliced cucumber
¼ cup sliced radishes (optional)
   Juice of ½ lemon
¼ teaspoon salt
¼ teaspoon coarsely ground pepper
¼ teaspoon celery salt
⅛ teaspoon garlic powder
½ teaspoon sugar
½ teaspoon or up to 1 full teaspoon dry mustard
2 tablespoons red wine vinegar
¼ cup vegetable oil

Put all the ingredients into a large salad bowl in the exact order given. Toss thoroughly and completely. If you wish a creamy dressing, add 2 tablespoons mayonnaise. After tossing, correct for salt if need be. There should be no dressing in the bottom of the bowl, and each particle of salad should be well coated. This is truly a salad worth mastering.

Vinaigrette Dressing   *1 quart*

This dressing is used at Carl Andersen's Chatam restaurant on all vinaigrette dishes, including mushrooms, asparagus, and tuna.

1 cup white vinegar
1 tablespoon salt
¼ teaspoon pepper
1 tablespoon Colman's dry mustard
1 teaspoon Accent or MSG (optional)
1½ teaspoons chopped fresh tarragon leaves
1 teaspoon garlic powder
1 tablespoon Worcestershire sauce
1 tablespoon capers
1½ tablespoons chopped chives
1½ tablespoons chopped parsley
1 teaspoon sugar
2 to 3 cups mayonnaise (homemade, Best Foods, or Hellmann's)

Put all the ingredients, except the mayonnaise, into a blender jar in the exact order given. Blend; add 1 cup mayonnaise; blend again; then add the last 1 or 2 cups mayonnaise and blend again.

Mushrooms Vinaigrette   *4 servings*

    1 pound *fresh* mushrooms
    1 cup Vinaigrette Dressing (preceding recipe)
    1 head lettuce
    4 lemon wedges

Be sure the mushrooms are very fresh with tightly closed bottoms. Wipe them with a clean damp cloth. Trim the ends. Slice the mushrooms ¼ inch thick, or thinner if you prefer. Put a layer of large lettuce leaves on four dinnerplates. Pile a cupful of shredded head lettuce in the center of each lettuce bed. Toss the mushrooms with the Vinaigrette Dressing and divide them among the four plates, piling the mushrooms on top of the shredded lettuce. Garnish each plate with a wedge of lemon.

Fresh Asparagus Vinaigrette   *6 servings*

    4 pounds *fresh* asparagus
    1½ cups Vinaigrette Dressing (see Index)
    1 head lettuce
    2 tomatoes, peeled and cut into sixths
    6 lemon wedges

Wash the asparagus. Snap off the tough ends and lay the asparagus in a large frying pan (*not* cast-iron or aluminum). Cover with water, add ¼ teaspoon salt, and bring to a rapid boil. Lower the heat slightly and cook at a slow boil until the color of the asparagus intensifies. Take out one stalk and test for doneness. The asparagus should still have some crispness to it. Don't cook the asparagus past its brightest color. When the asparagus is done, immediately run cold water over it until it is cool to the touch. Drain and chill.

Put one or two large lettuce leaves on six dinner plates. Shred the rest of the head of lettuce and divide it among the six plates. Divide the asparagus into six equal portions and lay the stalks on top of the shredded lettuce. Nap the center of the stalks generously with Vinaigrette Dressing. Garnish the plate with two tomato wedges and a lemon wedge.

Note: If you are serving Fresh Asparagus Vinaigrette as a main luncheon course or a light Sunday supper, top the dressing with a large sliced *fresh* mushroom and add a hard-boiled egg, cut in half, to each plate. Serve with rolls or bread and butter, then pass more dressing.

Celery Vinaigrette

6 servings

Cook celery hearts, quartered, or long thin strips of celery, as described for Celery Sauté (see Index), but omit the butter. When the celery is barely done, blanch it with cold water to stop all cooking action. Drain well and chill. Serve on a bed of shredded lettuce topped with the vinaigrette dressing of your choice. Garnish the plate with tomato wedges and a *fresh* raw mushroom, sliced and layered across the top of the celery.

GREAT-GRANDPA

My sparkling-eyed great-grandfather was French, from Alsace-Lorraine. Charles Yucker was his name. He came to southern California long before the postwar population boom, freeways, and smog and purchased a piece of land in the middle of a bean field. The closest road was called Wilshire Boulevard; the closest town, Los Angeles.

Great-Grandpa made his own wine. He raised deep purple Concord grapes and also bought from others. In late summer he filled the big Ford touring car with gas and a few grandchildren and took off for the San Fernando Valley by way of Beverly Glen. It was a long and beautiful drive through the hills and down into the vineyard-filled valley. Each one had lugs of grapes for sale, and Great-Grandpa would stop at each and every stand, taste the grapes offered, and either buy or drive on. Toward late afternoon the touring car would be piled high with red and white grapes. When the last purchase had been made, a large tarp would be thrown over all and the grandchildren would climb gingerly on top for the long journey home.

They say Charles Yucker made some very fine wines. I wish I'd been around in his wine-producing days, but I was only five years old when he died.

My great-grandmother, Caroline Yucker, was a great cook but extremely fastidious. She insisted that her only daughter (herself a mother of seven) scrub the stairs leading up to her apartment every day, and she refused to let her husband, Charles, bring the smelly cheeses he so loved into the house. So Charles would take a jar of wine and go into his workshop that was on the east side of the three-car garage, and there, in the cool shadows, he'd reach up to a high support and take down a second jar containing his beloved Limburger.

If Caroline Yucker had had a refrigerator rather than an old ice-box, and if there had been such things as foil and plastic wrap, perhaps she could have permitted Charles to drink his wine and eat his cheese in the comfort of his own home. But maybe that would have ruined everything. Perhaps those quiet moments in the coolness of his workroom were some of his best moments. He could sit back on an old chair he'd fixed with wire, drink his wine, and eat his cheese—all without hindrance from his loving wife.

Chatam Roquefort Dressing

1⅓ quarts

1 pint (2 cups) sour cream
1 pint mayonnaise (homemade, Best Foods, or
  Hellmann's)
1 cup garlic oil (see Note)
1 teaspoon salt
½ pound Roquefort or blue cheese

Blend all the ingredients except the Roquefort until smooth. Crumble the cheese and stir it into the dressing. Refrigerate.

This dressing is also great as a dip for raw vegetables.

Note: To make the garlic oil, crush 2 or 3 cloves of garlic and put them in a clean quart jar; fill with vegetable oil, cap, and store for at least a week. The oil is delicious for a dressing created directly on salad greens or for any dressing that calls for oil.

French Dressing

1 cup

⅔ cup vegetable oil
⅓ cup red wine vinegar
1 teaspoon salt
1 teaspoon sugar
½ teaspoon dry mustard
¼ teaspoon cracked pepper
1 clove garlic, minced

Mix all the ingredients together and allow them to sit for at least 2 hours. Strain to remove the garlic. You can omit the garlic clove if you use garlic oil (see the note after Chatam Roquefort Dressing).

Mayonnaise

1½ cups

There is no excuse for not having *real,* delicious, homemade mayonnaise in this day and age of blenders and food processors. I have never known this recipe to fail. You can use the oil of your choice (I prefer a bland vegetable oil) and the vinegar of your choice. You can even use all vinegar and no lemon juice, or all lemon juice and no vinegar. If you're going to use the mayonnaise with herbs, use an herb vinegar.

1 egg
½ teaspoon dry mustard
½ teaspoon salt
1 tablespoon cider vinegar
1 tablespoon lemon juice
1 cup vegetable oil

In the container of a blender or food processor place the egg, mustard, salt, vinegar, lemon juice, and ¼ cup of the oil. Cover the container and start machine (use low speed if using a blender). As soon as the machine has started, add the rest of the oil in a slow, fine stream; *do not* dump it in all at once. When all the oil has been added, stop the machine. The mayonnaise should be of the proper consistency. If it won't hold its shape, run the machine a few seconds longer until the mayonnaise has thickened.

Russian Dressing   *1 cup*

1 cup mayonnaise (homemade, Best Foods, or
    Hellmann's)
¼ cup chili sauce, the best you can buy

Blend and use. I know it sounds too simple to be true, but forty years of happy eaters can't be all wrong!

Bean Salad—Chatam   *16 servings (2 quarts)*

2 cups (1 can) dark red kidney beans
2 cups (1 can) cut green beans
2 cups (1 can) garbanzo beans
1 medium onion, chopped
1 cup finely julienned ham
¼ teaspoon salt
¼ teaspoon freshly ground pepper
¼ teaspoon dry mustard
⅓ cup vegetable oil
3 tablespoons red wine vinegar

Place all the beans in a colander and rinse very lightly with cold running water. Drain well. Place the beans in a bowl, top with all the other ingredients, and toss well to combine. Chill thoroughly.

Lentil Salad—Scandia

12 to 16 servings

> 1 pound dried lentils
> 4 ounces salt pork, cut into thin slices
> 1 large onion studded with 10 cloves
> 1 teaspoon salt
> 1 bay leaf
> 2 ribs celery
> 1 carrot
> 1 medium onion, chopped
> 12 scallions, chopped
> 1 cup julienned ham, *or* hot dog, *or* sausage, *or* tongue, *or* corned beef
> ¼ teaspoon salt, or to taste
> ¼ teaspoon freshly ground pepper
> ¼ cup vegetable oil
> 2 tablespoons red wine vinegar
> ¼ cup chopped parsley

Wash the lentils and soak them in cold water overnight. In the morning wash them again and cover with cold water at least 3 inches above the lentils. Add the salt pork, onion with cloves, salt, bay leaf, celery, and carrot. Bring to a boil, cover, lower heat, and simmer until the lentils are just tender, but not mushy. This usually takes up to 1½ hours, but start checking the lentils after 1 hour has elapsed. Remove the pot from the stove and allow the lentils to stand in their broth for 2 or more hours, or even overnight. Drain, discard the onion, vegetables, and salt pork, and rinse lightly under cold running water. Drain until dry. Place the lentils in a bowl and add the onion, scallions, meat, and seasonings. Toss lightly but completely, taste for seasoning, chill completely and serve.

Cucumber Salad

12 servings

> 6 firm cucumbers
> Salt
> ⅔ cup white vinegar
> ½ cup sugar, or enough to sweeten
> 1 tablespoon chopped fresh parsley
> ¼ teaspoon cracked pepper
> ¼ cup very thinly sliced red onion

Peel and slice the cucumbers thin. Layer the cucumbers in a bowl, and salt each and every layer. Put a plate on top of the cucumbers and a weight (such as a heavy can) on top of the plate. Refrigerate for a minimum of 5 hours or overnight. After the crisping time has elapsed, fill the bowl with cold water and swirl the cucumbers in the water, lightly rinsing off the salt. Drain well.

Stir the sugar into the vinegar until it is dissolved. Taste—it should be somewhat sweet and not have too much bite. If needed, add more sugar and stir until dissolved. Pour the vinegar-sugar mixture over the drained cucumbers, add the parsley, pepper, and onion, and refrigerate the salad for at least 2 hours.

This is truly a delicious salad and will keep in a covered glass container for days. It's great with duck, pork, cold cuts, barbecue, or just about any other meal.

Lorraine's Zucchini Salad   *16 to 20 servings*

1 tablespoon dehydrated onion
½ cup red wine vinegar
¾ cup white sugar
⅔ cup cider vinegar
½ teaspoon salt
½ teaspoon coarsely ground pepper
½ cup vegetable oil
1 cup diced green pepper
1 cup thinly sliced celery
8 slim zucchini, thinly sliced

Soak the onion in the red wine vinegar while you cut the vegetables and combine the sugar, cider vinegar, salt, pepper, and oil. Pour the onion mixture and the dressing over the vegetables and stir to coat them thoroughly. Refrigerate for a minimum of 24 hours.

This lovely marinated salad keeps well and is a delicious, crisp, and nutritious addition to any meal. Sometimes I substitute ½ cup thinly sliced red onion for the dehydrated onion and slice the green pepper in small julienne strips. Two tablespoons chopped parsley added just before serving is also excellent.

If you plan to make this salad for a small family, cut the recipe in half.

Celery Root Salad   6 to 8 servings

1 large celery root
1 tablespoon salt
2 tablespoons minced fresh parsley
Coarsely ground pepper
¼ cup white vinegar
2 tablespoons vegetable oil
2 tablespoons sugar

Rinse the celery root, put it in a pot, and cover it with cold water. Add 1 tablespoon salt and bring to a boil. Lower the heat, cover, and cook the celery root until tender. Drain and cool it. Cut away all the outer skin of the celery root until you have a peeled, light gray globe. Cut the root in half top to bottom, then each half top to bottom. Slice each quarter into ½-inch pieces and put them in bowl. Add the parsley and pepper to taste. Combine the other ingredients in a small bowl and stir until the sugar has dissolved. Pour the dressing over the celery root and toss thoroughly. Chill.

A small amount of red onion, sliced paper-thin, may be added for color and zest.

Red Tomatoes—Red Onions   6 servings

This is the quickest, prettiest, simplest, tastiest salad I know of. If you move very slowly, it may take you a maximum of 5 minutes to make.

3 medium-large tomatoes
1 medium red onion, preferably the same size as the tomatoes
Salt
Coarsely ground pepper
2 tablespoons vegetable oil
3 tablespoons red wine vinegar

Slice the tomatoes and onion. Make the onion slices half the width of the tomato slices. Alternate tomato slices with onion slices and arrange in overlapping layers in a white porcelain bowl or platter, or layer them on individual salad plates adorned with lettuce leaves. Sprinkle the tomatoes and onions with salt and pepper. Sprinkle with oil and then with vinegar. Chill and serve.

This salad is wonderful with fish, chicken, or beef, and it is particularly good with big broiled hamburger steaks.

Spinach Salad
8 servings

10 ounces fresh spinach
1 bunch fresh watercress (optional)
2 tablespoons chopped parsley
6 scallions, chopped
2 hard-boiled eggs, sliced
4 large mushrooms, thinly sliced
6 slices bacon, fried crisp and crumbled
¼ teaspoon salt
⅛ teaspoon celery salt
¼ teaspoon cracked pepper
⅛ teaspoon garlic powder
½ teaspoon dry mustard
½ teaspoon sugar
3 tablespoons red wine vinegar
1 tablespoon lemon juice
⅓ cup vegetable oil

Wash, trim, and fix the salad greens for the bowl. If the spinach leaves are large, tear them into edible-size pieces. Put the salad greens, eggs, mushrooms, and bacon in a large salad bowl. Sprinkle the seasonings over all, followed by vinegar, lemon juice, and oil. Toss *very* thoroughly and serve immediately.

This is such a delightful-tasting salad that it makes a superb meal when accompanied with good bread or hot rolls. As a main course it serves 4.

Sour Cream Coleslaw
12 or more servings

1 medium-size head cabbage
1 cup sour cream
2 tablespoons mayonnaise (homemade, Best Foods, or Hellmann's)
2 tablespoons sugar
1½ tablespoons cider vinegar
½ teaspoon salt, or to taste
¼ teaspoon coarsely ground pepper

Shred the cabbage. Mix all the other ingredients until totally combined. Mix the dressing thoroughly with the cabbage and chill. If you have a food processor, shred the cabbage with the slicing blade, turn the cabbage into a bowl, fit the processor with the steel or plastic blade, and blend the dressing ingredients. In less than 5 minutes you'll have delicious slaw.

Chatam Coleslaw
12 or more servings

1 head cabbage, shredded
1 tablespoon plus 1 teaspoon salt
¼ cup plus 1 tablespoon sugar
¾ cup white vinegar
2 tablespoons vegetable oil

Shred the cabbage into a bowl, sprinkle the salt and sugar over the top, and pour the vinegar and oil over all. Allow to stand for at least 1 hour. Mix well with the hands, squeezing the mixture as you turn it. Cover and refrigerate for 24 hours.

Chatam Coleslaw is great served as a dinner salad topped with a dollop of Russian Dressing (see Index).

If you don't want the slaw "wilted" as it's used in the Chatam Special sandwich (see Index), don't squeeze the cabbage as you mix it—simply stir with two forks.

Royal Copenhagen Salad
6 servings

1 8-ounce can artichoke hearts (*not* marinated)
1 small green pepper
1 cup julienned cooked ham
1 cup julienned cooked turkey
1 cup shredded lettuce (optional)
Lemon Dressing (see below)

Drain the artichoke hearts and cut them into thin strips. Core, seed, and wash the green pepper. Cut it into julienne strips. Julienne the ham and turkey and shred the lettuce. Make the Lemon Dressing.

Put all the julienned and shredded ingredients in a bowl. Pour ⅔ cup dressing over all and toss lightly but completely with two forks. Refrigerate until thoroughly chilled.

Serve the salad on buttered pumpernickel (or bread of your choice) as an open-face sandwich.

This is a special at the Chatam and must be tasted to be believed. It's marvelous served at a luncheon with a light white wine and a lovely dessert.

Lemon Dressing

1½ cups

2 egg yolks
2 tablespoons lemon juice
2 teaspoons white vinegar
1 tablespoon sugar
½ teaspoon dry mustard
¼ teaspoon salt
Pinch cayenne
½ cup sour cream
½ cup mayonnaise (homemade, Best Foods, or Hellmann's)

By blender or food processor:
Put the egg yolks into the processor bowl or blender jar along with the lemon juice and vinegar. Start the machine and add all the other ingredients in sequence. Try to have all ingredients ready as the total blending time should not exceed 2 minutes. Turn the machine off if you have to run back and forth to cupboard and refrigerator.

By hand:
Whisk the egg yolks with the lemon juice and vinegar until light and slightly thickened. Whisk in all the other ingredients and beat until very, very smooth.

Papaya and Crab Salad

PER SERVING:

½ papaya
½ cup king crab leg meat, cut into ½-inch slices

Select firm, ripe papayas. If you are serving a group, try to select uniform fruit so that one person doesn't get a small serving and his neighbor a large one.

Split the fruit in half lengthwise and discard the seeds and membranes connected to the seed pod. Slice the crab legs, making sure that all sinews have been removed. With a sharp-sided spoon, scoop the papaya flesh out of its skin, leaving at least ⅓ inch intact. Shape the flesh into uniform oval spoonfuls. Pile the papaya flesh back into the papaya skin, alternating crab with papaya. The fruit and crab should be well mounded.

Set each papaya half into a nest of cracked ice. Serve with a wedge of lime or lemon and Curry Dressing (see below). Serve this delicious dish as a main course at a luncheon or as a first course at an elegant dinner.

Curry Dressing   *1¾ cups*

¾ cup sour cream
¾ cup mayonnaise (homemade, Best Foods, or
      Hellmann's)
1 tablespoon curry powder
2 tablespoons cider vinegar
1 teaspoon lemon juice
2 teaspoons sugar
¼ teaspoon salt
1 tablespoon light cream

Mix all the ingredients together until smooth. A wire whip or blender does the job well. If the dressing is too thick, add more light cream.

Carrot Salad   *8 servings*

1 cup raisins
1 pound (about 5) carrots
4 ribs celery
2 large green apples
   Juice of ½ lemon
½ cup walnuts
2 tablespoons powdered sugar
¾ cup mayonnaise, *or* ½ cup yogurt and ¼ cup mayon-
      naise (homemade, Best Foods, or Hellmann's)

Cover the raisins with *hot* water and let them sit while you grate the carrots. Trim and thinly slice the celery, and peel and slice the apples, first into fourths and then across, forming small, almost triangular pieces. Put the grated carrots, celery, and sliced apples in a bowl. Squeeze lemon juice over the apples. Drain the raisins, and add them along with the walnuts and the other ingredients. Toss until well combined. Serve chilled.

Chopped pitted dates can also be added or used in place of raisins.

Chicken Salad
4 servings

In restaurants chicken salad is almost always made with turkey. Nowadays the new truth-in-menu laws prohibit restaurants from calling their turkey salad, chicken salad. It's a minor point, as the taste difference is small and turkey provides leftovers; whereas a chicken must be stewed and cooled, and then you have to pick the meat off all those small bones. Which fowl you use is strictly up to you.

> 3 cups chicken *or* turkey cut into small dice—not too small
> 1 cup diced celery
> 3 teaspoons lemon juice
> ½ teaspoon salt, or to taste
> ¼ teaspoon pepper
> 1 cup mayonnaise, or enough to bind (homemade, Best Foods, or Hellmann's)

Place the first five ingredients in a bowl. Add ¾ cup mayonnaise, then more, if you like, until all the ingredients are coated to your liking.

Note: Homemade mayonnaise makes a better salad; but if you use store-bought, be sure *not* to use a sweet mayonnaise. I recommend Best Foods, known elsewhere as Hellmann's.

Tuna Salad
4 sandwich or 2 salad servings

> 1 6½-ounce can white-meat tuna
> 2 teaspoons lemon juice
> ⅓ cup finely diced celery
> ¼ cup finely chopped scallions
> ½ cup mayonnaise, or enough to bind (homemade, Best Foods, or Hellmann's)

Drain the tuna and flake it into a bowl. Add all the other ingredients and toss well.

Use the salad either in sandwiches or piled into lettuce cups for a luncheon. It is also good piled into halves of avocado or scooped-out tomatoes.

Potato Salad

12 to 16 servings

3 pounds (about 5 large) potatoes
8 eggs
1 medium to large onion
2 cups sliced celery
2 tablespoons chopped parsley
1 tablespoon Colman's dry mustard
1½ teaspoons salt
½ teaspoon celery salt
½ teaspoon coarsely ground pepper
4 tablespoons white *or* cider vinegar
1½ cups mayonnaise (homemade, Best Foods, or Hellmann's)

Wash the potatoes, put them in a pot, cover them with water, add 2 teaspoons salt, and bring to a boil over high heat. Cover the pot, lower the heat, and simmer until the potatoes are done and easily pierced with the tip of a knife. Put the eggs in a pot, cover with cold water, add 1 tablespoon salt, and bring to a rapid boil. Lower the heat and simmer for 12 minutes, then rinse under cold water until the eggs are cool to the touch. Peel and chop the onion, put it in a strainer, and submerge it in boiling water for 1 full minute, then rinse thoroughly under cold running water. Wash and slice the celery and chop the parsley. Peel the potatoes while they are still hot; add the peeled eggs, sliced, and the onion, celery, and parsley. Sprinkle the warm mixture with the seasonings. Sprinkle the vinegar over all, then add the mayonnaise, and toss until all is completely mixed. Taste for seasoning and add more salt or pepper if needed. Since potatoes differ, the amount of seasonings can vary. It's best to go light on the salt at first and add the rest later. You should always make Potato Salad with *warm* potatoes, as the heat helps the seasonings be absorbed into the ingredients. Cover the salad and chill it in the refrigerator until ready to serve.

VEGETABLES

Kim E. Burroughs '81

The Most Healthful Vegetables

All vegetables contain a variety of vitamins and minerals, but some contain more than others. Here, in order, are the most potent vegetables you can consume: broccoli, spinach, brussels sprouts, lima beans, peas, asparagus, artichokes, cauliflower, sweet potatoes, and carrots. If you are partial to all or many of these and eat them regularly, along with a balance of proteins and whole grains, you should never need a vitamin pill.

If you want all the vitamins and minerals a vegetable contains, eat it raw. Even when cooked properly, a vegetable loses up to 25 percent of its nutrients. If you overcook a vegetable, forget it—the vitamins and minerals have left it. We used to think that all the nutrients went out of the vegetables and into the cooking liquid. We now know that some vitamins are leached into the liquid, but most of them are destroyed by prolonged heat. Minerals are different; they cannot be destroyed. Thus it is not only for flavor but for health that you should always use vegetable cooking liquid for soups and sauces.

The age of a vegetable is also very important. If you could sit in your garden with a bucket of cold water, pull a carrot from the ground, wash it, and eat it right then and there, you'd be assured of getting all that carrot had to offer. By the time you pick the carrots up at the market, however, their nutrient content has diminished. Still, they are good for you—so eat your vegetables.

How to Buy Vegetables

• Both asparagus and broccoli should be bought with tightly closed tips, or buds. If the tops of either vegetable have opened or discolored, leave them alone. Artichokes should also be closed, their leaves hugging the center. Any vegetable that feels limp or soft should be passed by. The firmer a vegetable is, the fresher it is.

• Onions and potatoes must be very firm to the touch, as should carrots and all their earth-grown cousins. Even corn should feel firm in the husk and should weigh in as heavy. If an ear of corn feels light, its juices have evaporated and it's too old.

• Vegetables that grow below the ground keep well and may be stored in the refrigerator for some time. Vegetables that grow above the ground should be bought with good color and firm bodies and used as quickly as possible. Unlike fruits, vegetables *do not* ripen off the vine. Bananas and avocados and all sorts of fruits are picked long before they're ripe and will then ripen, but once a vegetable is picked, plucked, or pulled, it gets old. Tomatoes are an exception—but then they're not vegetables. They're the fruit of a South American herb.

How to Cook Fresh Vegetables

A vegetable should be cooked until it's *just* done, *just* tender, and still a bit crisp. Beans (green or yellow), celery, carrots, cabbage, squash, turnips, parsnips, and pea pods can all have a bit of crunch when you serve them. Test for doneness with the thin tip of a paring knife. By the time you can easily insert the thick prongs of a dinner fork, the vegetable is dead.

Vegetables should be brought to the table "just done," and that means learning to handle them properly. If you plan to add butter and honey to the carrots, or butter and parsley to the beans, or brown sugar to the sweet potatoes, you must cook the vegetables until they're *almost* tender, as they will finish cooking with their allotted seasonings and condiments.

It's better for your waistline and your body to serve two vegetables and no bread; and if you can learn to treat vegetables correctly, you'll love dinner more each day.

Learn to cook vegetables ahead of time in the French manner—the way fine restaurants do. First, forget pots and lids except for potatoes, corn on the cob, artichokes, or whole cauliflower. Get out a frying pan; any kind other than cast-iron will do. The vegetable you're about to cook should fit nicely in the bottom of the pan to a depth not exceeding 1½ inches. (In the case of certain vegetables such as cauliflower floweretes, this is impossible; don't worry.) Barely cover the vegetable with water; salt with up to ½ teaspoon salt and bring to a rapid boil. Reduce the heat and lay a piece of aluminum foil over the vegetables. This "lid" should not cover the pan, just the center of the vegetable, and should be square to allow steam to escape on four sides.

Simmer the vegetable rapidly until its color has increased. Take out a bite and test. It should still have some crunch, but its taste should be that of a cooked, not a raw, vegetable. Immediately remove the pan from the fire and refresh the vegetable under *cold* water. No, you're not draining off all the vitamins, as you haven't cooked them away as yet. When the vegetable is completely cooled, drain and hold it until 5 minutes before serving time. If you're doing all this in the morning, refrigerate it.

You now have a perfectly cooked vegetable that needs only to be reheated with butter and herbs, or water, or all three. If you're putting the vegetable in a cheese sauce, a cream sauce, or a butter sauce, reheat it right in the sauce. If you want a plain, fresh "out-of-the-garden-tasting" vegetable, add 2 to 3 tablespoons water and a lump of butter and reheat until the water is gone and the vegetable is hot.

Vegetables that are fresh are obvious to the eye and *only* the freshest should ever be used. Sometimes you can make jams, jellies, and cobblers out of a little less-than-fresh fruits, but an old vegetable is an old vegetable, and you should simply forget it.

The following is a list of the vegetables that do their best cooked by the open-frying-pan method:

Asparagus: Wash, snap off ends.

Beans (snap or wax): Wash, trim ends, French cut or cut in desired lengths.

Broccoli: Wash, trim ends (pare stalks if necessary), cut so that stalks are no more than ¾ inch thick.

Brussels sprouts: Wash, trim ends, discard bad leaves.

Cabbage: Discard bad leaves, wash, cut in quarters, cut out core, cut in eighths.

Carrots: Wash, trim ends, peel if necessary, cut as desired.

Cauliflower: Wash, core, break into flowerets.

Celery: Trim ends, wash, cut to desired size.

Leeks: Trim ends, wash, wash, wash, cut as desired.

Onions: Peel, slice, or quarter. For brown-glazed onions, finish with butter and 2 teaspoons sugar.

Parsnips: Wash, peel, split into quarters.

Squash (summer, zucchini, etc.): Wash, trim ends, cut as desired.

Turnips: Wash, peel, cut into wedges or rounds.

How to Use Frozen or Canned Vegetables

There are times when fresh vegetables simply aren't available or you can't get to the market. At such times canned or frozen ones must be used. I prefer frozen to canned for color, taste, and nutritional value.

When heating frozen vegetables, follow the directions on the package, but in the case of peas I suggest adding a lump of butter and ½ teaspoon sugar to make them taste fresh. I heat frozen beans (from my own garden) in ¼ cup water and 1 tablespoon butter and salt to taste. The addition of butter (or margarine if you must) to a vegetable as it heats and finishes its final cooking enhances the taste. Be sure not to overcook frozen vegetables any more than you'd overcook fresh ones. They should be done during the last minutes of meal preparation.

When you are using canned vegetables, it's a good idea to drain the water from the can and add *fresh* water to heat the vegetables in. This is extremely important when heating sauerkraut. When using canned beans of several varieties for your favorite bean salad, rinse the beans under the cold water in a colander to give them a clean, fresh taste, and be sure to chill the salad completely before serving it.

There are always exceptions; beets should be heated in their own liquid.

The Artichoke

The artichoke is one of nature's most delightful vegetables. It has a delicate, distinctive flavor, but for some reason people are always out to smother its fine taste. They stuff it and stuff it and spread it with oil, then add lots of garlic and let it boil.

I prefer to love it—and leave it alone so that I may enjoy its true flavor.

To Cook an Artichoke

PER SERVING:

1 artichoke
Water
Salt
Clarified butter *or* mayonnaise (homemade, Best Foods, or Hellmann's)

Fill a pot with cold water (see Note). Cut the stem off an artichoke flush with its base; turn it on its side and cut about 1 to 1½ inches off the top. This will eliminate most of the spines on top of the leaves. Discard any outside leaves that are bruised or rusty, and trim the spines off the full leaves remaining with kitchen scissors. You can leave the artichoke whole, or you can scoop out the choke with a small knife and melon baller, or you can do what our family has done for years: Cut the artichoke in half, right through the center of the choke. Take a small, sharp paring knife and make a deep, half-moon cut beneath the choke just above the heart. Grab hold of the choke and pull it out. Put the two (choke-free) halves in the pot of water and continue the process until all the artichokes are trimmed and cut. Drain, and add fresh water to cover and 1 teaspoon salt distributed evenly over the vegetables. Bring to a boil, reduce heat, and simmer, covered, for 30 to 40 minutes, depending on size. Test for doneness by probing the heart with the end of a paring knife. Drain and serve hot or cold with an appropriate dip. If you're having artichokes as just another dinner vegetable, you might want to give each person just a half with a lump of butter melting into its hot little heart. Or serve cold with mayonnaise.

Note: Many fruits (apples and peaches, for example) and some vegetables, such as artichokes, avocados, and potatoes, turn brown when cut, peeled, or pared. When you work with them, have a bowl of acidulated water (water into which you've squeezed some lemon juice) by your side in which to put the cut fruits or vegetables.

Kim E. Burroughs '81

🍃🍃🍃🍃🍃🍃🍃🍃🍃🍃🍃🍃🍃🍃🍃🍃🍃🍃🍃🍃🍃🍃

DIGGING FOR ASPARAGUS

Some girls long their whole life through for a mink coat. Some boys dream of flying around in their own plane. My husband always wanted a backhoe, and our newly acquired ranch gave him the perfect excuse to get his long-dreamed-of toy.

Oh, joy! The immense truck and trailer rolled up the road with the bright orange backhoe lashed to its back. My husband was taking moving pictures of the backhoe; I was taking pictures of him taking pictures of the backhoe; and the truck driver was shaking his head.

After the backhoe had lumbered off the flatbed, a nice man in a pickup came driving up with a smile, books, and a free lesson. When the man left, he said he'd check back later, as the first day was usually eventful.

Snow was still on the ground—not much, but large patches were everywhere, and the asparagus roots were sprouting. I knew they wouldn't last long if they weren't planted soon, so the first task for the backhoe was a trench for the asparagus.

My husband maneuvered the bright orange monster through the east corrals and through the gate into the back garden. He swung the seat around. Within three minutes, ten feet of trench were dug. He moved the machine back and began to dig again, but the thin frozen crust he'd driven over (and was now sitting on) had melted, and I watched in horror as the backhoe and my husband sank into spring's incredible muck.

The man with the nice smile came back. He showed us how to extricate a backhoe from muck, and eventually I planted the asparagus.

When you get asparagus home from the market or bring it in from the back garden, wash it well and then *snap off* the tough ends. The asparagus knows where its tender part begins and its tough part stops. If you take a stalk of asparagus by its middle and its end and bend—*voilà!* The asparagus will break at the magic point your knife can only guess at.

🍃🍃🍃🍃🍃🍃🍃🍃🍃🍃🍃🍃🍃🍃🍃🍃🍃🍃🍃🍃🍃🍃

Asparagus, Fresh and Simple

⅓ pound asparagus per person
¼ teaspoon salt
Butter

Wash the asparagus, snap off the tough ends, and lay it in a 12-inch Teflon, stainless-steel, or enamel frying pan. All heads should be at the same end of the pan. Add water just to cover, salt, and bring to a rapid boil. In the restaurant we lay a clean towel over the asparagus to keep it submerged. A piece of foil cut the width of the pan, leaving four open spaces on the sides of the foil, will do as well. Cook the asparagus until its color is enhanced. Take out a stalk and test the end. If it's still too crunchy, return it to the pan and boil for another minute or two. Do not allow the asparagus to lose its color. When served, it should be tender but never limp or mushy. When the point of a sharp knife goes in easily and it tests almost done, remove the pan from the stove and rinse the asparagus under cold running water in order to stop the cooking process. At serving time, add 2 tablespoons water and a good lump of butter to the frying pan and reheat the asparagus until it's piping hot. Don't allow it to sit and cook.

If you're using the asparagus for Fresh Asparagus Vinaigrette (see Index), cook as above, then rinse well under cold water and refrigerate until ready to use.

To Cook Cabbage
4 to 8 servings

Discard any battered or old leaves from the outside of a head of cabbage. Wash the cabbage, cut it in half, then in half again. Cut the core from each quarter. Place the wedges in a pot of cold water, add ½ teaspoon salt, and bring to a boil. Cover, lower the heat to medium, and cook the cabbage for 11 minutes—use a timer. Drain it as soon as the cooking time is up, and serve it with butter. Or make Creamed Cabbage (following recipe).

Creamed Cabbage

Clean and cook one head of cabbage as described above. Make a *roux* of 3 tablespoons butter and 3 tablespoons flour. Add 1 cup milk and 1 cup broth from the cooked cabbage; add salt and pepper to taste. Simmer the sauce for 5 minutes, stirring occasionally. Add the cabbage and gently combine with the sauce.

When you make Creamed Cabbage, you may wish to cut the head into eighths or even sixteenths.

Red Cabbage
12 servings

1 medium head red cabbage
1 medium onion
1 large green apple
½ teaspoon salt
½ cup packed brown sugar
½ cup red wine
2 tablespoons butter
1 tablespoon cider vinegar

Remove any old or damaged leaves from the cabbage. Wash and cut it into four sections. Cut out the core, then shred the cabbage, peel the onion and apple, and shred or chop them fine. (A food processor makes all this very easy.) Place the cabbage, onion, and apple in a large pot. Sprinkle with the salt and brown sugar. Pour over the wine and toss well with two forks. Cover the pot tightly with a lid, turn the heat on low, and simmer the cabbage for 1 hour. After an hour add the butter and vinegar, toss again, and cook for another 30 minutes over very low heat. Correct for salt and serve.

Red cabbage is so compatible with pork, duck, or any other fowl and is so easy to make. It can be reheated with no change in character and keeps well in the refrigerator in glass jars. In fact, this dish tastes better the next day.

𝕭𝕭𝕭𝕭𝕭𝕭𝕭𝕭𝕭𝕭𝕭𝕭𝕭𝕭𝕭𝕭𝕭𝕭𝕭𝕭𝕭𝕭

CARROTS

Autumn at the ranch is like a spell that befalls the land and its people. As I dig autumn carrots for storage, the trees try to hang onto their leaves, and the dry wild flowers dance in gusts of wind that strain to dislodge all foliage. The horses get randy; and although geldings, they prance and rear in a mock ritual of sexual play. Slowly their coats thicken, readying them for the long, long winter ahead.

Here in the northwest corner of Wyoming, frosts come long before the first snowfall and the gardener must work many hours to harvest all her vegetables before the onset of winter.

Carrots are a pretty hardy bunch. They store so well that they're in our markets the whole year round. They are also easy to grow; and they provide the treat of eating baby carrots, freshly pulled from the garden, to allow the rest of the crop to mature into the big heavies that are pulled in the fall.

𝕭𝕭𝕭𝕭𝕭𝕭𝕭𝕭𝕭𝕭𝕭𝕭𝕭𝕭𝕭𝕭𝕭𝕭𝕭𝕭𝕭𝕭

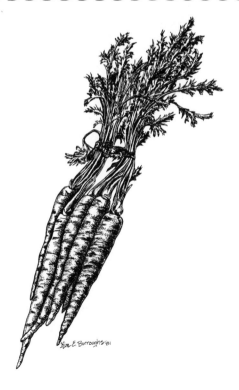

To Cook Carrots
6 servings

Sweet young carrots are wonderful cooked in an open frying pan with water to cover, ½ teaspoon salt, and a lump of butter. By the time the water has boiled away, the carrots should be just right.

This method can be used on market carrots, too. If the carrots are winter-storage carrots, you might wish to give them a little boost. When the water has cooked away, test the carrots for doneness. Remember, don't let them cook until they're mushy—they should still be firm. If they're underdone, add more water and allow it to cook away. When the carrots are done, add 2 tablespoons honey and another lump of butter to the pan. Shake over a high flame until the butter and honey are melted, hot, and have coated the carrots with a lovely glaze.

Creamed Carrots
6 servings

> 1 pound carrots
> ½ teaspoon salt
> 2 tablespoons butter
> 2 tablespoons flour
> 1½ cups chicken stock *or* broth from carrots
> ¼ cup cream *or* half-and-half
> ⅛ teaspoon pepper
> 1 teaspoon chopped parsley (optional)

Wash, peel, and trim the ends of the carrots. Cut in slanting diagonal pieces or sticks not exceeding 3 or 4 inches in length. Put the carrots in a frying pan, cover with water, add salt, and boil until not quite tender. Put a half-lid of foil over the carrots while they cook. When the carrots are almost tender, remove them from the heat. In a saucepan make a *roux* with the butter and flour; cook for 2 minutes, stirring—do not allow the *roux* to brown. Slowly add the stock or broth from the cooked carrots. Stir with a wire whip until smooth and creamy. Add the cream, pepper, and parsley. Correct for salt, add the carrots, and allow them to simmer for 5 minutes; or pour into a flameproof serving dish, cover, and put in a 350° oven for 15 minutes. Remember, flour takes 5 minutes to cook. Even if you're in a hurry, be sure the flour cooks the required time.

To Cook Cauliflower

In choosing a fresh cauliflower, look for white flesh, fresh green leaves, and no rust or brown spots. When you get the head of cauliflower home, wash it, then peel back and break off all the leaves with your hands.

With a short, sharp knife cut the stem flush with the lowest flowerets. Then make a conical cut into the base of the stem. With the point of the knife cut a cross in the bottom of the conical cut.

Place the cauliflower, base down, in a pot and sprinkle it with salt. Add water to a depth of 1½ inches. Cover tightly, bring to a boil, lower the heat, and simmer for 10 to 15 minutes, or until the cauliflower is tender. The time depends on the freshness and the size of the head.

When the cauliflower is just done, drain it completely. It's lovely served with melted butter poured over all and topped with sautéed bread crumbs or that wonderful old favorite, Cheese Sauce (see Index).

Celery Sauté   6 *servings*

    1 bunch celery
    2 tablespoons butter
       Salt and pepper to taste

Wash the celery and trim the ends and tops. Please don't trim the ends *off;* simply pare them so that the clean white meat shows. The white end part of the celery is excellent in both taste and vitamins. Don't waste it. If the outside stalks of your celery bunch look tough or a bit worse for wear, peel them with a potato peeler to remove the outer tough layer. When the celery is washed and trimmed, lay it on a chopping block and cut it into 1-inch diagonal slices. Lay your knife almost horizontal to the chopping block in order to produce good diagonal cuts. Put the butter in a large frying pan. When the butter has melted, add the celery plus enough cold water barely to cover. Bring to a boil and boil over very high heat until the water has evaporated down to a few tablespoons. Season the celery with salt and pepper to taste and test one piece of celery. It should be done but still have a lot of crunch to it. If you feel that the celery needs more cooking, add more water and repeat.

Celery is delicious cooked and served this way all by itself, topped with nothing but some chopped parsley. It is also an excellent stretcher. When snow peas are $3 a pound, but you can't resist, buy ⅓ pound and add them to the celery when the water has reduced to half. Stir as the rest of the water cooks away. The celery lends itself to the pea pods, and you now have enough for company. Celery Sauté is also excellent combined with string beans, wild rice, peas, or carrots. How about zucchini? Diced cabbage? Stir-fried asparagus?

Perfect Corn

Like most other vegetables, corn is too often overcooked. Unlike the vegetables that are best when their color peaks, corn is overcooked and sometimes tough by the time it develops a deep golden yellow color. This method of cooking corn is foolproof, and you'll never serve tasteless, tough, dark yellow corn again if you'll just try it.

Allow one ear of corn per person—more if you've just picked it out of the garden. Husk and wash the corn, and put it in a large pot. Cover it with cold water, add 1 teaspoon salt, and bring to a boil over high heat, leaving the lid of the pot *off*. As soon as the water boils, remove the pot from the heat, put a tight lid or cover on it, and allow the corn to sit for 3 to 5 minutes.

Note: If the corn you're cooking is more than two days old, add 1 teaspoon sugar to the water.

Fresh Corn Sauté   *6 servings*

This is my mother's recipe and the best corn I've ever eaten.

    4 medium to large ears fresh corn
    4 tablespoons (½ stick) butter
    ¼ teaspoon salt
    ¼ teaspoon pepper
    2 teaspoons sugar
    ½ cup light cream

With a large knife slit the kernels of corn by running the knife down each row. When all rows have been slit, stand the ear on its bottom and cut the corn from the cob. With the blade of the knife scrape the cob downward, thus extracting all the tips of the kernels that remain in the cob. Melt the butter in a frying pan or saucepan and add the corn, salt, pepper, and sugar. Sauté the corn in the butter for 2 or 3 minutes, stirring frequently. Add the cream, lower the heat, and allow the mixture to simmer for another 5 minutes. Add more cream if the consistency seems at all dry.

If you have leftover corn on the cob, you can make this dish with the leftover ears. It'll be very good if you cooked your fresh corn properly (see Perfect Corn). Since the leftover corn has already been cooked, it won't be necessary to recook it. Melt the butter, add the cut corn and all the other ingredients, and simmer only until just hot.

Carl's Corn Fritters
6 servings

>   2 tablespoons butter
>   2 cups fresh corn cut from the cob (2 large ears usually give 2 cups; frozen or canned corn can be used but fresh is best)
> ½ cup light cream
>   Salt and pepper to taste
>   3 tablespoons flour
>   1 teaspoon baking powder
>   2 egg yolks
>   2 egg whites, beaten stiff

Melt the butter in a saucepan and add the corn, cream, salt, and pepper. Cook for 5 minutes, stirring occasionally. Remove the pan from the heat. Beat the flour and baking powder well into the corn mixture with a wooden spoon. Add the egg yolks and beat again. Fold in the egg whites until all is totally combined. Spoon the batter onto a hot griddle, making fritters about 2½ inches wide. Bake the fritters, browning them on both sides, just as you would pancakes.

These have a wonderful consistency and are simply delicious. They're great with chicken, ham, pork, barbecue, and brunch and are especially good served with fresh stewed tomatoes.

If you bake corn fritters in silver-dollar size, they make an excellent hors d'oeuvre. Serve with a small bowl of heated Salsa Roja (see Index). They can even be reheated. As you bake them, place them in overlapping layers on a small cookie sheet. Reheat in a 325° oven until hot.

Corn Pudding   8 *servings*

2 or 3 cups fresh corn, cut from cob (at least 4 ears)
4 large eggs
1½ cups light cream
½ teaspoon salt
¼ teaspoon coarsely ground pepper
1 tablespoon sugar

Run a sharp knife down the rows of kernels lengthwise, thus splitting each kernel in half. Stand the ear on its bottom and cut the corn from the cob. Scrape the cob with the blade of the knife to force the heads of each kernel from the cob.

When all the corn is cut, beat the eggs in a bowl, add the other ingredients, and beat well. Add the corn, stir, and pour into a well-buttered soufflé or baking dish. Bake in a 350° oven for 35 minutes, or until a knife comes out clean and the top starts to take on a bit of color.

Corn Pudding goes well with most meat, poultry, and fish dishes.

THE MUSHROOM

It took me more than fifteen years to get my first husband to like mushrooms. About the time he thought they were really great, we divorced. I'm telling you—sometimes you just can't win!

A lot of people can't win with mushrooms. I see them every time I go to the market. They carefully pick out the old mushrooms and take them home to lose. They lose texture, taste, and the chance of making a fantastic dish.

A fresh mushroom is *closed*. If the underside of a mushroom (the part connected to the stem) has opened up and separated from the stem, forget it. Think of a mushroom as an umbrella; if it's open, it'll rain on your parade. The more tightly closed the mushroom, the sunnier your dish.

When you get your tightly closed mushrooms home, treat and cook them correctly. If you must hold them a day or two, keep them in a plastic bag in the refrigerator. When you're ready to use them, take them out and wipe them with a damp cloth unless you're going to sauté them. In that case, follow the instructions for Sautéed Mushrooms.

🌿🌿🌿🌿🌿🌿🌿🌿🌿🌿🌿🌿🌿🌿🌿🌿🌿🌿🌿🌿🌿

Sautéed Mushrooms   *1/6 pound makes 1 serving*

Pour 1 tablespoon salt into the plastic bag your mushrooms are in or into a bowl in which you've placed the mushrooms; add water and roll the mushrooms around for about 5 seconds. Drain, rinse, and put the mushrooms on a towel.

Heat 2 tablespoons butter for every ¼ pound mushrooms in a *large, wide* frying pan. Trim the ends and slice the mushrooms to desired thickness (at least ⅓ inch); add them to the pan when the butter begins to bubble. Squeeze ½ lemon over the mushrooms and sauté over brisk heat, turning them frequently, until they are delicately browned.

Adding lemon juice, but never salt, during the sautéing of mushrooms is the secret every lover of these delicious morsels should know.

Fried Onions   *4 to 6 servings*

4 large yellow onions
2 tablespoons vegetable oil
2 tablespoons butter
2 teaspoons sugar

Peel and thinly slice the onions. This task is made easier if you slice a small piece off one side of the onion you're about to slice. Place the flat cut-off portion on your cutting board and proceed. The cut-off section will give the onion a flat edge on which to rest.

In a very large skillet heat the oil and butter. When they are hot, add the onions and sauté them over high heat until they are transparent and begin to take on color. Sprinkle the sugar over the onions and stir-fry them over high heat until they are well browned.

These onions are marvelous with a steak or even a hamburger steak.

Note: To remove gas from onions, soak chopped or sliced onions in white vinegar for 15 minutes. Drain, rinse, and use in any way you wish.

🥦🥦🥦🥦🥦🥦🥦🥦🥦🥦🥦🥦🥦🥦🥦🥦🥦🥦🥦🥦

PEAS AND PAWS

I saw the squall stalking up the valley as I picked peas. The wind tore at my hair as our big hound, Captain, pressed against me with the first rumble of thunder.

I cleaned out one pea patch and decided to shell the peas on the back porch so that I could watch nature's summer show of clouds, lightning, and marching rain.

As the thunder's clamor increased, Captain's brother, Major, joined us, followed by Stinky, my daughter's hybrid husky (Stinky isn't afraid of thunder or lightning, but she hates to miss a party).

Soon the tiny storm was getting close, and Captain could stand it no more. Despite my protest, he climbed right up into my lap.

By the time the rain came, all three dogs were there. Captain was doing fine with his head tucked under my right arm, his eyes tightly shut, and his right paw in the pea pot.

Fresh peas are marvelous either in a salad, just as they come from the pod, or put out *au naturel* in their pods as a snack. If you must cook them, do it quickly, and please don't let them lose that beautiful color.

Since becoming a farmer of sorts, I've found that vegetables right out of the garden cook in half the usual time. The fresher the pea, the shorter the cooking time.

🥦🥦🥦🥦🥦🥦🥦🥦🥦🥦🥦🥦🥦🥦🥦🥦🥦🥦🥦🥦

REDS AND OTHERS

Ever grow a potato? It's great fun! Take a piece of potato with an eye in it and stick it in the ground. Push it down to a depth of about four inches, cover it nicely, and in three to four months you can go on a treasure hunt beneath your potato plants. With my trusty pitchfork I've found up to fifteen potatoes under one plant. The method is more work than going to the market, but it's much more fun and exciting.

If you want to plant your own potatoes, see your county agent. He may give you free seed potatoes that are pest- and disease-resistant in your area. If not, he'll be able to tell you where to get some. A seed potato has many eyes in it and has not been treated for the prevention of growth. When you cut your seed potatoes for planting, be sure that each piece has at least one eye in it.

If you live where the summers are hot, you'd best stick to spring-grown red potatoes, or new potatoes as they're often called. Potatoes don't like excessive heat.

Red potatoes can be dug five or six weeks after planting when they're not much bigger than a quarter, but russets or baking potatoes are best dug after a killing frost that actually kills the top plant. This helps "set" the skin of the russets, which allows them to be stored over the long winter.

If you go to the work of planting some red "new" potatoes and get to have the thrill of finding the little devils, then you'll be in for a taste treat you won't believe. After digging the reds, wash them carefully. The skins are so tender when first dug that they will slip off with a rub of your fingers, but you want those beautiful skins to stay on. Boil the reds in their jackets until just tender, drain, cover, and shake the pan over high heat until *all* moisture has left the pan. Pass the bowl with butter, salt and pepper, and sour cream.

Denmark actually has a "new potato" season which last for two weeks or so. During the season every home and restaurant serves quarter- to fifty-cent-size new potatoes. They are buttery, smooth, and delicious.

Baked Potatoes

Allow 1 medium baking potato per person. Scrub the potatoes—that's dirt on the skin. They grow in the ground, and if the farmer washed them they'd rot by the time you got them, so you must wash them. A plastic or nylon kitchen scrubber does a quick and excellent job. Stab each potato once with the point of a knife. Put the potatoes in a 400° oven. Test for doneness after 45 minutes. Few potatoes take longer than 1 hour.

Serve with all your favorites: butter, sour cream, chives, crumbled bacon, chopped scallions, and of course salt and pepper.

Unless you're partial to wet potatoes, don't wrap potatoes in foil when you bake them. That steams the potato rather than baking it and makes for a damp, unattractive skin, to mention nothing of a watery interior.

Note: Green potatoes are poisonous. They've grown up to the surface of the soil and poked their little ends up to the sunlight. A poisonous chlorophyll has then developed within the skin and meat, so, like yellow snow, don't eat green potatoes.

Roast Potatoes

1 medium potato (russet or new) per person
2 tablespoons vegetable oil
Salt and pepper

Scrub the potatoes. Put them in a covered pot, cover with cold water, add 1 teaspoon salt, and bring to a boil. Boil for 5 minutes. Remove the pot from the stove, drain the potatoes, and rinse them under cold water until cool enough to handle. With a paring knife peel the potatoes and cut them into pieces of the desired size. Toss the peeled and cut potatoes with the oil and place them in a baking dish. Sprinkle with salt and pepper and bake in a 400° oven until golden brown, usually 30 minutes or more. You may add small peeled onions to the potatoes when you toss them with the oil; they will come out crunchy sweet after roasting.

Stuffed Baked Potatoes   *8 servings*

4 uniformly large baking potatoes
3 tablespoons butter
½ cup sour cream
2 tablespoons chopped chives
Salt and pepper to taste
⅓ cup milk
1 cup grated sharp Cheddar cheese
2 tablespoons grated Parmesan cheese

Scrub the potatoes and bake them in a 400° oven for at least 1 hour, or until they are done. While the potatoes are still very hot, cut them in half and scoop the insides into a bowl. Mash with a potato masher; add all the other ingredients except the cheeses, and mash again or beat with an electric mixer. When the mixture is smooth, stir in the Cheddar. Spoon the mixture back into the potato skins, sprinkle the Parmesan over the tops, and reheat in the oven until piping hot and the tops are slightly browned.

Stuffed potatoes can be fixed in the morning or the day before and then rebaked just prior to serving.

It's imperative that you bake potatoes to be stuffed without foil, as you need a skin worth stuffing.

Scalloped Potatoes   *12 servings*

 4 cups very thinly sliced potatoes (peeled)
 ¾ cup thinly sliced scallions
 ½ teaspoon salt
 ¼ teaspoon pepper
 3 tablespoons butter or margarine, melted
 1 tablespoon finely minced parsley
    Whole milk to cover barely

Gently toss together all the ingredients except the milk. Place in a buttered baking dish, add the milk, and bake in a 350° oven for 1 hour and 15 minutes, or until the potatoes test done. This dish reheats well.

To Cook Yams and Sweet Potatoes

I find it hard to understand women who buy canned yams or sweet potatoes in a supermarket when twenty feet away are fresh fat yams and sweet potatoes. The flavor of these nutritious roots is marvelous when their meat is nicely baked within their skins. Simply place the yams or sweet potatoes on a cookie sheet or in a pie tin and bake them in a 350° oven for 45 minutes to 1 hour and 15 minutes. The large time difference is due to the variation in size. Some sweet potatoes are huge and take well over an hour. When the tip of the knife slides easily into the vegetable, it's done. Remove from the oven, cool, peel, and use. Baking yams and sweet potatoes in their jackets gives them a sweeter taste and keeps all their vitamins and minerals within. If you have a food processor, you can process the meat of either vegetable and make a yam or sweet potato pie using your favorite recipe for pumpkin pie.

Candied Yams and Sweet Potatoes

Allowing one tuber per person, bake as many as you need in the above manner. Peel and slice the vegetables into a well-buttered baking dish. Alternate layers with brown sugar; the more you use, the more candied they'll be. Dot the top of the dish with butter and bake in a 350° oven for 30 minutes, or until it bubbles.

Beautiful Rice—Every Time   *4 servings*

Do yourself a favor and buy some long-grain white rice. You'll find it much cheaper than "quick" rice in a box, and much better. If you like cold rice salads, or if you wish to make rice ahead of time, it's imperative that you cook it properly to ensure perfect rice every time. Here's how.

3 quarts water
1 tablespoon salt
1 cup long-grain white rice

Bring the water to a rolling boil. Add the salt and rice; stir. Cook the rice, uncovered, for 13 minutes. It's a good idea to set a timer. When the bell rings, remove the pot from the stove and set it in the sink. Allow a slow stream of cold water to run into the pot. I tip the pot slightly so that the overflow runs out one side. Allow the water to run slowly into the pot for at least 4 minutes, or until the rice is cold and the water runs clear when you swirl the rice with a spoon or your hand. To keep the rice, put it in a glass container, cover it with cold water, and refrigerate. Cooked rice will keep this way for at least a week. To serve, drain the rice in a sieve or colander. Boil a pot of water and plunge the rice (in the sieve) into the water for 1 or 2 minutes, or until hot. Or drain the rice and toss it with melted butter and seasonings in a large frying pan. Keep turning the rice until it's piping hot.

Carl's Stir-Fried Rice   *10 servings*

When I was a child I wasn't too fond of rice. But my father's stir-fried rice changed my mind.

3 tablespoons vegetable oil
6 scallions, finely chopped, including part of the green
½ cup minced crisp bacon *or* ham *or* cooked shrimp
4 cups cooked white rice

6 eggs
¼ cup chopped parsley
2 tablespoons soy sauce

Heat a wok or large frying pan. Pour the oil around and down the sides of the wok or pan to coat. When the oil is hot, add the scallions. Stir-fry until they look as though they're about to color. Add the bacon (or ham or shrimp) and rice. With two spatulas toss the rice until heated through. Make a well in the center of the rice and break in the eggs. When their bottoms start to cook, break the yolks and stir them into the rice mixture. Using a spatula, stir and lift the rice constantly until the eggs are totally dispersed and set. Add the parsley and soy sauce. Toss to combine completely and serve. This may be kept in a partially covered dish or pan in a warm oven for up to 1 hour, but it's best when served immediately.

Note: Leftover cooked pork or chicken or sautéed mushrooms can all be used in this rice dish.

RICE VERSA

My daughter Kim is a health nut who eats nothing but brown rice or wild rice. On my last trip to Los Angeles Kim reprimanded me for following the instructions on the brown rice package. "I don't know why they all call for so much water; it simply isn't necessary and makes for lousy rice," she said. We discussed the cooking of brown rice, and when I got back home to Wyoming I tried her method. The kid was right. Her way produces light, dry brown rice, cooked to a turn, ready for butter, seasonings, or the incorporation of other foods.

Brown Rice   *4 servings*

1½ cups water
1 cup brown rice (not the quick type)
Salt
Butter

Put the water into a pot with a tight-fitting lid. Add the rice and bring to a boil, immediately lower the heat to the lowest possible setting, and cook for 40 minutes, tightly covered. In high altitudes add 10 or 15 minutes to the cooking time. When the rice is done, toss it with butter and salt to taste, or make Fancy Brown Rice.

Note: Never cook brown rice with salt.

Fancy Brown Rice   *4 servings*

4 tablespoons (½ stick) butter
1 cup thinly sliced mushrooms
1 small onion, diced
1 tablespoon chopped parsley
¼ teaspoon celery salt

Cook brown rice as described above. Melt the butter in a frying pan. Wash, dry, and slice the mushrooms and set them aside. Peel and chop the onion, add it to the butter, and cook until transparent. Add the mushrooms, turn up the heat, and cook, stirring with a wooden spoon, until the vegetables begin to take on color. Add the rice, salt, and parsley. Heat over moderate heat until the rice is piping hot and all is combined. Correct for salt.

Note: Be sure to add the celery salt *after* the rice is cooked, not to the cooking water.

Wild Rice   *8 servings*

Wild rice is not actually a rice at all, but the seed pod of a North American wild grass that used to grow in many states but is now found only in Minnesota.

I love wild rice as so many do, but it was only recently that I found out that I was losing out on a good portion of each dish of the lovely stuff that I fixed. I used to boil wild rice for 20 to 30 minutes. It tasted done and was delicious, but then I found out that the "rice" should be simmered for 40 to 45 minutes, or until the seeds open up. Then you should drain the rice, sauté it in butter until hot, and combine it with any other ingredients you wish.

Wild rice should also be washed numerous times before you cook it. Choose a fairly large, heavy pot with a good lid. After washing the rice (1 cup will end up serving six people), put it in the pot and cover it with 5 cups water. After 30 minutes check the water; if the rice is dry, add more water.

1 cup wild rice
Water
2 tablespoons butter
½ pound mushrooms
1 tablespoon lemon juice
½ cup finely chopped onion
½ cup celery, cut into thin diagonal strips
4 tablespoons (½ stick) butter
1 tablespoon chopped parsley
Salt and pepper

Cook the rice in 5 cups water for 45 minutes, or until opened. Sauté the mushrooms in 2 tablespoons butter. Add the lemon juice halfway through cooking and stir until lightly browned. Set aside. When the rice is done, drain it well. Cut the onions and celery; melt 4 tablespoons butter in a large frying pan. Add the vegetables. Stir-fry until the onion starts to lose its opacity. Add the parsley, the mushrooms with their liquid, and the drained rice. Salt and pepper to taste and toss with two rubber spatulas over high heat until all is combined and hot. Recheck for salt.

Wild rice is excellent with any kind of fowl, veal, lamb, and some fish. If you love it as I do, you'll find you love it with almost anything.

To Cook Spinach

People love to tell you to bring a big pot of water to a boil and then plunge in the spinach, but spinach is mostly water and will steam itself done in a matter of minutes with little help from you. When the spinach is in its second sink bath, get out a large pot and set it by the sink. As you rewash the spinach, deposit the leaves in the pot. The water clinging to the leaves will be more than enough to cook the vegetable. When all the spinach is washed and in the pot, sprinkle with salt, cover with a lid, and put it over medium-high heat. When the lid rattles, the liquid is boiling; lift the lid and stir the spinach with a long fork, replace the lid, and cook for no more than 3 to 5 minutes more, depending on the amount in the pot. Drain and nap with butter. Reserve the liquid in case you have any leftover spinach; then you can make Cream of Spinach Soup (see Index).

🌿🌿🌿🌿🌿🌿🌿🌿🌿🌿🌿🌿🌿🌿🌿🌿🌿🌿🌿🌿

SPINACH

Spinach is one of my all-time favorites. It's wonderful simply cooked, chopped, in crêpes, Italian dishes, or soup, and it is marvelous served raw in a salad. Its only failing is that it likes to pick up dirt and sand as it grows, so you must wash it and then wash it again. This is best done in a sink full of cold water. Wash the spinach leaves in the water, deposit them in a colander, drain them, then refill the sink and do it all again.

If you buy fresh spinach and find the leaves large and heavily veined, simply fold each leaf in half, using the center vein as a guide. With a small paring knife cut along the center vein and discard it. The deveined leaves will cook like tender spring spinach.

🌿🌿🌿🌿🌿🌿🌿🌿🌿🌿🌿🌿🌿🌿🌿🌿🌿🌿🌿🌿

Creamed Spinach   *6 servings*

    1 pound spinach
    3 tablespoons butter
    2 tablespoons flour
    ¼ cup light cream
      Spinach broth
      Salt and pepper

Wash the spinach in two changes of water. Discard any bad leaves, the roots, and any large stems. Cook according to the rules in To Cook Spinach. Drain the spinach well in a colander, then chop it fine on a chopping block, or process it quickly in a food processor, turning the machine on and off until the desired texture is achieved. Melt the butter in a saucepan or medium-sized frying pan. Add the flour and cook the *roux* for a minute or two. Add the cream and about ¼ cup spinach broth, stirring until smooth. Add the spinach and cook until all is combined, hot, and smooth. It may be necessary to add more spinach broth to achieve the proper consistency. The mixture should be thick but not able to hold its shape. Season with salt and pepper to taste and serve.

Note: I love the Dutch people and I love nutmeg, but I hate nutmeg on vegetables. The Scandinavians and the Dutch decided a long time ago that this spice that's so good on top of eggnog would be great on vegetables. If you've never had spinach without nutmeg on it, please try it; you might find out that you like it. If you happen to love vegetables with nutmeg, I can only say what Steve Martin says: "Well, excuse me!"

To Cook Banana Squash

This versatile squash of immense size is delicious when treated in the same manner as yams or sweet potatoes. It also freezes beautifully. Cut it into chunks, boil it for 10 minutes, drain and cool it, and cut off the outer skin. Set the pieces on a cookie sheet, freeze until solid, and then store them in plastic bags. Banana squash can also be cooked until very soft, drained of its water, and mashed like a potato with lots of butter and salt and pepper, but *no* milk, please. I love it mashed with nothing but butter, salt, and pepper, but many people like to add brown sugar or honey to taste; it's up to you. Candied baked banana squash can have pecans or walnuts added to the dish. Be sure to boil the squash before layering it into the baking dish with the butter and brown sugar, just as you must bake yams or sweet potatoes first.

Tomatoes

Tomatoes add the tang and the liquid needed in many dishes, but the peel of a tomato never helped any dish, so before you add a tomato to your stew, your sautéed zucchini, or your best meat sauce, please peel it. A *peeled* tomato makes a great deal of difference in salads, or in any cooked or baked dish. Put the tomatoes into a vessel just big enough to hold them, pour boiling water over them, and allow them to sit for 1 or 2 minutes—never longer—then rinse under cold water and peel. Once you cut out the core, the skin will simply slip off.

Canned tomatoes can be dressed up by melting 2 tablespoons butter in a saucepan. Add 2 tablespoons flour and stir the *roux*, add the juice from a large can of stewed tomatoes and 1 teaspoon sugar. Add tomatoes. Check for salt. Simmer for 5 minutes. These stewed tomatoes are wonderful on or next to corn fritters, zucchini pancakes, or alongside a big helping of macaroni and cheese. As I recall, we ate a lot of macaroni and cheese with stewed tomatoes during the war . . . it was very good and there was never any left.

🍃🍃🍃🍃🍃🍃🍃🍃🍃🍃🍃🍃🍃🍃🍃🍃🍃🍃🍃🍃🍃

TURNIPS

My adorable grandmother said she hated turnips. I'd just arrived in L.A. for a visit and had brought a whole suitcase full of fresh vegetables from the ranch. Among those delectable legumes was a big bunch of turnips. Mom and I love turnips, but Grandmom kept saying that she hated them and that even if I had grown them she wasn't going to like them. We told her that was all right and proceeded to cook the turnips and mash them exactly like mashed potatoes. At the table everyone ohed and ahed, and even my turnip-hating son-in-law said that mashed turnips passed the test. My poor little grandmother, a master in the kitchen in her own time, couldn't stand it anymore. "Give me just a tiny spoonful of those things," she said. We did, and then we helped her to two more helpings. After the third helping she looked up, wiped her mouth with her napkin, and said, "I still hate turnips."

🍃🍃🍃🍃🍃🍃🍃🍃🍃🍃🍃🍃🍃🍃🍃🍃🍃🍃🍃🍃

Fried Zucchini   *6 servings*

¾ cup fresh bread crumbs
½ cup grated Parmesan cheese
½ teaspoon salt
¼ teaspoon pepper
½ teaspoon Accent
1 tablespoon finely chopped parsley
¼ teaspoon basil and ⅛ teaspoon oregano leaves, *or* ½ teaspoon Italian seasonings
½ cup flour
1 egg
1 tablespoon water
2 large zucchini
2 tablespoons butter
¼ cup vegetable oil

Combine the bread crumbs, Parmesan, salt, pepper, Accent, parsley, and seasonings. Put the flour in a saucer. Beat the egg and water together. Wash the zucchini and trim the ends. Cut the zucchini on a sharp diagonal into ¼-inch-thick slices. Because of the diagonal cut, you'll end up with two triangular end pieces; discard them, or grate them into a salad. Heat the butter and oil in a large frying pan, preferably nonstick. Dip the zucchini slices in the flour, then the egg, and then the bread-crumb mixture. Fry them over moderate heat, browning lightly on both sides. Keep the zucchini warm in a slow oven until all pieces are fried.

Zucchini Pancakes   6 *servings*

½ pound zucchini
2 tablespoons grated onion
Scant ½ teaspoon salt
⅛ teaspoon coarsely ground pepper
1 tablespoon chopped parsley
2 tablespoons grated Parmesan cheese
¼ cup flour
1 teaspoon baking powder
2 eggs

Grate the zucchini into a colander. Grate the onion onto the zucchini. Sprinkle the vegetables with salt and toss with fork. Allow to stand for at least 20 minutes.

Squeeze any excess liquid from the zucchini-onion mixture and put the mixture into a small mixing bowl. Add the pepper, parsley, and Parmesan. Stir well with a fork. Sprinkle the flour and baking powder over the mixture and stir again. Break the eggs on top of the mixture and *beat* with a fork until all is totally combined and light.

Bake the zucchini pancakes on a hot griddle. Make them small—around 2 to 2½ inches in diameter. Brown on both sides and keep them warm on a plate in a warm oven.

Zucchini Pancakes should be the last thing you fix for your evening meal. When the last one is done, serve them immediately.

Mom's Zucchini   *4 to 6 servings*

2 medium zucchini *or* other summer squash
1 medium onion
2 medium tomatoes, peeled
2 tablespoons butter
  Salt and pepper
1 tablespoon chopped parsley (optional)

Wash the zucchini and slice it into ⅓-inch slices. Peel the onion and cut it in half, then into quarters, then into thin slices. Peel the tomatoes. In a heavy saucepan with a tight-fitting lid layer the onion, then the zucchini, and then the tomatoes. Cut the tomatoes into small slices over the pan with a paring knife. By cutting the tomatoes up over the pan you'll be sure of getting all the juice in the pot. Dot the vegetables with the butter, salt, and pepper, and add the parsley if you wish. Sprinkle the contents of the pot with 1 or 2 tablespoons water, put the lid on tight, and cook over medium-low heat for 5 minutes. Lift the lid and gently stir the vegetables with a wooden spoon or rubber spatula. Continue cooking the vegetables, tightly covered, for another 10 minutes, or until the zucchini tests done.

ENTRÉES: MEATS

Veal—a Bit of Opulence

True veal is a by-product of the dairy business. According to the U.S. Department of Agriculture, veal cannot be over three months old. Let your butcher read that statement and watch him blush.

Dairy cows must be "freshed" every few years, meaning they must bear young in order to replenish their milk supply. In Europe the calves are left on the mother's teat for the full three months, which produces marvelous, creamy white veal. In America the dairymen are too eager for the cow's milk, so they put Junior on a milk replacer.

There are various reasons for our dairymen not taking the time to produce fine veal. First of all, few Americans know or appreciate the qualities of fine veal, so the market is limited. Second, the European dairy breeds, such as the Swiss Simmentals, are much larger than our Holsteins and Guernseys. Thus the European dairyman produces a lot more veal in three months than his American counterpart does.

Calves who are fed a good, iron-free milk replacer become America's best veal, commanding a price of $8 to $10 per pound. If the farmer allows the calf to graze just a little, the calf's meat immediately turns dark pink and then red. These calves are often sold as veal or "baby beef." Though the price for this red veal may be low, it simply isn't worth the money at any price, as it does not taste like veal and tends to be quite tough.

Veal has little fat; therefore it should be cooked with moist heat or sautéed in a good amount of butter and oil over moderately high heat. Large roasts should be larded and/or cooked with low heat.

Veal's delicate flavor takes kindly to sauces, but care must be taken not to go overboard with the spice cabinet or you'll outsauce your veal.

You may have wondered why restaurant veal is often so much more tender and better in quality than the kind you cook at home. There are two reasons. Many times a fine restaurant is able to procure the finest-quality veal available, which is often held in special reserve to be sold only to restaurants and hotels, just as some prime beef is held for the same reasons. Second, some cuts of veal, such as cutlets, must be pounded properly. The unfair practices of the wholesale meat trade may hinder you, but you can pound your meat as well as any chef, thus guaranteeing yourself more tender veal.

Always pound from the center out, using a wooden mallet or heavy wooden rolling pin. Don't be shy. Not until a cutlet is twice as large as it was when you started pounding it should you even consider cooking it. If your pounding produces a hole or two, fear not; it will all cook back together.

Veal Cutlets   *4 servings*

 1 4- to 6-ounce veal cutlet per person
 ½ cup flour
  Salt and pepper
 2 tablespoons butter
 2 tablespoons vegetable oil
 2 tablespoons butter
 1 tablespoon lemon juice

Pound the cutlets as described above. Season the flour with salt and pepper. Heat 2 tablespoons each of butter and oil in a large skillet over moderately high heat. Dip the cutlets in the flour and sauté them for 4 or 5 minutes, turning often. When the cutlets take on a tinge of color, transfer them to a heatproof platter and keep them warm in a 250° oven. If the cutlets are large, you may have to sauté them in batches.

Drain the skillet of butter and oil. Add another 2 tablespoons butter and place over the heat. When the butter bubbles and starts to brown, add the lemon juice and swirl. Pour the lemon butter over the cutlets and serve.

Breaded Veal Cutlets

If you wish to extend your priceless veal cutlets, thus providing a heartier meal, bread them in the following manner.

Pound the cutlets and dip them in seasoned flour, as for Veal Cutlets. *Then* dip the cutlets in well-beaten egg, and then in fresh bread crumbs. Lay the breaded cutlets on a cookie sheet and place in the freezer for 10 to 15 minutes; this sets the breading and makes for finer frying. Once the breading is set, fry the cutlets in 2 tablespoons each of butter and oil. Allow the breaded cutlets to brown lightly on both sides. Turn them only once.

Breaded Veal Cutlets may be served with the lemon butter used for Veal Cutlets, or they can be further enhanced with Paprika Sauce.

Paprika Sauce   *1 cup*

After sautéing the cutlets and transferring them to a warm oven, drain the skillet. Add 2 tablespoons butter. When it has melted, add 2 tablespoons flour. Stir the *roux* over moderate heat for 1 to 2 minutes. With a wire whip blend in ¾ cup chicken stock, veal stock, or carrot broth. When the sauce is thick, remove the skillet from the stove and whisk in ¾ cup sour cream and 1 to 2 teaspoons paprika, or to taste. Reheat the sauce almost to the boiling point. Do not let it boil, however, as the sour cream will curdle. Nap the cutlets with the sauce, or serve it on the side.

Kalvfilet Oscar—Scandia   *6 servings*

Kenneth Hansen, the founder of Scandia restaurant of Hollywood, used to say, "Next to the smorgasbord, no finer dish ever came out of Sweden. It will make the *pièce de résistance* of a dinner for that very special festive occasion." He was complimenting the Swedes on Kalvfilet Oscar, which is a main course that serves forth meat, seafood, vegetables, and sauce in one magnificent tier.

     6 veal cutlets
       Salt and pepper
     ½ cup flour
     3 tablespoons butter
    24 asparagus tips, cooked and kept warm
    30 crab legs (Dungeness preferred), sautéed in butter
     ¼ cup water
       Béarnaise Sauce (see below)

Pound the veal cutlets until slightly flattened. Season them with salt and pepper, then dip them in the flour. Sauté the cutlets in the butter over brisk heat, turning them several times until they are done to a golden brown. Place the cutlets on a warm platter. On each cutlet place 4 asparagus tips and top the asparagus with 5 crab legs. Add ¼ cup water to the pan in which you browned the cutlets. Reduce the resulting stock and pour it over the tiered cutlets. Place in a warm oven until the sauce is made and you're ready to serve it. At serving time nap each Kalvfilet Oscar with Béarnaise Sauce.

Béarnaise Sauce—Scandia   *1½ cups*

    8 peppercorns, crushed
    2 shallots, chopped, *or* 4 scallions, chopped, white part
       only
    1 bay leaf
    5 sprigs parsley, chopped
    ½ cup tarragon vinegar
    5 egg yolks
       Juice of ½ lemon
    1 tablespoon water
    ½ pound (2 sticks) clarified butter)
       Salt
       Cayenne
    1 teaspoon chopped parsley
    1 teaspoon chopped tarragon leaves

In a small saucepan place the pepper, shallots, bay leaf, parsley, and vinegar. Boil until reduced to one-fourth its volume. Beat the egg yolks with the lemon juice and water in a double boiler until thick. *Very* slowly add the butter, whisking continuously. When all the butter has been added, stir in the vinegar and spices, season with salt to taste, and add a few pinches of cayenne and the chopped parsley and tarragon.

Beef

Beef, or meat in general, is an essential part of our diet. It provides proteins that our bodies need, along with many other nutrients that few other foods provide. Vegetarians must be very careful about their diets as proteins are vital for a healthy functioning body.

The filet is the tenderest part of the cow. Next comes the New York. T-bone and Porterhouse steaks are simply a combination of the filet and the New York, with the small side being the filet and the bigger piece of meat on the other side of the bone being the New York. Porterhouse steaks are always very thick, whereas T-bones can be cut thin and still take the name.

After the tenderest cuts of the loin we have the prime rib and the sirloin. The eye of the prime rib is often cut for steaks and listed on menus as Spencer steaks or eye-of-round steaks. From there to the oxtail it's downhill in the tenderness department, but not in the flavor department. The lesser cuts of meat can provide fantastic flavor and variety to your meals. Learning to fix some really good short ribs or a succulent pot roast is an absolute necessity if you plan to eat anything other than steak and hamburger.

The charts tell us that we should roast beef 15 to 20 minutes per pound for rare, but that 5-minute variable can mean an hour's difference on a 10- or 12-pound roast. If you aren't an expert at testing a roast, I strongly suggest that you buy a good meat thermometer and learn to use it. Remember that the tip of the thermometer should be in the center of the roast but should never touch a bone. Meat thermometers are needed only for roasts that should be served rare to medium (except for pork, which see). Well-done or long-simmering pieces of beef are cooked for so long that the timing is less important.

Other Points to Remember

• Salt toughens meat. Never add salt to a marinade, and try salting a roast only during the last hour or 30 minutes of roasting.

• Bacon is a good substitute for salt pork.

• If you can't taste the meat, you've gone overboard on the seasoning. You can always add more salt and seasonings to a pot, but once they're in, they're in. It's best to go light on the spices and then recheck for seasoning 30 minutes before a dish is done.

• When browning hamburger, or any meat that's going into a sauce, always tilt the frying pan at the end of the browning process and push the meat to the uphill side of the pan. Discard all the fat that flows to the bottom. It's bad for your health and adds nothing but calories to your dish.

• You can brown stew meat, pot roast, or short ribs under the broiler rather than frying them in oil—less fuss and fewer calories.

• Always have meat thoroughly defrosted and at room temperature before roasting it. Once a roast is done, allow it to stand for 20 minutes in a warm spot. This facilitates carving and allows the meat to retain its wonderful juices.

• Always roast meats with the fat side up and the bone side down. If there's no bone in the roast, place the fat side up. If you are roasting a blade-cut pot roast, check both sides of the meat and place the side that shows more bone down.

• Meats that have bones roast faster, as the bone conducts heat.

• Meat is marinated for two reasons: first, to season the meat and penetrate the flesh with flavor, and second, to tenderize the meat.

• If you're fat-conscious, cool spaghetti sauces, stews, and soups and remove the congealed fat before reheating.

About Steak

At the risk of insulting some of my readers, here's a note about the finer cuts of beef, especially the filet, New York, etc. If you like your meat well-done, *please* eat other cuts of the cow. Anyone who orders a filet mignon well done is wasting a lot of money and upsetting the chef and should be disappointed in the steak when it arrives. The tender cuts of meat have less fat content within the muscle itself and tend to dry out the longer they're cooked. The tender cuts of meat also have less flavor, and the intensity of flavor quickly diminishes the longer you cook them. If you could afford the following test, you'd understand what I'm saying.

Cook 5 filet mignons, 1½ inches thick—1 rare, 1 medium rare, 1 medium, 1 medium well, and 1 well. Now take a bite out of the center of each steak, starting with the rare and ending with the well-done. Chew, taste, and swallow each bite. It will be impossible for you not to notice that the rare steak is moist, juicy, tender, and flavorful. As you go down the line toward well-done, the moistness diminishes, the juiciness leaves, the meat begins to toughen, and by the time you get to the well-done filet the flavor resembles last week's discarded pot roast that you overcooked and left uncovered in the refrigerator.

Now that I've gotten that off my chest, let's talk about steaks and the lovely things you can do with them.

You can learn to test steaks for doneness just as the professionals do. A good fry cook can tell the doneness of a steak by poking at its center with his index finger. Does that sound silly or hard to do? It's really very simple, and anyone can learn to do it. The principle is self-explanatory. As a steak cooks, the meat contracts, starts to dry out, and thus becomes more resistant to the touch. A rare steak can be poked like a soft pillow; a well-done steak gives about as much as a wood plank. To start learning this simple technique, cook your next steak by the clock, and poke at it with your index finger before you cook it, after you've cooked the first side, and when it's done. You will begin to get an idea of what a steak should feel like when it's done just to your liking. The first few times you try this method of testing, cut into the center of *your* steak (not your guests') to see if you've judged correctly. Once you've mastered the "feel," it won't matter how thick or thin your steaks are or whether you're pan-frying them, broiling them, or barbecuing them, for you'll always be able to determine their doneness correctly.

Pan-Fried Steak

Americans seem to think that a steak must be broiled or barbecued. Any Frenchman can tell you that both ways tend to dry out even a rare steak. This is especially true of barbecuing. That's why it's so important to turn a steak with tongs rather than with a fork. Otherwise, juices will escape from those beautiful morsels of beef.

A frying pan is about as close as you can come in your kitchen to the large griddles found in restaurants. The best is a cast-iron skillet. If you don't have one, use the heaviest frying pan you own. Heat the pan over medium-high heat. Sprinkle the pan very lightly with salt. When the pan is good and hot, run a lump of butter over the bottom. The butter should sizzle immediately and start to brown. Immediately add your steaks. Don't crowd them; this is very important, because if the steaks touch each other they will stew instead of sauté.

Put your kitchen stove fan on and keep the heat at medium-high. If the steaks stop making noise during their cooking time, the heat is too low—turn it up. The steaks should sing all the while they cook. You'll need to pan-fry 1- to 1¼-inch steaks approximately 5 minutes to a side for medium-rare.

Test the steaks with your finger as described above. If you must, cut into one steak to check its degree of doneness.

If you've never pan-fried a steak, please try it; you'll end up time after time with beautifully browned, juicy steaks cooked to perfection.

Steak Tartare—Chatam

The original Steak Tartare was scraped steak mixed with an egg yolk, chopped onions, chopped beets, capers, and seasonings. Rarely is a steak trimmed and scraped for this wonderful dish anymore; instead, the meat is trimmed and ground. The taste is the same, but the consistency is different. People either love Steak Tartare or turn up their noses at it. Some have a total mental block about eating raw meat, let alone a raw egg yolk. What they don't realize is that raw steak gives off the total flavor of the meat and is simply delicious, and a raw egg yolk has a very buttery flavor. The two together with some seasonings are marvelous and oh, so good for you! Athletes should all be Steak Tartare lovers on those days when they want to stock up on protein.

For Steak Tartare you, or your butcher, must trim all the fat from the steak you're going to use. The original scraping (as opposed to grinding) of the steak was done to produce sinew-free meat. As the large knife was scraped across the meat, it would expose, but not gather, any sinews hidden in the flesh of the steak. Oh, well, we not only don't get scraped steak anymore, we usually don't even get one of the finer cuts of steak. Thousands of restaurants use round steak, which has a delightful flavor but more sinews to watch out for. If the chef who cuts the round steak for the grinder knows what he's doing, he can cut away all sinews and give you some very good Steak Tartare.

Our family's restaurant doesn't mix your Steak Tartare for you unless you request it. So when the Steak Tartare is placed in front of you, it is up to you to add as many onions, capers, and other goodies as you wish. Then, with

Aquavit and beer at your side, you dive in. Naturally, many people ask us to mix their Steak Tartare for them, which we gladly do, but being Scandinavian, I delight in incorporating nothing more than the egg yolk, onions, and salt and pepper. I enjoy the other ingredients, but when I feel like a purist I stick with the basics.

PER PERSON:

2 slices pumpernickel *or* rye bread (or your choice)
6 ounces finely ground steak, *no fat or sinew*
1 raw egg yolk
3 lettuce cups
2 tablespoons finely chopped onion
1 tablespoon capers
2 tablespoons finely chopped cooked beets
Salt, pepper, Worcestershire sauce, Poupon mustard, and other condiments of your choice

Butter both slices of bread and put one in the lower center of a dinner plate. Cut the other piece of bread in half, corner to corner, forming two triangles. Put the long cut sides of the triangles up against either side of the bread on the plate. Form the meat into a round patty and place it on the center slice of bread. Make a small, rounded depression in the center of the meat patty and put the egg yolk in it. Place three small lettuce cups above the bread slices. Place the onions in one, the capers in the center cup, and the beets in the last one. Serve with condiments.

If you're fixing Steak Tartare for a party, it's best to mix it, as it's almost impossible for your guests to fix their own at a buffet or hors d'oeuvre table.

Mixed Steak Tartare   *16 hors d'oeuvre servings*

2 pounds finely ground steak, *no fat or sinew*
5 raw egg yolks, *or* 2 whole eggs plus 2 egg yolks
⅔ cup chopped onion
⅓ cup capers
½ cup chopped beets
Salt and pepper to taste
1 tablespoon Worcestershire sauce
1 teaspoon Poupon mustard

Mix all the ingredients together until very well combined. Mound into a bowl or on a platter. Serve with hors d'oeuvre–size bread and a fancy spreading knife.

Beef Stroganoff

6 servings

It was many years ago that my father, Carl, cooked Beef Stroganoff for parties given by the late Sigmund Romberg, the Hungarian composer who delighted us with *The Student Prince, Desert Song, New Moon,* and many others. Dinner was always formally served in the large oval dining room which seated thirty-five. It was always an elegant occasion.

Stroganoff is a great party dish and one that deserves being mastered. Our family has never enjoyed the addition of tomato to the smooth and delicate sour cream sauce that makes this dish so popular. Tomato paste (the substance added in most recipes calling for tomato) has a strong and spicy taste to it and tends to overpower the subtlety of other flavors. Thus, I shall proceed to give you the recipe for what I can only think of as *real* Beef Stroganoff.

2 pounds beef, julienned
¼ cup (½ stick) butter
1½ pounds mushrooms
Juice of ½ lemon
½ cup white wine
3 tablespoons vegetable oil
2 tablespoons butter
Flour, salt, and pepper
1 medium onion, chopped
3 tablespoons flour
2 cups chicken *or* beef stock
½ teaspoon chicken base
¼ teaspoon garlic powder, *or* 1 clove garlic, pressed
¼ teaspoon coarsely ground pepper
2 tablespoons brandy
¾ cup sour cream

Stroganoff is usually made with filet mignon or the ends of a filet, but it can be made with New York steak just as well. If those prime cuts are out of reach of your wallet, round steak can be used if you just give it some time and care. Instructions I are for making Beef Stroganoff with the tenderest of steaks. Instructions II are for making it with a good piece of round steak.

Instructions I

Have 2 pounds filet or New York steak cut ¾ inch thick and trimmed of all fat. Pound the meat with the side of a cleaver or a rolling pin. Cut the meat into ¼-inch strips. (If the meat is slightly frozen, it is easier to cut. Also, if you cut it on a slant across the grain, it will be tenderer.) Sprinkle with salt and pepper and allow to stand, lightly covered in your refrigerator, for at least 1 hour.

Melt the butter in a large frying pan. Wash or wipe the mushrooms, trim the ends, and slice them ½ inch thick into the butter. Sauté the mushrooms over medium-high heat, squeeze lemon juice over them, and cook until the mushrooms begin to take on color. Add the wine and simmer 2 minutes more. Remove from the heat and transfer the mushrooms and their liquid to a bowl. Put the oil and butter in the pan and heat. Dredge the meat in seasoned flour and brown it over medium-high heat. Do the meat in batches so as not to crowd the strips and to allow for maximum browning. As the meat browns, remove it to a 3- or 4-quart pot with a slotted spoon. When all the meat has been browned and transferred to the pot, add the onion and garlic (if using fresh) and cook until transparent. Add 3 tablespoons flour and cook the onion *roux* for 2 minutes, stirring and scraping the pan to get all the brown particles you can. Add the stock and chicken base and whisk the sauce until smooth. Add the liquid from the mushrooms and whisk again. Simmer the sauce for 5 minutes. Add the mushrooms to the meat in the pot (top with the garlic powder). Add the brandy. Correct the sauce for salt and strain it over the meat and mushrooms. This can all be done in the morning and will actually enhance the flavor of the Stroganoff; however, it is not mandatory. Whether you cook the Stroganoff in the morning or go from start to finish just before dinner, you'll need to simmer the meat mixture with the wine sauce for 5 minutes, then remove the pan from the heat and stir in the sour cream. When thoroughly blended, return the pan to the stove and heat over very low heat until piping hot, but do not allow it to boil. It may be held in a double boiler. Serve with buttered rice or buttered noodles.

Instructions II

Have round steak cut ½ inch thick and trimmed of all fat. Pound the meat and cut it lengthwise so that the strips are no more than 3 or 4 inches wide. Cut these into ¾-inch strips. Follow Instructions I to where the sauce is strained over the mushrooms and meat. *Do not* add the mushrooms to the meat. Strain the sauce over the meat only, cover, and simmer for 20 minutes, stirring occasionally. After 20 minutes, check to see if the steak is tender. If not, simmer it until it is. (If more cooking time is required, you may have to add more stock. The sauce should be quite thick but not so thick that it will burn.) When the steak is tender, add the mushrooms and proceed as if the best of all steaks were in your pot.

Boeuf Bourguignon   *6 to 8 servings*

Boeuf Bourguignon is a deliciously glorified beef stew that is well worth the little extra care and time it requires.

3 pounds boneless chuck, cut into large cubes
  Flour
3 tablespoons vegetable oil
3 tablespoons butter
  Salt and pepper
6 strips bacon, julienned
2 cloves garlic, minced
2 carrots, sliced
2 medium onions, chopped
1 tablespoon chopped parsley
¼ teaspoon thyme leaves
¼ teaspoon celery salt
1 teaspoon chicken base
1 bay leaf
2 cups Burgundy
2 tablespoons brandy
½ pound mushrooms
3 tablespoons butter
2 tablespoons lemon juice
12 pearl onions
¼ teaspoon salt
1 tablespoon butter
1 teaspoon sugar
2 tablespoons butter
1 tablespoon flour

Dredge the beef in flour and brown it in the oil and butter. Transfer the meat with a slotted spoon to a large covered baking dish. To the fat left in the pan add the bacon, garlic, carrots, and onion. Sauté over high heat until the bacon is done and the vegetables start to take on color. With a slotted spoon transfer the vegetables to the baking dish, distributing them evenly over the meat. Top with parsley, salt and pepper, thyme, celery salt, chicken base, and bay leaf. Over the seasonings pour the Burgundy and brandy. If the liquid doesn't quite cover the contents of the dish, add water so that the liquid equals the height of the meat and vegetables. Cover the baking dish tightly and bake in a 325° oven for 2 hours, or until the meat tests done.

While the Bourguignon is cooking, wash and sauté the mushrooms whole in the butter and lemon juice (*no* salt) until they are nicely browned. Set them aside. Peel the pearl onions and put them in a frying pan. Cover them with water, add ¼ teaspoon salt, and boil them until all the water has evaporated. Test for doneness; if the onions aren't cooked enough, add more water and repeat. When they test done, discard any remaining water and add 1 tablespoon butter and 1 teaspoon sugar to the pan. Cook the onions over high heat, shaking the pan until the onions are evenly browned. Set aside.

When the beef tests done, carefully pour as much liquid from the baking dish as possible. Thicken it with 2 tablespoons butter mixed with 1 tablespoon flour. Simmer the sauce for 5 minutes and then strain it back over the meat. Decorate the dish with the mushrooms and onions. Reheat in a 350° oven for 10 minutes and serve.

This recipe is equally good when prepared with moose or elk.

Flank Steak Mignonettes   *4 to 6 servings*

>   1 large flank steak
>   ¼ cup soy sauce
>   2 tablespoons Worcestershire sauce
>   ¼ cup oil, olive preferred
>   ½ cup dry red wine
>   Juice of ½ lemon
>   2 cloves garlic, minced
>   1 teaspoon sugar
>   Salt and pepper
>   8 or more strips bacon

Combine all the ingredients except the salt, pepper, and bacon. Marinate the steak overnight, or a minimum of 5 hours. Score one side of the steak in a diamond pattern. Sprinkle with salt and pepper.

Roll the steak lengthwise with the scored side in.

Wrap the bacon (as many strips as it takes to cover the steak) around the meat. Secure with wooden toothpicks. Slice the roll between the strips of bacon and barbecue it over hot coals, or broil it. Figure up to 5 minutes per side.

Serve with a large sautéed mushroom cap on each steak if you wish. Crisp brown onions also go well.

Or you can barbecue or broil the entire flank steak, rolled without the bacon. Cut between the wooden picks after the steak is done. It will take up to 30 minutes to broil the whole steak if it is placed 8 inches from the broiler. It will take less time over hot coals. This is a cheap, tender way to have a delightful steak.

Boiled Brisket of Beef with Horseradish Sauce   6 to 10 *servings*

    1 beef brisket, 3 to 5 pounds depending on the number
      of persons to be served (figure ½ pound per serving)
    ½ teaspoon salt
    ¼ teaspoon celery salt
    ¼ teaspoon cracked or coarsely ground pepper
    1 bay leaf
    4 sprigs parsley
    1 clove garlic
    2 large onions, peeled and cut in half
    1 large carrot per person, peeled, ends trimmed
    1 medium potato per person

Take out your largest pot. If the brisket is too large for the pot, cut it in half. Cover the meat with cold water and bring it to a boil. When the froth comes to the top, pour off all the water and add fresh cold water to cover along with all the other ingredients except the potatoes. Be sure the water covers everything. Cover the pot and simmer the brisket and vegetables over very low heat for 3 hours. Taste the broth and add salt as needed. Add the potatoes, peeled and cut in half; cover and continue to simmer over slightly higher heat until the potatoes test done, usually about 20 minutes. Remove the meat from the pot to a cutting board. Slice it against the grain and layer it neatly down the center of a large platter. Arrange the vegetables around the meat, cover lightly with foil, and put the platter in a 225° oven.

Horseradish Sauce

    3 cups broth from the brisket
    3 tablespoons flour
    1½ teaspoons prepared horseradish, or to taste
      Salt and pepper

Ladle 3 cups broth from the simmering pot into a saucepan. Sprinkle the flour over the top and whisk with a wire whip until smooth. Add the horseradish and salt and pepper to taste. Simmer the sauce for 5 minutes. Taste, add more horseradish or salt if needed, and strain. Remove the platter from the oven, nap the meat with the sauce, and serve the rest of the sauce in a gravy boat.

Served with homemade bread, this makes a wonderful one-pot meal. Don't forget to strain the sauce, and if it gets too thick while simmering, thin it with more broth from the cooking pot.

Corned Beef and Cabbage

1 4- to 5-pound corned beef brisket
2 medium onions
4 large carrots
2 ribs celery, leaves included
5 sprigs parsley
1 bay leaf
5 whole cloves
1 large clove garlic
¼ teaspoon cracked pepper
1 medium potato per person
1 head cabbage

Rinse the corned beef under cold water. Place it in a 6- to 8-quart pot with a lid. Cover with cold water and bring to a boil. Drain off the boiling water and rinse the corned beef once more under cold running water. Again cover with cold water; add the onions, carrots, celery, parsley, bay leaf, cloves, garlic, and pepper. Bring the meat and vegetables to a slow boil and simmer for 4 hours with the lid slightly ajar. Most corned beef briskets will become tender in 4 hours, but taste a little sliver to make sure. Half an hour before the corned beef is due to be done, add the potatoes, peeled and cut in half, to the pot. Wash the cabbage, cut it into quarters, and cut out the core. Cut the quarters in half and place them in a pot that will just accommodate the pieces. Ladle 1½ cups of the cooking broth from the corned beef over the cabbage. Cover the pot and cook the cabbage at a slow boil for 11 minutes. It should still have some crunch to it. Drain the cabbage. Arrange the corned beef on a large platter and surround it with the potatoes, carrots, and cabbage (discard the garlic). Run a lump of butter over the vegetables and sprinkle the potatoes with chopped parsley. Serve with more butter, sour cream, a variety of mustards, and some horseradish.

Note: If the pot you cook the corned beef in is big enough, you can lay the cabbage right on top and cook it for 11 minutes with the lid on. Spoon it out with a slotted spoon when it is done so as not to overcook it.

Swiss Steak   *6 servings*

3 pounds round steak, 1 inch thick
Flour
¼ cup vegetable oil
3 large onions, sliced thick or thin
½ pound mushrooms, washed and sliced (optional)
2 tablespoons butter (for mushrooms)
2 teaspoons lemon juice (for mushrooms)
½ teaspoon salt
¼ teaspoon pepper
2 tablespoons chopped parsley
3 large tomatoes
1 teaspoon chicken base
½ cup water
½ cup red wine

Sift a thick layer of flour onto a chopping block. Dredge the meat in it, and with the largest butcher knife you have, pound the flour into the meat, making thousands of little cuts. Turn the meat and do the other side; then turn again and rotate the meat so that your next cuts will cross the ones you made before. Once you've pounded both sides twice and have worked out all your aggressions for the day, cut the meat into serving pieces.

Heat the oil in a large frying pan and brown the meat well on both sides over a medium-high flame. As the meat browns, transfer it to a baking dish that can accommodate the pieces in one layer. Add the onions to the pan, separating the rings as you do so. Stir-fry until barely transparent. Tilt the pan to drain the onions and distribute them over the meat. Add the mushrooms to the pan along with the butter and lemon juice. While the mushrooms are cooking, sprinkle half the salt and pepper over the onions. Sprinkle 1 tablespoon of the parsley over the seasonings. When the mushrooms begin to take on color, tilt the pan; drain and distribute the mushrooms over the onions. Pour boiling water over the tomatoes. Let them sit for 10 to 15 seconds; drain them and slip off the skins. Cut the tomatoes into ⅓-inch slices and place at least one slice over the onions and mushrooms on each piece of meat. Again add salt and pepper and add the last tablespoon of parsley. Dissolve 1 teaspoon chicken base in ½ cup water and add the wine; stir and pour over all. Cover tightly with a lid or foil and put the dish in a 275° oven for 5 hours, or all day if you've a job to go to.

If you can't start your Swiss Steak in the morning and it's three o'clock when you hit the kitchen, bake it in a 350° oven for 3½ to 4 hours, depending on the tenderness of the steak; it should melt in your mouth.

Serve with mashed potatoes, parsleyed potatoes, or buttered noodles, plus a green vegetable or green salad or both. Add some french bread and a bottle of red wine and you're eating in style.

The husband of a friend of mine thinks he doesn't like onions, although he eats them without knowing it all the time. When making her Swiss Steak in the manner described, she adds 1 cup sliced celery to the onions. It's delicious, and he thinks it's all celery. You might wish to experiment by adding celery or green pepper or leeks to yours. The obvious secret is fresh vegetables on top of the meat and long, slow cooking. The same procedure is used for pot roast, but in that case sautéing the vegetables isn't necessary.

Pot Roast   *6 to 8 servings*

1 pot roast *or* chuck roast *or* round bone roast (figure ½ pound per person)
2 large onions
2 large carrots
2 stalks celery (optional)
½ cup sliced mushrooms
1 large or 2 small tomatoes (optional)
½ teaspoon salt
¼ teaspoon pepper
¼ teaspoon celery salt
1 tablespoon chopped parsley
½ teaspoon chicken base
½ cup water *or* red wine

Put the roast in a deep-sided baking dish and brown it under the broiler. While the meat is browning, slice all the vegetables thin; I run them all through my food processor. When the meat has been browned on both sides, pile the sliced raw vegetables on top. Sprinkle the salt, pepper, and celery salt over the vegetables; top with parsley and add ½ teaspoon chicken base dissolved in ½ cup water or wine. Cover tightly and bake in a slow (225°) oven all day, or bake in a 350° oven for 2 to 3 hours, depending on size. The roast can be transferred after browning to a slow cooker which will do the same job. I've taken a frozen chuck roast out of my freezer, shoved it under the broiler, cut my vegetables, and had the whole works in a slow oven in 10 minutes.

Braised Short Ribs of Beef   *4 servings*

3 pounds short ribs
¼ teaspoon salt
⅛ teaspoon pepper
1 onion
2 carrots
1 clove garlic (optional)
¼ cup red wine
½ cup water
½ teaspoon chicken base (optional)
1 tablespoon flour
1 tablespoon butter

Put the short ribs in a baking dish and cook, uncovered, in a 400° oven for 45 minutes. Remove from the oven, drain off the fat, and sprinkle with salt and pepper. Peel the onion and cut it into large dice. Peel the carrots and cut them into quarters lengthwise and then in half. Add the onion, carrots, and garlic to the baking dish. Add the liquids, cover tightly, and bake in a 325° oven for 2½ hours, or until tender. All this can be done in the morning and the dish reheated later. Fifteen minutes before you're ready to serve, remove the vegetables with a slotted spoon and set them aside, discard the garlic, and drain the liquid into a saucepan. Return the short ribs to a hot (450°) oven to crisp and brown while you knead the flour and butter together until well blended. Add the flour-and-butter mixture bit by bit to the liquid. Simmer until thickened, adding water or stock to the gravy to attain the consistency of heavy cream; strain. Arrange the short ribs on a serving platter, garnish with vegetables, and nap with gravy. Serve the rest of the gravy on the side.

Biff à la Rydberg—Scandia

2 servings

The name is exotic and the dish is delicious. The serving of it (if done as suggested) is marvelous and impressive. Kenneth Hansen of Scandia gave me this delightful recipe and suggested that it be served as a light midnight snack or at a luncheon to be enjoyed with Aquavit and beer or perhaps Black Velvets.

1 pound filet of beef *or* top sirloin steak, all fat removed
1½ cups white potatoes, cooked, peeled, and diced
1 cup diced onion
5 tablespoons butter
Salt and pepper
2 tablespoons Worcestershire sauce
2 teaspoons Dijon mustard
4 egg yolks

Cut the meat into ½-inch dice. Dice the potatoes the same size. Have all the other ingredients ready and at room temperature. Brown the onions in 1 tablespoon butter in a small frying pan. In another frying pan fry the potatoes in 2 tablespoons butter. Season both the onions and potatoes with salt and pepper. Season the meat and brown it in 2 tablespoons butter in a separate frying pan over high heat. Place the three ingredients in separate piles in the top of a chafing dish or crêpe pan. Place the Worcestershire, mustard, and egg yolks (separated and brought to the table in their half shells placed in a low bowl of salt) on a platter and bring the platter and the chafing dish to the table. Light the flame under the chafing dish. With a serving spoon and fork lightly mix the meat, onions, and potatoes together. Add the Worcestershire and mustard and mix. Add pepper to taste (a few grinds of a pepper mill is just about right) and the egg yolks. Mix lightly to combine. As soon as the egg yolks have coated all the ingredients, Biff à la Rydberg should be served. The heat in the ingredients will be enough to take care of the buttery egg yolks.

If you're not trying to impress guests or neighbors, you can do all the final cooking in the privacy of your kitchen, by adding the potatoes and onions to the frying pan that contains the meat and going from there over very low heat.

Prime Rib Hash   *4 servings*

I have never enjoyed what is commonly referred to as hash in this country. The recipe I'm about to give you is for a hash, but it has little resemblance to the fatty mess you normally meet. To begin with, it is made with leftover prime rib roast beef which was ideally cooked rare or medium rare. Though prime rib is best, any leftover cooked beef will do. I have made a marvelous dish of this hash from steaks brought home in doggie bags from the finest restaurants where we all ordered too much. This recipe is great for using up leftovers, and even someone who doesn't like leftovers will love it and ask for more.

2 tablespoons vegetable oil
2 tablespoons butter
1 medium onion, diced
2 cups cooked, peeled potatoes, cut into ½-inch dice
2 cups leftover prime rib roast, cut into ½-inch dice
  Salt and pepper to taste

In a large, heavy skillet heat the oil and butter. Add the onion and cook over medium heat until transparent. Add the potatoes, turn up the heat, and cook until the potatoes are lightly browned. Add the meat and stir-fry the mixture until the meat is browned and all is piping hot. Spoon into a hot serving dish and enjoy, or put portions on plates and top with a fried egg.

Grand Pirozhki   *4 entrée servings*

1 pound ground beef, *or* veal, lamb, elk, or moose (there should be some fat in the meat)
1 medium onion, chopped
½ teaspoon salt
¼ teaspoon pepper
4 hard-boiled eggs, chopped
⅓ cup chopped parsley
2 tablespoons butter
1 tablespoon flour
½ cup milk
⅔ cup stock
¼ teaspoon celery salt

½ teaspoon rosemary leaves
½ teaspoon chicken base
1 recipe Infallible Pie Crust I, II, *or* III (see Index)
1 egg yolk
1 tablespoon milk

Brown the meat and onion together. Add the salt and pepper and cook until the meat is brown and the onion transparent. Drain off any fat, and transfer the meat and onion to a bowl. Add the hard-boiled eggs and the parsley to the bowl. Melt the butter in a saucepan, add the flour, and stir the mixture for a moment or two over moderate heat. Slowly incorporate the milk and the stock, stirring with a wire whisk until very smooth. Add the celery salt, rosemary leaves, and chicken base. Add the sauce to the bowl and stir until all ingredients are blended together.

Roll two-thirds of the pie dough into a rectangle, rolling from its center out. (Never roll back and forth, as this toughens dough.) When the dough is thinly rolled, place the meat mixture down the middle, lengthwise, leaving 2 inches at each end. The mixture should be piled and rounded and resemble a small log, but don't make it more than 2 inches high or it will tend to settle down during the baking process and split the crust. Fold the two short ends up over the meat, then take the long side closest to you and fold it over the meat. If the long back edge is ragged, trim it with a knife and then fold it over the meat toward you, thus totally encasing the meat mixture. Seal this final seam with water. With two long spatulas transfer the whole thing to a lightly greased cookie sheet. (Some people like to roll the dough, put it on the cookie sheet, and do the rest right on the sheet; however, I've never had any trouble with the transfer. It's up to you.)

Roll the remaining dough thin, and with a knife cut long, thin stems, some pointed oval leaves, and some flowers. (I often cut small circles of dough and then cut the circles to form tulips.) Wet the back of the stems and apply them to the top of the crust. Do the same with the leaves and flowers, forming your own design. This decoration is optional, but it makes a very beautiful dish. When you've completed your design, beat the egg yolk with milk and brush the entire creation with the mixture. Bake in a 400° oven for 30 minutes, or until golden brown.

This is not only an impressive dish but a delicious one, and even your standard meat-and-potatoes eater will love it. It can be cut into several pieces for an appetizer, or served as a main course along with parsleyed potatoes, a green vegetable, and either soup or salad. It's economical, too.

Carl's Stuffed Zucchini   8 *servings*

4 large (8-inch) zucchini
4 ounces Swiss cheese
4 ounces Cheddar cheese
4 ounces mozzarella cheese
1 cup bread crumbs
2 sweet Italian sausages
½ pound ground beef
1 medium-sized onion, chopped
1 6-ounce can V-8 *or* tomato juice
½ teaspoon salt
¼ teaspoon pepper
¼ teaspoon thyme leaves
½ bay leaf
3 tomatoes
6 medium-sized mushrooms
2 shallots, *or* 1 teaspoon dehydrated shallots, *or* 4 scallions, white part only
1 tablespoon butter
1 tablespoon chopped parsley

Wash the zucchini and trim the ends. Cut the zucchini in half lengthwise. Simmer them in a large frying pan with water almost to cover for 5 minutes, skin side down. While the zucchini are simmering, grate the cheeses and lightly toss them with the bread crumbs; set aside. When the zucchini have cooked for 5 minutes, their skin should be bright green and the flesh still firm. Remove from the heat and rinse under cold water until all cooking action has stopped; set aside. Remove the skins from the Italian sausages and put the meat in a frying pan with the ground beef and onion. Brown the meat mixture over moderately high heat, turning and breaking it up as it cooks. When the beef is done, tip the pan and push all the ingredients to the uphill side. Allow the fat to drain; discard all you can. Add the V-8, salt, pepper, thyme, and bay leaf to the drained meat mixture and simmer until the juice has been completely absorbed. Pour boiling water over the tomatoes; allow them to sit for 2 minutes, then drain, peel, seed, and cut them into julienne strips. With a spoon scoop the pulp from the zucchini to within ½ inch of the skin. Be careful not to break through the flesh. Wash the mushrooms, cut them in half, turn, and cut them into thin slices. Peel and mince the shallots or substitute. Melt 1 tablespoon butter in a large frying pan; add the tomatoes, zucchini pulp, mushrooms, and shallots. Cook the vegetable mixture over medium-high heat, stirring until the mixture is smooth and loses all its moisture. This will take about 15 minutes. Cook both the beef and vegetable mixtures; remove the bay leaf. If liquid accumulates in either, drain it.

Put the zucchini shells into a buttered baking dish; combine the beef and vegetable mixtures; add the chopped parsley and 1 cup of the cheese-crumb mixture. Fill the zucchini, heaping the mixture into the scooped-out cavities. Pile the cheese-crumb mixture onto the stuffed zucchini. If you can't get all the cheese on top, save what's left for topping other dishes or for open-face toasted cheese sandwiches. Cover the stuffed zucchini tightly with plastic wrap until ready to heat and serve. To serve, remove the plastic and heat the zucchini in a 350° oven for 20 minutes, or until thoroughly hot and the cheese is melted. Serve with a green salad, french bread, and red wine.

Kalldolmars—Scandia   *6 servings*

Every European country has its rendition of stuffed cabbage leaves. The following recipe is from Kenneth Hansen of Scandia. His customers have been enjoying them for years, and now you can do the same in your own home.

½ cup long-grain white rice
1½ cups milk
1 head cabbage
½ pound ground veal *or* beef
½ pound ground pork
1 small onion, grated (about ¼ cup)
1 egg
1 tablespoon flour
½ teaspoon salt, or to taste
¼ teaspoon coarsely ground pepper
2 pinches nutmeg
   Pinch ground allspice
   Salt, pepper, and paprika
2 tablespoons butter
2 tablespoons molasses
1 tablespoon flour
1 tablespoon butter

Cook the rice in the milk in a covered pot over low heat for 25 minutes. Uncover the pot and allow the rice to cool. Wash and core the cabbage. Submerge it in boiling water for 5 minutes, drain, and cool it. Save 2 cups of the cabbage broth. Beat the meat, onion, rice, egg, flour, and seasonings together until very well combined. Remove the leaves from the cabbage, spreading out the largest ones for stuffing. Cut the tough central core from the bottom of each leaf. The filling will fill from 8 to 24 cabbage leaves. Determine how many cabbage rolls you need and how large you wish them to be, and divide the meat filling among the number of leaves you need. Fold the leaves over the meat mixture and roll them up in traditional cabbage-roll fashion and tie with string. Place the cabbage rolls in a buttered baking dish. Season with salt, pepper, and a sprinkling of paprika. Melt 2 tablespoons butter with 2 tablespoons molasses and pour over the cabbage rolls. Braise in a 350° oven for 30 minutes, turn, and braise another 30 minutes. Turn the Kalldolmars again, add 1 cup of the cabbage liquid, turn the oven up to 450°, and let the rolls brown.

When they are golden brown, place them in a serving dish and keep them warm in a low oven. Put the pan juices in a saucepan, add another cup of cabbage liquid, and reduce by half over high heat. Thicken the gravy with 1 tablespoon flour kneaded into 1 tablespoon butter. Correct the seasoning and add a few drops of Kitchen Bouquet, if desired for color. Strain the gravy over the Kalldolmars and serve with fluffy whipped potatoes and lingonberries.

Beef Enchiladas   *6 servings*

  1 pound ground beef *or* other ground meat of your choice
  1 onion, chopped
  ½ teaspoon salt
  ¼ teaspoon pepper
  1 4¼-ounce can black olives, chopped
  ½ teaspoon chili powder
  ¼ teaspoon cumin
  ¼ cup vegetable oil
  1 10-ounce can enchilada sauce
  8 ounces Jack cheese, grated
  6 ounces Cheddar or American cheese, grated
10 scallions, chopped
12 corn tortillas

Brown the meat and onion in a large frying pan. Sprinkle with salt and pepper. When the meat is cooked, tilt the pan, drain the fat, and discard it. Add the olives, chili powder, and cumin to the meat mixture, plus 2 tablespoons enchilada sauce. Mix well.

Grease a 14-inch baking dish. Have the baking dish, the grated cheese, the chopped scallions, and the meat mixture arranged by the stove, plus one dinner plate. Heat the oil and 2 tablespoons enchilada sauce in a frying pan big enough to hold the tortillas.

Working in succession, put one tortilla in the oil mixture. When it softens, turn it to moisten the other side. Put the tortilla on a dinner plate. Put 2 tablespoons of the meat mixture down the center of the tortilla, top with 2 tablespoons Jack cheese and a good teaspoonful of scallions. Roll the tortilla tightly around the stuffing and place it seam side down in the baking dish. Repeat until all the tortillas are used.

If you have any scallions left, sprinkle them over the enchiladas, then pour any remaining enchilada sauce over all. Top with any remaining Jack cheese and all of the Cheddar. Bake in a 350° oven for 20 minutes, or until very hot. The baking time will vary, depending on whether you go from start to finish with the recipe or make them ahead of time, thus putting them into the oven cold.

This is an excellent enchilada recipe, but it is only mildly spicy. If you like your enchiladas fairly hot, use *hot* enchilada sauce rather than the mild, and if you like your enchiladas *very hot,* crumble 1 or 2 dried hot chilies into the meat mixture and use the *hot* sauce to boot—then have the beer at the ready.

This is a fabulous way to use up leftover meat. To replace the ground beef, you'll need 1½ to 2 cups thinly julienned meat.

If you're on a tight budget, or are serving another meat course, omit the meat altogether and have cheese enchiladas only.

Chili

    2 pounds ground beef
    2 large onions, chopped
    2 15-ounce cans tomato sauce
 1½ teaspoons salt
   ¼ teaspoon pepper
 1½ tablespoons chili powder
 1½ teaspoons cumin
   ½ teaspoon oregano leaves
    2 small hot chilies, crumbled (use only 1 if you don't like your chili too hot)
    1 clove garlic, minced, *or* ½ teaspoon garlic powder
    1 teaspoon chicken base, *or* 1 bouillon cube
    1 can beer
    4 cans kidney *or* chili beans, *or* ½ pound cooked kidney *or* pinto beans
    3 tablespoons flour
   ¼ cup water

Brown the meat and onions over high heat in a large frying pan. When the meat is done, tip the pan, scoop the meat and onions to the high side, and discard the fat that drains off the mixture. Put the meat in a slow cooker or large pot. Add all the other ingredients except the beans, flour, and water. Simmer for 2 hours. When the simmering process begins, add any leftover meat you might have, diced fine. You might also like to add green pepper or dehydrated sweet peppers. When your chili has simmered for at least 2 hours, add the beans, which you have drained, and strain the flour and water that you have mixed together into the chili. Stir to combine completely, and simmer for at least another 30 minutes. During the last simmering check for salt content and, if desired, add 1 cup grated Jack or Cheddar cheese. Or serve finished chili with grated cheese and chopped onions.

Chili is a fantastic dish in which to hide leftovers. Whether you add beef, lamb, pork, veal, or fowl, you will enhance the flavor of your chili. Chili freezes well, too.

Note: If your chili seems too dry, or if you like more sauce, add another can of tomato sauce or more beer. Correct for salt.

Lasagna

2 pounds ground beef
2 large onions, chopped
2 15-ounce cans tomato sauce
1 teaspoon salt
¼ teaspoon pepper
1 large clove garlic, minced
1 teaspoon dried basil leaves
½ teaspoon dried oregano leaves
¼ teaspoon celery salt
½ teaspoon sugar
⅛ teaspoon thyme
1 bay leaf
1 tablespoon chopped parsley
⅓ cup dry red wine
1 teaspoon chicken base mixed with ½ cup water

1 8-ounce package lasagna noodles

1 pint ricotta cheese
6 ounces mozzarella cheese, thinly sliced
6 ounces Jack cheese, thinly sliced
2 ounces Parmesan cheese, grated

Brown the beef and onions over high heat until the meat is brown and the onions are transparent. Tip the pan, push the meat mixture to the high side, and allow the fat to drain. Discard it. Put the meat mixture in a large saucepan and add all the other sauce ingredients. Allow it to simmer for a minimum of 2 hours. Stir occasionally. Discard the bay leaf.

Boil the lasagna noodles according to the package directions. Drain them. Butter a large baking dish approximately 14 by 8 inches. Put a layer of sauce in the bottom of the dish, top with a layer of noodles, then meat, Jack cheese, noodles, meat, ricotta, noodles, meat, and mozzarella. Finish with Parmesan. (That's four layers of meat sauce, three layers of noodles, and a different cheese in each layer.)

Bake in a 350° oven for 25 minutes, or until hot and all the cheese is melted.

Variations

You can use cottage cheese in place of the ricotta.

You can substitute Cheddar for the ricotta and have American Lasagna, or use Jack, mozzarella, and Parmesan only.

A layer of sautéed mushrooms is marvelous, or add the mushrooms to the sauce.

If the Lasagna isn't going to be a main dish or if you wish to go meatless, make the sauce without the ground beef.

Lamb

When I was fourteen, I spent a summer in the tiny town of Candor in upstate New York. My mother's sister Mickey had moved there with her husband right after World War II. It was there that I picked my first sun-ripened vegetables and husked fresh corn that was cooked and eaten 10 minutes later. I made jam and canned berries we'd picked in the morning and gorged on a wild berry pie that made my tongue blue for hours. I also hunted night crawlers (large worms) late at night by flashlight for bait.

Aunt Mickey was a wonderful cook, and besides the fish we caught with the night crawlers, we had succulent pork, which had been born and fattened on a brother-in-law's farm, plus beef, also locally raised.

"When are we going to have lamb chops?" I asked.

"Never!" my aunt replied. I didn't understand. Mickey explained that her husband wouldn't eat lamb.

For years I was mystified by this prejudice. The only time I ever heard of anyone refusing to eat lamb was in movies and books about the Old West when the cattlemen warred with the sheepherders and never touched a lamb chop.

Then it happened—we moved to Wyoming and had a dinner party. A king's ransom of leg of lamb graced the table. One guest said, "Oh, I've never tasted lamb." She explained that she was from cattle country and that people from her part of the country simply didn't eat lamb. She was very gracious, tried the lamb, and loved it. She now serves it in her own home.

Months later I was having another dinner party. The allergies of some of my guests narrowed my choice of entrées, so I decided on lamb. But first I checked with one of the wives whose husband is a cowboy through and through. Embarrassed, but honest (thank God), she explained that serving lamb to her husband would be like serving a whole roast pig to a group of rabbis. "Yes," she agreed, "the range wars were over years ago, but still . . ." I changed my menu one more time.

I am reminded of an old friend of the family who loved mountain oysters and ate them often at his favorite Basque restaurant south of Bakersfield, California. One evening when we were all enjoying his favorite dish, he asked my father, "Carl, you're the food expert. Where the hell do they catch these? I've been to every stream and lake around here and have never seen any." We all laughed and said that he must surely be joking; everyone knew that mountain oysters were sheep's testicles. At that point he went white and rushed out of the restaurant clutching his mouth.

I can understand his being shocked, since he'd always thought them to be something else; but where was his logic in the years that followed when he never again ate one of his favorite foods?

If you don't know what you're eating, the chances are you'll like it. Our background and upbringing cause our culinary prejudices, not our taste buds or our bodily nutritional needs. If you discard some of your prejudices and expand your eating habits, you'll broaden your palate and pleasure.

Lamb Facts

• Lamb must be fresh. If you use frozen lamb, cook it as soon as it's defrosted. Don't keep it in the refrigerator for three days. (This holds for pork also.)

• If you don't care for the smell of roasting lamb, turn down the heat. Lamb has what butchers call hard fat, and high heat causes it to give off more of an odor. The French like to pop their lamb into a very hot oven and then lower the temperature (so do I), but you can cook lamb at 325° from start to finish and end up with a beautiful juicy roast and almost no odor.

• Only lamb over eight months old, which should be called mutton, need be cooked well-done. Mutton is not sold in American markets, so unless you live on a sheep ranch, cook lamb so that it is slightly pink to get the best possible flavor. This is especially true with loin or French (rib) chops.

• Lambs these days are born almost the year round. So "spring" lamb only means one less than six months of age.

• Many people ask the butcher to remove the "oil" or "musk" gland from legs of lamb, thinking the gland gives the lamb a bad odor. The identical glands are found in beef and pork but are never removed. I don't bother with it.

• Breast of lamb is very fatty but delicious. Brown it in butter, season it with salt and pepper, and braise it in the oven for several hours until the fat has melted out of the tissue, leaving you juicy morsels to strip from the bones.

• When you roast a leg or shoulder of lamb, never remove the thin membrane that covers the meat. It is a natural casing that protects the meat and keeps it juicy and tender during the cooking process. This membrane is often referred to as the fell.

• When roasting lamb, figure 25 to 30 minutes per pound for leg cuts and 40 to 45 minutes for shoulder cuts.

• If you don't like garlic with roast lamb, try squeezing the juice of a lemon over it instead.

Baked Irish Lamb Stew

PER SERVING:

1 shoulder chop, *or* the equivalent amount of stew meat *or* neck meat *or* lean breast meat
1 medium potato
¼ cabbage (if cabbage is large, 1/6 or ⅛)
Salt and pepper
Butter

Butter a large flameproof casserole. Be sure to use a lot of butter and spread it clear to the rim. Place the lamb in the bottom of the casserole in a single layer. Salt and pepper the meat. Peel the potatoes, cut them in half lengthwise, and place them on top of the lamb in a single layer. Again salt and pepper. Wash and core the cabbage, cut it in wedges or slices, and place it on top of the potatoes. Dot with butter. Cover the casserole tightly. If the lid is not extremely tight-fitting, cover the casserole with foil, crimp it tightly, and add the lid. Bake in a 350° oven for 1½ hours. Check the lamb; if it's not tender, cook it a bit longer. Shoulder chops will be done in this time.

That's all there is to it. It's almost too easy and delicious. You add no liquid, yet you end up with a lovely broth in the casserole. If you wish you may drain the broth, thicken it, and season it to your liking, but this stew simply spooned into hot bowls and served with crusty bread is a delight.

Note: If you like onions, add them between the potato and cabbage layers, along with salt and pepper. Add small peeled pearl onions if company is coming.

Stuffed Grape Leaves (Dolmades)   *12 servings*

2 cloves garlic
2 pounds ground lamb *or* beef
1 large onion, chopped fine
½ teaspoon salt
¼ teaspoon pepper
3 eggs
½ cup chopped fresh parsley
½ teaspoon cinnamon
1 cup uncooked rice
1 cup tomato sauce
2 8-ounce jars grape leaves (if fresh grape leaves are available, blanch them for 30 to 40 seconds in boiling water a few at a time)
6 eggs, separated
1 cup lemon juice

Press the garlic cloves with the broad side of a large knife to break their skins. Peel and mince them, or put them through a press. Put the garlic in a bowl along with all the other ingredients except the grape leaves, separated eggs, and lemon juice. Be sure your hands are clean and dive in. Work the ingredients together until they're evenly distributed and blended to a consistency that will hold together.

Rinse the grape leaves under cold running water and set them in colander to drain. Take the grape leaves one at a time and pinch off the stem. Place the leaf on a cutting board with the snipped-off stem pointed toward you. Place a teaspoonful (large or small, depending on the size of the grape leaf) of the meat mixture on the leaf just in back of the place where the stem was removed. Fold the right part of the leaf (at the end closest to you) over the meat mixture, then the left. Start rolling away from you, all the while tucking the side leaf edges over the center where the meat mixture is. When you come to the end of the leaf, you should have a neat bundle with the meat mixture snugly confined within. It's important that none of the mixture should ooze out or show. As you roll the Dolmades (as they are called in the Near East), place them seam side down in a large, wide, flat-bottomed pot with a lid. Fit them in tight next to each other. When they have all been rolled and put in the pot (they may be two deep if necessary), cover them with water and put two or three heatproof plates on top of them to keep them submerged while they cook. Cover the pot with the lid, bring to a boil on top of the stove, reduce the heat to a temperature that'll keep the water just simmering, and cook for 35 to 40 minutes. Remove the plates.

Beat the 6 egg whites until frothy, add the egg yolks, and beat. Add the lemon juice and the broth from the cooking pot. Blend well and pour the lemon-egg mixture back over the Dolmades. Cook another 10 minutes. Remove from the heat and allow to sit at room temperature until completely cooled. Refrigerate.

The following day arrange the Dolmades in a pretty ovenproof dish, spoon as much of the sauce as desired over them, and reheat (covered) in a moderate oven until bubbling and hot.

Serve as an hors d'oeuvre or as one of the main courses at dinner. They're great for parties, fine with fish or roast lamb or on a buffet. Dolmades will keep in the refrigerator for a week or more; and if you're like the Italian-Greek who gave me this recipe, you may snitch them out of the refrigerator cold. She says she loves them that way best.

Pork

A filet of beef may be delicious rare; a medium-rare rack of lamb may be a delight; but *pork must* be cooked well-done. There is no exception to the rule that pork must cook a minimum of 30 minutes to the pound, whether you're roasting it or frying it or simmering it in a kettle.

Danish Roast Pork Loin

  1 6- or 7-pound loin of pork
  Salt and pepper
  ½ medium onion per person
  1 cup water
  3 prunes per person
  1 green apple per person
  ½ cup sugar
  ½ cup white wine

Have the butcher trim the loin so as to leave ¼ inch of fat on top. Then ask him to saw through the bottom of each chop in the loin so that you can easily carve the roast into chops after roasting. Place the loin on a rack in a roasting pan. Sprinkle it liberally with salt and coarsely ground pepper. Add the onions to the pan, plus 1 cup water. Put the roast in a preheated 400° oven, immediately lower the heat to 325°, and cook it for 3½ hours. Meanwhile, stew the prunes in water to cover until just tender. Pare the apples, cut them into quarters, cut out the cores, and put them in a saucepan. Add the sugar and wine, cover, and bring to a rapid boil. Boil for 2 minutes, remove from the heat, and drain. Drain the prunes and put the prunes and apples in a buttered baking dish. When the roast is almost done, put the prunes and apples in the oven to heat. When the roasting time is up, place the roast on platter, surround it with onions, prunes, and apples, and set it in a 200° oven while you make the gravy.

Pork Gravy

  3 tablespoons pan drippings
  3 tablespoons flour
  2½ cups water
  Salt and pepper to taste
  2 tablespoons currant jelly

Drain all but 3 tablespoons fat from the roasting pan and place the pan on a burner over medium heat. Sprinkle in the flour and stir with a wire whip. When the flour is well incorporated, add the water, a small amount at a time, and continue stirring. With the wire whip scrape all the brown particles from the pan. When the gravy is thickened and smooth, taste it for salt and pepper. Add the jelly and stir until it is melted. If the gravy is too thick, add water. It should be the consistency of thick cream, not of library paste. Simmer 3 more minutes, then strain it into a heated gravy boat.

Glazed Ham   20 or more servings

1 cured ham, preferably Hormel Cure '81
1 cup packed brown sugar
¼ cup dry mustard, Colman's preferred
  Water or dry sherry or white wine

Place the ham on a rack in a roasting pan. Combine the sugar and mustard
in a bowl. Choose the liquid you wish to use and add some to the sugar
mixture; start off with about 2 tablespoons. You should get a thick heavy
paste. Do not add enough liquid to produce a runny mixture. Pile half of the
glaze on top of the ham, smoothing it down the center with a knife. Don't
spread the glaze; it will run down over the ham on its own. Place the ham in
a 350° oven for 1 hour, remove it from the oven, cut a diamond pattern ¼
inch deep into the top, spread it with the remaining glaze, and return the
ham to the oven for another 30 minutes.

If you use a Cure '81, you'll have very little fat and no waste. Since a ham
of this type has so little fat, it's a good idea to put ¾ cup water in the bottom
of the roasting pan to keep the glaze that drips from burning.

Danish Fricadeller—Scandia   6 servings

There are as many recipes for Danish Fricadeller as there are recipes for
American meat loaf, but no one made them better than Kenneth Hansen of
Scandia.

½ pound ground veal or beef
½ pound ground pork
1 medium onion, grated or very finely chopped
1 tablespoon butter
1 egg
3 tablespoons flour
½ cup lukewarm milk
½ cup club soda
  Salt to taste (about ½ teaspoon)
  Pepper to taste (about ¼ teaspoon)
  Pinch nutmeg
1 scallion, chopped
2 tablespoons butter
1 tablespoon oil

By hand:
Have the butcher grind the veal and pork together twice. Sauté the grated onion in 1 tablespoon butter; do not allow it to brown. Place the meat, onion, and egg in a bowl and beat vigorously with a wooden spoon. Add the flour, then the milk and soda, a little at a time, beating continuously after each addition. Add the seasonings and chopped scallion and beat again. Taste and correct for seasonings. Cover the mixture with plastic wrap and refrigerate it for at least 1 hour.

Heat the butter and oil in a large frying pan. With a tablespoon form the meat mixture into oblong patties and fry them, turning and browning them until well cooked. If you can keep turning them a third or a fourth of their circumference each time, you'll be able to maintain their lovely egg shapes. When the Fricadeller are well browned and thoroughly cooked, transfer them to a warm platter. Serve with 3 tablespoons browned butter poured over all. You should get from 12 to 18 Fricadeller from this recipe, depending on how large you make them. If your frying pan won't hold all of them, do them in two batches, keeping the first batch in a warm oven while you fry the second batch.

Kenneth suggested that Fricadeller be served with lingonberries (available at imported food stores), cranberries, or currant jam. He also suggested a creamed vegetable and fried potatoes. I love mine with lingonberries, creamy mashed potatoes, and a fresh green vegetable. The sweet fruit is important; the rest is up to you.

By electric mixer:
Follow the hand method, but put the ingredients in the work bowl of an electric mixer and allow it to do the beating.

By food processor:
With a food processor you needn't have the butcher grind the meat twice. Add the ingredients in the order given, and turn the machine on and off until they are well combined.

Fricadeller II   *10 to 12 servings*

My old recipe differs from Kenneth's in that it uses all pork, and the meat mixture is first poached and then browned. Whichever recipe you choose, you should be aware of the fact that Fricadeller freeze well and that they are just as delicious cold as hot. The Danes make open-face sandwiches out of leftover Fricadeller. They slice them at an angle in order to get the biggest possible slices and layer them onto dark buttered pumpernickel with thinly sliced pickled watermelon rind, thinly sliced onion, or crisply fried bacon as a garnish. Being an American girl, I love Fricadeller sliced cold on rye bread with lots of mayonnaise, thinly sliced onion, and lettuce. I'm sure you'll invent other exciting variations on the Fricadeller sandwich theme.

Note: Fricadeller is a delicious cold luncheon meat that contains no chemicals, food dyes, or additives.

1 good-sized onion
2 tablespoons butter
2 pounds ground pork
4 slices bread, trimmed and cut or torn into small pieces
6 eggs
1 teaspoon salt
¼ teaspoon coarsely ground pepper
1 tablespoon chopped parsley
Milk or half-and-half
3 quarts water
1 tablespoon salt
1 teaspoon chicken base, or 1 bouillon cube
2 tablespoons butter
1 tablespoon vegetable oil
2 tablespoons flour

By food processor:

Peel and chop the onion fine, and sauté it in butter until it is transparent. Put the pork, onion, and bread into the work bowl of the food processor fitted with the steel blade. Start the machine and add the eggs and seasonings. Process until the mixture is very smooth. If it becomes very thick, add milk or half-and-half until the dough is soft and will *just* hold its shape when spooned onto a plate. If the mixture becomes too thin, continue to process until the proper consistency is reached.

Bring the water, salt, and chicken base or bouillon cube to a boil. Taste the Fricadeller batter; it should taste good. Correct for salt and pepper if necessary. Keep the water at a simmer as you gently spoon egg-shaped spoonfuls of batter into it. Simmer the Fricadeller for 15 minutes. Remove them from the water with a slotted spoon. Reserve the broth. In a large frying pan melt the 2 tablespoons butter with the oil. When hot, brown the Fricadeller over high heat, shaking the pan and turning the Fricadeller to brown all sides. With a slotted spoon remove the Fricadeller to an ovenproof serving dish. Stir 2 tablespoons flour into the oils left in the frying pan and stir with a wire whisk. When the flour has been totally absorbed, add 2 cups poaching liquid. Whisk until smooth and thickened. Correct for seasonings. Simmer 5 minutes. Strain the sauce over the Fricadeller and reheat in the oven when ready to serve.

Fricadeller are excellent served with noodles. Don't forget the lingonberries or cranberries, though I've been known to substitute applesauce. If you wish your sauce to be a rich brown, add a few drops of Kitchen Bouquet.

Note: If you wish to freeze Fricadeller, brown and freeze without sauce. Naturally, you can serve Fricadeller without sauce or pass it on the side.

Oven-Barbecued Country Ribs   6 *servings*

6 pounds country-style ribs, or one large piece per person
1 recipe Brad's Barbecue Sauce (see Index)

Place the ribs on a rack in a roasting pan. Add ¼ inch of water to the pan. Bake the ribs in a 350° oven for 1 hour. While the ribs are baking, make the barbecue sauce. After 1 hour remove the ribs and pour off all the fat. If the ribs don't fit fairly closely in the roasting pan, remove them to a closer-fitting baking dish. Pour half of the barbecue sauce over the ribs and return them to the oven for 30 minutes. Again pour off any excess fat and pour over the other half of the barbecue sauce. Return to the oven and cook for another 30 minutes.

Pork and Sauerkraut

This recipe is so easy that I include it only because it's so good.

Use any cut of pork, as long as it's fresh—pork chops, country-style ribs, loin, shoulder, or fresh ham. Plan on enough for the people who will be supping with you.

One can of sauerkraut—if only two of you are dining; two or three if you're having guests or you have a large family and you all love kraut. Take a nice deep pot with a tight-fitting lid. Put the pork in the bottom of a pot; sprinkle with cracked pepper if you like pepper, but add *no* salt. Drain the sauerkraut well and put it on top of the pork. Use enough sauerkraut to cover the pork thoroughly. Add water just to cover; put a lid on the pot and let it simmer for at least 2 hours. If it happens to simmer for 4 hours, don't worry. Serve with mashed potatoes and enjoy.

Note: The reason you drain the kraut is to get rid of the tin-can taste of the water, which sometimes lessens the goodness of the kraut. You should always use fresh water on canned kraut.

𝒝𝒝𝒝𝒝𝒝𝒝𝒝𝒝𝒝𝒝𝒝𝒝𝒝𝒝𝒝𝒝𝒝𝒝𝒝𝒝𝒝

OH SAGE–NO SAGE

I do not stand among the sage lovers of the world. My dislike for sage came about when I was quite young. (I still needed a pillow or pile of books on my chair to elevate me to the proper height for eating at "the big table.")

My parents and I were at the home of a very dear friend. The hostess had roasted a large turkey and had stuffed it with sage dressing. I remember with great clarity that first bite of sage dressing. The sage exploded over my taste buds, its fumes filled my nostrils, my eyes watered, and I began to choke. I joined the other guests in leaving my dressing on the side of my plate. It was many years before I could eat anything seasoned with sage.

Whenever you cook, go easy on the seasoning. You can always add more, but you can never extract an overdose.

𝒝𝒝𝒝𝒝𝒝𝒝𝒝𝒝𝒝𝒝𝒝𝒝𝒝𝒝𝒝𝒝𝒝𝒝𝒝𝒝

Homemade Sausage   *12 patties*

Making your own sausage patties is a snap if you have a food processor or a really good blender. Like homemade breads, there is something very special about homemade sausage. You can spice it to your own satisfaction and you can, as I do, leave out the sage.

The following recipe contains no sage, but I think you'll find it delicious. When you make sausage, remember that the ratio of fat to meat should not exceed one part fat to two parts meat. Any cut of fresh pork can be used, however; shoulder cuts or country-style ribs are used most often and contain the correct amount of fat. I prefer country-style ribs; they're easy to bone and are usually one-third fat, which is the way I like it.

1½ pounds fresh pork, fat included
1½ teaspoons salt
½ teaspoon coarsely ground pepper
⅓ teaspoon paprika

⅓ teaspoon thyme
Pinch ground cloves
¼ teaspoon ground allspice
¼ teaspoon chicken base

Bone the pork if necessary. Grind it in a food grinder, processor, or blender. Add the seasonings, sprinkle with 2 teaspoons water, and mix with the hands until totally blended. If the mixture seems dry, add a bit more water. Be sure you work the mixture well in order to distribute the spices throughout. Shape the sausage meat into 3-inch patties, ½ inch thick. Fry over moderate heat for 15 minutes, browning well on both sides.

These freeze beautifully and will go from the freezer to the pan with no trouble. Add a few minutes to the cooking time to compensate for the frozen state. This recipe can be doubled.

Other Meat Dishes

Rudy Vallee's Wild Meat Marinade   *about 2 quarts*

The Rudy Vallee I know isn't a singer; he's a French chef who is the owner of Le Grange restaurant in southern California. His grandmother's culinary expertise so influenced Rudy that he went to school to become a master chef. When friendly patrons bring Rudy venison from their hunting trips, he makes a marinade according to the same recipe his grandmother used. Once the marinade has cooled, he rinses the meat and submerges it in the marinade, where it may stay for a day, a week, or a month. The marinade will keep the meat for a considerable time, and if it must keep longer, one need only drain the marinade, reboil it, and pour it over the meat again once it has cooled.

When you marinate meat you want to think about its weight and size. If you're marinating steaks, 24 hours will do. If you're marinating a hindquarter or a large roast, you'll want to give it a week or two. Whatever the size, whatever the time period, remember to turn the meat in the marinade at least once a day, preferably twice.

2 cups white wine
3 quarts water
4 large cloves garlic, cut lengthwise
2 medium onions, sliced
2 large carrots, sliced
2 ribs celery, sliced, *or* ½ cup top leaves of celery
1½ cups cider vinegar
½ teaspoon thyme leaves
2 bay leaves
1 tablespoon chopped parsley (fresh or dried)
½ teaspoon sweet basil leaves
8 whole cloves
1 tablespoon cracked pepper
½ teaspoon salt

Combine all the ingredients in a large pot (not aluminum) and bring to a brisk boil. Boil for 30 minutes, cool completely, and pour over the meat. Refrigerate. Turn the meat at least once a day. The recipe may be cut in half or doubled. This quantity is enough for a large roast.

When you're ready to use the meat, remove it from the marinade and wipe it dry, then proceed to sauté, roast, or stew as you wish. If you are making a stew or dish with a gravy, add some of the strained marinade to the cooking liquid. If you're roasting the meat, strain the marinade and add the marinade vegetables to the bottom of the roasting pan, and don't forget to lard the meat or cover it with a layer of fat. Regardless of the way you cook the marinated meat, this marinade moderates completely any gamy flavor and makes the dish come out tasting mighty fine.

Rabbit
4 servings

My Great-Great-Uncle Ohler bought ten acres on the edge of the Mojave Desert in a place that is now known as Lancaster, California. The time was the late 1930s. Uncle Ohler was elderly, retired, almost entirely deaf, and widowed when he purchased the property. He set himself up a nice cabin, got his water from the Kern County Irrigation Ditch, grew a few vegetables, picked pears for extra cash, and ate a lot of rabbit. Uncle Ohler never shot his rabbits. As he would explain, he had lots of time and he didn't like his game shot up.

Uncle Ohler would sit on a rock by a fresh rabbit hole, stick in hand. He didn't mind if the wait was 20 minutes or 4 hours. He knew that the rabbit would get nosy sooner or later, and when it did—*whack!* Food for dinner.

Though wild rabbit and hare make fine eating when jugged (another term for marinated), a tender domestic rabbit rivals chicken in taste and quality and can be used in place of chicken in most recipes.

Rabbit is high in food value and protein, low in fat, cholesterol, and calories. Rabbit has been a favorite in Europe, Canada, and South America for centuries, but Americans are stand-offish. This recipe could change their minds.

¼ cup vegetable oil
3 tablespoons butter
1 domestic rabbit, approximately 3 pounds, cut up
½ cup flour
½ teaspoon salt
¼ teaspoon coarsely ground pepper
1 medium onion, chopped
½ pound fresh mushrooms
1 carrot
1 stalk celery, *or* some celery leaves
2 tablespoons flour
1 can chicken stock, *or* 1⅓ cups homemade chicken stock
⅓ cup dry white wine (optional, but it makes a difference)
½ cup light cream
¼ cup chopped parsley

Heat the oil and butter in large frying pan. Dredge the rabbit pieces in flour seasoned with salt and pepper. Sauté the rabbit over medium-high heat until nicely browned. Remove the rabbit pieces to a casserole and pour off all but 2 tablespoons of the oil and butter. Add the onion, and when it is semitranslucent add the mushrooms, either whole or sliced. While the onion and mushrooms cook, peel the carrot and wash the celery. Cut them into large pieces and add them to the casserole. When the onion and mushrooms are cooked, sprinkle them with 2 tablespoons flour and stir with a wooden spoon to combine. Slowly add the chicken stock and blend until smooth. Add the wine and simmer 2 minutes. Add the cream, stir, and taste for salt and pepper; season accordingly. Pour the sauce over the rabbit, cover the casserole tightly, and bake in a 325° oven for 2 hours. When the rabbit is fork-tender, transfer the meat to a heated platter. Add the parsley to the sauce and recheck for seasoning. Pour the sauce over the rabbit and serve with buttered noodles.

Note to chicken lovers: This recipe is wonderful made with chicken.

Carole's Curry Sauce   6 *servings*

2 tablespoons butter
1 tablespoon vegetable oil
1 large or 2 small green apples, peeled, cut into eighths, and sliced thin
1 medium onion, chopped
½ cup raisins, golden preferred
2 tablespoons curry powder
3 tablespoons flour
2 cups chicken stock, *or* 2 cups hot water plus 1 teaspoon chicken base
½ cup light cream
1 clove garlic, minced, *or* ¼ teaspoon garlic powder
Pinch paprika
Pinch ground cloves
⅓ teaspoon coriander
⅛ teaspoon onion salt
¼ teaspoon celery salt
3 tablespoons chopped parsley
¼ cup sherry
Salt, if needed

Melt the butter with the oil in a large frying pan or a 2-quart saucepan. Add the apple and onion and sauté until transparent. (If you use fresh garlic, as opposed to powder, add it along with the onion and apple.) Stir in the raisins, curry powder, and flour. Stir the mixture for 2 minutes over moderate heat. Add the chicken stock a cupful at a time, blending completely after each addition. When the sauce is smooth, add the cream followed by all the other ingredients in the order given. Stir and blend the sauce after each addition. When all is combined, simmer the sauce over low heat for 15 minutes.

This sauce is great as is, or it can be processed in a food processor or blender until smooth. For a totally creamy sauce, put it through a sieve after processing.

For a milder, different curry add ½ cup sour cream or yogurt when the sauce is finished, or if you like your curry *hot*, add a dehydrated small red chili, crumbled into the sauce right.after the stock has been blended in.

Variations

SHRIMP: Add cooked shrimp or shrimp that have been cleaned, deveined, and sautéed in butter and shallots until their color is bright and their flesh is opaque. Heat shrimp and sauce until piping hot; serve over rice.

LAMB: Add cubed, leftover leg of lamb or lamb stew meat that has been simmered until tender. Heat lamb and sauce until hot; serve over rice if desired. Chutney is especially good with lamb curry.

CHICKEN: Spoon the hot sauce over sautéed, baked, or broiled chicken, or stir in boned and skinned cooked chicken and heat until the chicken is hot through. Serve over rice or noodles.

TURKEY: Add cooked turkey cut into chunks or wide julienne strips to the sauce and heat until the meat is hot through, or slice two pieces of white-meat turkey per person. Heat the slices in a tightly crimped foil package in a 350° oven for 20 minutes. Fry four slices of bacon per person. Arrange the plate in this order: 1 slice turkey, 2 slices bacon, 1 slice turkey, 2 slices bacon. Then ladle the curry sauce down the middle of the overlapping turkey slices between the bacon slices.

This curry sauce is good all by itself, but of course you can accompany it with all of the goodies that are traditional. Chutney is the only one I really crave, but you may also serve coconut, peanuts, more raisins, cashews, chopped scallions, or chopped hard-boiled egg (yolks only are preferred).

Sweet-and-Sour Sauce   *4 cups*

The Chinese were creating marvelous dishes while the French were still charring wild boar steaks over an open fire. Unfortunately, many of America's Chinese restaurants fail to live up to their country's fine culinary reputation. The exceptions are always busy and fun to visit. When good Chinese food isn't around the corner, don't get sullen and dour—go make some sweet-and-sour. A fine sweet-and-sour sauce is a delight to the palate and fabulous for enhancing leftover pork roast, chicken, or seafood.

⅔ cup catsup
½ cup white *or* malt vinegar
⅓ cup sugar
2 tablespoons soy sauce
2 tablespoons sweet rice wine from Kikkoman *or* sherry *or* any sweet wine
½ cup pineapple juice from a 14-ounce can of chunk pineapple
1 medium-sized white or yellow onion, cut into ¾-inch chunks
1 green pepper, cut into ¾-inch squares
1 14-ounce can chunk pineapple
2 tablespoons cornstarch dissolved in remaining pineapple juice

Combine catsup, vinegar, sugar, soy sauce, wine, and pineapple juice in a saucepan. Bring the mixture to a boil. Lower the heat and simmer 2 minutes. Add the onion, green pepper, and pineapple. Dissolve the cornstarch in the remaining juice and stir it into the simmering sauce. Cook, stirring carefully, until slightly thickened and clear (the cornstarch has done its job when the mixture goes from opaque to translucent). Remove from heat. Add any of the following and get the chopsticks ready.

Variations
SHRIMP: Sauté shrimp in half butter and half oil until they lose their opacity, or deep-fry them in batter. The Chinese always use batter-fried shrimp, but I love them plain. They're less fattening too.

CHICKEN: Use leftover stewed chicken cut into uniform pieces or left in whole jointed pieces. Cut pieces of skinned and boned chicken in uniform sizes, and sauté in butter and oil until just done; or go completely American and dredge chicken parts in seasoned flour and sauté them until nicely browned and cooked through. Place a heatproof baking dish and spoon sauce over all. Heat in the oven until the sauce bubbles.

PORK: You can use any cut of pork. Remove all the fat and cube the meat. Dredge in seasoned flour (1 teaspoon salt, ¼ teaspoon pepper, 1 cup flour) and fry in half butter and half oil until done. Or you can cube and use any cut of leftover cooked pork, but heat it before adding it to the sauce.

BEEF: Make your favorite meatballs and season them with finely minced scallion, garlic, and ginger.

FISH: Cut firm, white-fleshed fish filets into cubes. Dip them in batter and deep-fry in 375° oil. When brown, remove the fish from the fat and drain it on paper towels. When all the fish has been fried, add it to *hot* Sweet-and-Sour Sauce and serve immediately.

Note: Do not overcook Sweet-and-Sour Sauce or the onions and pepper will lose their crispness and color and the vinegar will lose its oomph!

Dipping Batter for Shrimp and Fish   *2 cups*

    1 cup flour
    1 teaspoon salt
    1 teaspoon baking powder
    1 egg
    1¾ cups ice water

Mix the dry ingredients in a bowl. Add the egg and water and beat until very smooth. Dip shrimp or fish in the batter and fry in 375° oil. Oil is hot enough for frying when a bread cube browns in 1 minute.

Sweet-and-Sour is a dish and meal unto itself. The only company it may crave is rice.

ENTRÉES: CHICKEN AND OTHER FOWL

Chicken

Chicken is one of the most versatile of all meats, as it adapts to a wider range of recipes than any other kind of flesh that we consume.

You can stew today's fast-fed, no-exercise, tender chickens in an hour and make a low-cholesterol, high-protein meal fit for a king. Unless you raise your own chickens, you probably couldn't find an old hen to stew all day even if you wanted to. You can, however, select various weights of chickens: a 5- to 6-pounder for roasting, 2- to 3-pounders for frying, and under 2 pounds for broiling.

A cut-up chicken bakes in 40 minutes to 1 hour, depending on the thickness and weight of the bird. Roasting a whole bird takes longer. You can test for doneness by piercing the leg of the fowl with a sharp knife. If the juices run clear, the bird is done. Another sign of doneness is to see if the leg of the fowl can be easily moved.

A wonderful-tasting dish of very few calories, little cost, and very little trouble can be made by cutting the boned and skinned meat of a whole chicken breast in julienne strips. Sauté it quickly with fresh sliced mushrooms in a mixture of butter and oil, add slivers of celery and some Chinese pea pods, and stir-fry over high heat until the vegetables are cooked but still crisp. Season with salt, pepper, and soy sauce if desired.

If you wish to serve baked boned breasts of chicken, put the breasts in a buttered baking dish, brush with melted butter, and bake in a 350° oven for 15 minutes, or until the flesh loses its opacity. Remove from the oven and allow to cool. Run your fingers beneath the breastbone and down along the rib cage. The breast meat will come completely away, giving you an intact piece of meat. To complete your chicken dish, spoon sauce over the breasts, or combine them with any other ingredients called for in a recipe. Rebake the chicken in a 350° oven for 15 to 20 minutes, or until piping hot.

This is a simple way of giving your guests no bones to wrestle with.

Ducks, Geese, and Other Fowl

Whereas a turkey or chicken should have its breast pierced only once or twice to keep the juices in while preventing the skin from bursting, a duck or goose needs many piercings to allow the heavy fat layer a means of exit.

When you prick the skin of a duck or goose, do so at a slant so that the fork prongs enter the fat layer sideways. Do not allow the prongs to penetrate the meat, as doing so will cause the flesh to dry out during roasting. Basting ducks, geese, or turkeys with white wine during the roasting process produces a wonderfully brown skin.

A more thorough way to rid your bird of its fat is to follow the Oriental method of blanching the duck or goose three times in boiling water. A stout cord is tied around the tail of the bird, and it is hung for at least 1 hour between dunkings. The third blanching usually calls for honey and wine to be added to the water along with any seasonings. The honey causes the bird to roast to a beautiful brown.

The blanching is usually done early in the morning and then the third is allowed to hang all day until ready to be roasted. Then the tail and all the fat around it are cut away to give the bird's fat a way out. There is no need to pierce the skin or stuff the bird. Ducks that have been blanched and hung are seemingly devoid of fat, yet are tender and moist.

Goose fat is a treasure to the cook. It's wonderful in pâtés, great for making *roux* for soups, and lovely when frying potatoes. Duck fat is not as versatile but will do many of the same jobs.

Guinea hens, Rock Cornish game hens, and squab, along with all wild fowl, lack fat, so it is necessary for you to supply it. Salt pork, bacon, butter-drenched cheesecloth, or a *roux* of butter and flour should be put over these thin birds in order to keep them moist while roasting. The smallest of these will roast in 25 to 30 minutes.

Whatever fowl you prepare for your table, be sure it's fresh. Your nose will give you the answer.

Kenneth Hansen's Chicken Louise for Two   *2 to 4 servings*

1 2½-pound chicken, split in half
  Salt and pepper
1 tablespoon butter
½ teaspoon chopped shallots, *or* 2 teaspoons finely
  chopped scallions, white part only
8 medium-sized mushrooms
½ cup sherry
¾ cup heavy cream
  Pinch nutmeg
  Pinch paprika
  Dash Tabasco

1 egg yolk
2 tablespoons heavy cream
Puff paste *fleurons, or* fancy-shaped toast sautéed in butter

Remove the bones from the breast, the back, and the thigh. Each half chicken should have only the leg bone and wing bones in it. If you aren't a boning artist, have your butcher do it, or buy boned chicken breasts. Salt and pepper the chicken. Heat the butter in an ovenproof skillet and sauté the chicken over moderate heat until golden, but do not allow it to brown. Turn the chicken and cook the other side. Add the shallots and mushrooms. When the shallots are lightly cooked, pour over the sherry and ignite. Turn the heat up and reduce the liquid in the pan to half its volume. Add ¾ cup heavy cream, shake the pan, and put it in a 375° oven for 15 minutes. Return the pan to the stove, transfer the chicken and mushrooms to a serving casserole, and place it in a warm oven. Reduce the sauce in the pan to half its volume, or until it is creamy. Season the sauce with nutmeg, paprika, and Tabasco. Check for salt. Mix the egg yolk with 2 tablespoons cream. Remove the pan from the heat, whisk in the egg-yolk mixture, and stir the sauce well. Return the pan to low heat and stir the sauce until it is thickened. Do not allow it to boil. When it is thick, strain it over the chicken and mushrooms. Serve with *fleurons* or toast. This is a beautiful dish accompanied by fresh asparagus and a lovely Chenin or Pinot Blanc.

If you use four chicken breasts instead of two half chickens, you could make this for four. Use 4 mushrooms per person and proceed according to the recipe. The sauce in the proportions given here should be just enough.

CHICKEN À LA KING

One sunny morning Floss put on her old pedal pushers, her sneakers, and one of her husband's shirts and wrapped her blond curls up Aunt Jemima style in an old red bandanna. She'd decided this was the day to strip and rewax the floors.

She took all the furniture she could handle into the dining room, then swept the kitchen and back porch, got out the mop and bucket, and began the long job of stripping the wax.

She was into her second coffee break when the phone rang. It was Harold, her husband, who sold Cadillacs in downtown Burbank. "Honey? I've got a fella here who's just bought a nice new convertible. Is it all right if I bring him home for lunch while they service her up?"

Harold often brought customers home for lunch while they waited for their cars. It was good business—but today of all days! "All right, Harold, but I'm doing the floors and there's not much around here to eat."

Floss was backing out of the porch door on hands and knees as Harold and his guest came around the corner of the house. All she could see was Harold's polished shoes followed by a pair of old sneakers topped by some worn jeans. As she started to mumble her apologies, Harold told her to take her time, adding that they'd go around to the side porch, have a drink, and enjoy the sunshine.

While the wax dried, Floss watered out front, then she ran in and added some cream, a can of mushrooms, and some more seasonings to the Chicken à la King from the night before. As the dish heated on the stove, she shoved the furniture back into the dinette area, set the table for three, made a salad, and put in some toast.

"I'm a mess, but Chicken à la King is now being served," she yelled out the side window. But her face became ashen and her knees weak when she saw that it was the King himself—Clark Gable—who walked in with her husband to partake of the leftovers.

Chicken à la King

Chicken à la King has gotten an old and tired reputation over the years, but made with fresh mushrooms and a bit of sherry, it's a lovely dish.

    2 cups stewed chicken *or* leftover turkey
    ½ pound fresh mushrooms
    2 tablespoons butter
    Juice of ½ lemon, at least 2 tablespoons
    1 recipe Cream Sauce (see Index)
    1 teaspoon chicken base, *or* 1 bouillon cube
    2 tablespoons sherry
    ¼ cup pimientos, *or* ¼ cup finely julienned green pepper
    Puff paste patty shells *or* toast

Cut the chicken or turkey into wide julienne strips or chunks. Cut the mushrooms into ½-inch slices. Put them into a pan with the butter and squeeze the lemon juice over them. Sauté until the mushrooms begin to take on color; set aside. Make Cream Sauce, add to it the chicken base, and simmer the sauce for 5 minutes, stirring it frequently. Put the chicken and mushrooms in a saucepan, strain the sauce over it, and stir in the sherry. Bring the mixture to a low boil, add the pimientos (rinsed) or green pepper, and heat for 1 more minute. Ladle it over toast or patty shells. The pimientos or green peppers are traditional, but optional.

Note: If you wish to make Chicken à la King ahead of time for a party, make the sauce and keep it separate from the chicken. Boil the chicken, and refrigerate both. Just before serving, heat the sauce and the chicken *separately*, then combine and heat until piping hot. These simple rules will keep away any possibility of contamination.

Honey-Baked Chicken

    1 large or 2 medium-sized broiling chickens (depending
        on the number of people you're serving)
    ½ cup (1 stick) butter *or* margarine, melted
    ½ cup honey
    ¼ cup prepared mustard, *or* 2 tablespoons dry mustard
    1 teaspoon salt
    1 teaspoon curry powder (2 if you like it spicy)

Cut up the chickens and place them skin side up in a large baking pan. Be sure the chicken is in one layer and not too crowded. Combine all the other ingredients and pour them over the chicken. Bake the dish in a 350° oven for 1 hour, basting often. Be sure you or the butcher trims all excess fat from the chicken, as the melted fat will create too much juice in the pan and the chicken will stew rather than bake.

Chicken Paprika   *4 servings*

    3 tablespoons vegetable oil
    2 tablespoons butter
    1 chicken, cut up
    ½ cup flour
    ½ teaspoon salt
    ¼ teaspoon pepper
    2 tablespoons butter
    ¼ cup flour
    1 cup stock, *or* 1 cup water plus 1 teaspoon chicken base
    ¾ cup milk
    1 tablespoon paprika
    ¼ teaspoon celery salt
    ¼ teaspoon onion salt
    2 tablespoons sherry or white wine
    ½ cup sour cream

Heat the oil and butter in a large frying pan. Shake the chicken pieces in the flour, salt, and pepper. Fry over medium-high heat until browned on both sides. As you brown the chicken, place it in an ovenproof casserole with a cover. When all the chicken is done, pour off the fat left in the frying pan, but don't scrape out the pan. Add 2 tablespoons butter and ¼ cup flour, and cook the *roux* over medium heat for 2 minutes. Add the stock and stir until smooth. Add the milk and seasonings, and continue stirring over medium heat. Add the sherry or white wine and cook 2 minutes more. Pour half of the sauce over the chicken and bake it in a 350° oven for 45 minutes. Arrange the chicken on a platter and heat the other half of the sauce. Add the sour cream to the heated sauce, whisk until smooth, and pour over the chicken.

Chicken Paprika reheats well, but don't overheat, as the sour cream will break down and separate. Serve Chicken Paprika with buttered noodles, or by itself with vegetables next to it.

Chicken Enchiladas   6 to 8 servings

 1 onion, chopped
 2 tablespoons butter
 3 cups cooked chicken or turkey, julienned or chopped
 2 tablespoons chopped parsley
   Sprinkling of salt
10 scallions, chopped
 6 ounces Jack cheese, grated
 6 ounces mozzarella cheese, grated
24 pitted black olives
¼ cup vegetable oil
 1 can enchilada sauce
 8 flour tortillas, or 12 corn tortillas

Sauté the onion in the butter until it is transparent, add the chicken, parsley, and salt, stir until all is heated, and remove from the heat.

Chop the scallions and grate the cheese. Have all ingredients ready and a plate on which to roll the tortillas. Grease a 14-inch baking dish.

Heat ¼ cup oil in a frying pan and add 2 tablespoons enchilada sauce. When the oil is hot, add a tortilla, heat it on both sides, and remove it to the plate. Place 2 tablespoons of the chicken mixture down the center of the tortilla and top with mozzarella, 3 olives (2 if you are using corn tortillas), and scallions. Roll up the enchilada and place it in the baking dish with the seam side down. Repeat until all tortillas are used. Top the enchiladas with any leftover scallion, the remaining sauce, and the Jack cheese. Heat in a 350° oven for 25 minutes, or until piping hot. You can get fancy by heating some black olives in a little oil and placing them down the center of the enchiladas when they come out of the oven.

These make a mild and lovely Mexican-tasting dish. You can make it hotter by using hot enchilada sauce or by adding chili peppers to the chicken mixture.

Rock Cornish Game Hens   6 to 8 servings

Salt and pepper	2 tablespoons flour
1 game hen per person	1 teaspoon salt
1 onion	½ teaspoon pepper
Parsley	½ teaspoon basil leaves
½ cup (1 stick) butter	½ teaspoon thyme leaves

Remove the giblets from the body cavity and save them for making stock. Cut off the bird's tail and any excess fat. Tie the legs together with string. Salt and pepper the cavity. Stuff with a wedge of onion and some parsley. Mix the butter, flour, salt, pepper, basil, and thyme until well combined; a food processor or blender will produce a wonderfully smooth paste. With your hands, smear the butter paste all over the breasts and legs of the hens. Put the birds on a rack in a large roasting pan. (I put two overlapping cooling racks in my rectangular roaster.) Roast the birds in a 400° oven for 15 minutes. Lower the heat to 350° and continue roasting for another 45 minutes. During the last 30 minutes of cooking time, baste the birds with their own pan juices. I usually don't stuff these little birds.

Stuffing   *12 servings*

This stuffing can be used to stuff any fowl, pork chops, saddle of lamb, flank steak, crown roast, breast of lamb, or what have you. Remember: *never* put warm stuffing into a cold bird and then let it sit. Once you stuff any fowl, *put it in the oven.* This is one of those simple rules which, if followed, will eliminate all possibility of food poisoning.

> ½ cup (1 stick) butter
> 2 medium onions, chopped
> 4 cups diced celery
> ¼ cup chopped parsley
> 3 quarts dry bread crumbs
> 4 large eggs
> 1 quart milk
> 1 teaspoon salt
> ¼ teaspoon celery salt
> ¼ teaspoon onion salt
> ¼ teaspoon coarsely ground pepper
> 1 teaspoon rosemary leaves (2 if fresh)
> ½ teaspoon thyme
> 1 teaspoon chicken base
> 1 cup chopped cooked giblets *or* mushrooms *or* sausage

Melt the butter in a large frying pan. Add the onions and celery. Cook over moderate heat until the onion is transparent. Do not allow the vegetables to brown. While the vegetables sauté, sprinkle the parsley over the bread cubes. Beat the eggs in a separate bowl and heat the milk to scalding. When the milk is hot, pour it into the beaten eggs in a thin stream, whisking all the while. Add all the seasonings to the onion and celery, plus the giblets, mushrooms, or sausage. Stir the mixture well to combine, then pour it over the bread cubes and add the egg-milk mixture. Toss and mix thoroughly. Turn the stuffing into a well-buttered 4-quart casserole and bake in a 350° oven for 45 minutes, or until a knife comes out clean.

I always bake stuffing separately from the turkey or capon, as most stuffings do little for the bird and the bird does little for the stuffing. Stuffings that are placed between the skin of the fowl and the breast meat do keep the bird moist, and if you go in for very spicy stuffings you can influence the taste of the birds. But otherwise you're better off baking the stuffing separately—then you can bring both a beautiful bird and beautiful stuffing to the table.

Bread Cubes

Use any leftover bread you have. Stack the bread four to five slices high. Cut it into ¾-inch strips, turn, and cut the strips into cubes. Allow the cubes to dry overnight or for 2 to 3 hours. I use a combination of breads in my stuffing, including the crust. The varied breads produce a better stuffing.

Giblets

Simmer giblets (the liver, heart, gizzards, and neck) in a pot with water to cover. Add ¼ teaspoon salt and a pinch of pepper. If you have some chicken base, add some; about ½ teaspoon will do. After the giblets have simmered for 15 minutes, remove the liver and continue to cook the giblets for 1 hour, or until they are tender. Trim the gizzard and chop it. Chop the liver and heart. Remove the skin from the neck and remove whatever meat you can; chop. In the stuffing recipe I call for 1 cup chopped cooked giblets, mushrooms, or sausage, but if you end up with 2 cups, use it; the added amount will only give you more flavor.

Mushrooms

Wipe clean ½ pound mushrooms and chop them. Sauté them in 2 tablespoons butter. Squeeze 2 tablespoons lemon juice over the mushrooms as they begin to cook, turn the heat to high, and cook, stirring with a wooden spoon, until the mushrooms begin to brown and the moisture is reduced. Add to the stuffing.

Sausage

Use the sausage of your choice. Brown it in a frying pan, breaking it up with a wooden spoon. When the sausage is browned and cooked through, tip the pan and remove all the fat. Add it to the stuffing.

Note: My children don't like giblets, but they *love* my stuffing. Get the idea? They get good taste, vitamins, and minerals, and I keep from wasting good food.

Turkeys

The big-bosomed white-meated turkey you serve on Thanksgiving and Christmas bears almost no resemblance to the wild American turkey that the Pilgrims knew. The modern-day bird is bred and never wed. Kept in tight quarters with too much food, it quickly matures into a roasting giant. It is also incredibly stupid. People who raise sheep are often heard to say that a herd of sheep has one objective in life, and that's to die. The turkey of today is so stupid that it doesn't even have an objective. No matter; dumb as it is, a turkey has a lot to offer nutritionally. Turkey contains more protein than any other cooked meat we consume. It's high in riboflavin and niacin, but low in calories and cholesterol.

Some people are hunting the wild turkey again, but you and I can simply buzz on down to our local market and pick a hefty turkey out of the freezer section, let it defrost for 24 hours, and have a big bird golden brown and succulent.

Some points to remember:

• Do not wrap leftover turkey in airtight foil or plastic. Turkey will keep far longer if loosely wrapped and covered with a damp cloth. If your refrigerator isn't frost-free, the cloth isn't necessary.

• Leftover cooked ham or turkey freezes well. Use it within two months.

The Precarved Turkey   *12 or more servings of breast meat*

On a cold buffet there are few foods that can equal the beauty and servability of a turkey. Best of all is the fact that you can precarve a large turkey, glaze it with its own juices, and serve it "seemingly" whole and untouched by human hands.

A turkey that will be precarved should be a minimum of 22 pounds. This is very important, as a smaller bird will not yield enough white meat and will be too difficult to work on.

If you have bought a frozen bird, be sure to let it defrost for at least 24 hours. *Do not* remove the plastic bag your frozen bird comes in until it's time to put it in the oven. *Do not* start the cooking procedure until the bird is totally defrosted.

To prepare the bird for roasting, cut off the tail and put it in a stockpot along with the giblets and neck. Be sure to extract the giblets and neck from the two body cavities. I've known people who've roasted their bird with the giblets still neatly tucked inside the bird, and I somehow doubt that the paper bag in which they rested added much flavor. To the giblets, neck, and tail add some carrots, celery, onion, parsley, salt, and pepper. Cover all with cold water and set to simmer on top of the stove.

Back to the bird. Cut off the excess skin flap at the base of the neck opening. Since the bird won't be stuffed, the flap isn't needed and it prevents the browning of any skin it touches. Add it to the stockpot. Now salt and pepper both body cavities. Use coarsely ground pepper and use the salt shaker liberally.

Place the turkey on a rack in a shallow pan and put it into a preheated 325° oven. After 1 hour, pierce the bird once on each lower side of the breast and once more on each front end of the breast. These four small piercings will keep the breast from bursting open but keep enough of the juices in to produce a juicy bird.

Then, run a large lump of butter all over the breast and legs. Continue roasting, allowing a total time of 12 to 14 minutes to the pound. Since the bird isn't stuffed, roasting time is greatly reduced. A 24-pound tom will roast in 4½ to 4¾ hours.

Turkeys love attention. Check your bird often. When the breast looks perfect and has reached just the color you desire, place a piece of foil on top to keep it from getting any browner. If the bird's skin looks dry, butter it again. You must remember that turkeys, like any other piece of meat, may vary because of feed, age, and other factors. Most of the big birds you buy today are of excellent quality, but do check it often.

When the roasting time is up, pierce the bird's leg with one prong of a sharp meat fork. If the juice runs clear and is not bloody, the bird is done. Remove it from the oven. With rubber gloves or pot-holder mittens, gently pick up the bird and tip it so that all the excess juices run from the body cavities. Tip it up both ways—get all the juices. Once you've drained the turkey, place it on a platter and pour the juices in the pan into a straight-sided glass container. If there's a great amount, use two containers.

Set the glass container to cool with a knife under one side of the bottom to allow air to flow freely underneath. The debris from the pan will sink to the bottom and the fat will come to the top. When cool enough to handle, refrigerate the juices so that they may jell.

Cool the bird thoroughly. This can take several hours, and you may roast the bird the night before if you wish. If you wish to do it all in one day, put the bird in the oven by 8:00 A.M. By 3:30 in the afternoon you should be able to carve it successfully.

The stock you put on the stove at the very beginning should simmer for 3 hours and be cooled in the same manner as the juices were, then refrigerated. The stock is used for meals made with leftover turkey.

When the turkey is cool, build it a nest of foil and place it on your most beautiful platter. If you don't have a big beautiful platter, cover a piece of board with foil, or if the board is good-looking, oil it and use it *sans* foil. An oiled board can be cleaned with a hot damp rag and stored until next time.

To build your bird's nest, tear off a 3-foot strip of foil. Crumple the foil into a 3-foot-by-6-inch strip. Now simply bring the ends around to meet, crimp them together, and squeeze the foil into an oval that will fit *under* the bird. Don't pack the foil down; the bird must do that job. Place the bird on the foil collar and settle it onto its nest. Stuff any foil that protrudes under the turkey and resettle the bird so that it is stable.

Remove the leg clamps and cut the skin away from both cavities. Cut off the wing tips. Now you are ready to carve, which is easier than it sounds. You'll need a slim knife; a boning knife is the best as it is slender and stiff. Locate the breastbone. You can't miss it, because it runs down the top of the breast dead center. Run the knife along one side of the breastbone in a perpendicular motion. Don't be bashful; you must stab your knife in there and cut along the bone. The object is to cut down 3 to 4 inches, but not so far as to cut the breast completely from the bird. The breast needs to be attached to the lower part of the rib cage. Now make the same cut on the other side of the breastbone. Be sure in making these two cuts that you cut all the way from the front to the back.

Next, make an incision between the breast and the leg. Cut *only* the skin; do not cut any meat. You simply wish to detach the leg skin from the breast skin so that when you're finished the bird will look whole and beautiful.

Now it's time to carve. Starting at the top of the breast, work one side at a time. Slice the breast meat parallel to the floor. You can slice the meat as thick or as thin as you desire, but I suggest that you make the slices ¼ inch thick, as slices of that thickness make for a generous serving.

Your first cut on top of the breast will be small. Hold that top piece with one hand as you cut the next and the next and so forth. Take your time and make sharp, smooth sawing cuts through the breast meat. Be sure that you cut the breast meat all way through, or the meat won't come away for your guests. Again, cut from front to back. Don't be afraid of your bird; you're cutting parallel to the floor and good old gravity will keep all intact. When you've cut one side of the bird as far down as you can reach with your knife, turn the bird and carve the other side. This whole procedure will be easy and go quickly if you use a *sharp* knife. No carving job can be done decently with a dull knife.

If you've held onto your turkey while you carved and if you moved your knife in clean, smooth strokes, you should end up with a seemingly intact bird with approximately 24 to 26 ¼-inch slices of breast meat ready for your guests.

Since the legs are full of tendons and splinter bones, save them and all the rest for other meals. If you're planning on a large party, you might consider roasting two turkeys and carving the dark meat from the second bird; or you might bake a ham and surround the carved turkey with him slices.

After carving the bird, it's time to dress it for the party. Skim all the fat from the juices you placed in the straight-sided glass container. With a large spoon ladle out the jelled juices, leaving the debris in the bottom. Discard the fat and the debris. Place the jelled juice in a small saucepan and heat it over a low flame until it melts. Put the pan in the freezer and leave it there for 10 minutes. In the meantime cut the stems from 2 mushrooms of uniform size. Dip the caps in lemon juice and secure them with toothpicks to the places where you cut off the wing tips. If fresh mushrooms aren't available, or if you prefer, secure cherry tomatoes to the wing tips.

After 10 minutes, remove the turkey juice from the freezer. It should be cold and almost jelled again. With a pastry brush, spread the juice over the entire breast of the carved turkey. Repeat the process until the entire bird is well glazed. You may wish to keep the saucepan in a bowl of ice to keep the juice thick. Brush the bird from stem to stern. Return any leftover juice to the refrigerator to jell completely. When it is set, cut it into ½-inch squares with a sharp knife and put the jelly around the base of the bird, or serve it in a side dish. It's a delicious jellied consommé. Just before serving your masterpiece, stuff lots of fresh green parsley into both body cavities. You may wish to get fancy and add some daisies, roses, or other flowers. The entire carving and glazing process shouldn't take more than 45 minutes.

The best part of this project is that the bird can be roasted and carved and glazed the day before and set in the refrigerator overnight. It's not mandatory (because of the glaze), but you might wish to put some toothpicks in the high points of the turkey and cover it with plastic wrap. Take the bird out of the refrigerator at least 1 hour before serving.

When you serve the bird, your guests won't realize that it's already carved, so it helps if you take a pretty carving knife and fork and remove the first slice or two until they get the idea. Be ready for many compliments.

This procedure is the simplest and easiest method of serving a precarved turkey. It is wonderful for a buffet, but will not do for hors d'oeuvres. Carl does an hors d'oeuvre precarved turkey that is much harder to achieve and an art to master. But I'm sure that any of you can do a buffet turkey. When you get good at it, you can manage to cut the slices so that they are hinged at one end where you haven't quite cut through. Practice makes perfect.

With the turkey's own juices brushed back onto it, you'll find your carved bird one of the tastiest and juiciest you've ever cooked.

Whether you carve your turkey before or attack it at the buffet table, this procedure of roasting an unstuffed turkey will give you a great bird, whether served hot or cold.

ENTRÉES: EGGS, CHEESE, CRÊPES, QUICHE

Eggs

With all the talk of cholesterol, you'd think the egg had nothing else in it. The egg has always been a food favorite, not only for its versatility and good taste, but for its high protein, vitamin, and mineral content. Eggs are also economical.

Even the best cookbooks tell you to add milk or cream instead of water to scrambled eggs. But when making an omelette or scrambled eggs or french toast, please try water instead so that you can have the full flavor of the egg and no milk solids to cook up hard, often leaving their water content behind. For each egg you plan to use, beat in 1 teaspoon water. You'll love it, and you'll save yourself some calories to boot.

To hard-boil eggs, put them in a pot (not aluminum) and cover with cold water. Add 2 teaspoons salt and bring to a boil. Reduce the heat and simmer for 12 minutes. Immediately pour cold water over the eggs, and continue running cold water over them until cool to the touch. Cooked in this manner, hard-boiled eggs should peel and not have that overcooked gray ring around the yolk.

Don't be distressed if some eggs simply won't peel—it's the chemical composition of the egg. In most cases the above method works.

· Peeled hard-boiled eggs keep beautifully for at least a week if covered with water and kept in a glass container in the refrigerator.

· When poaching eggs, add a tablespoon or two of vinegar to the simmering water to keep the whites from breaking into fragments.

· To clear soup stock, mix 1 egg white and 1 eggshell thoroughly into *cold* stock. Heat slowly to the boiling point, simmer 5 minutes, then strain through a strainer lined with cheesecloth.

· If there is even *one drop* of egg yolk in your egg whites, they will *never* whip up stiff.

· Do not use a food processor to beat egg whites.

- Egg whites beat up better when at room temperature and placed in a steep-sided narrow bowl.
- When beating eggs for dipping (as before breading), beat the egg with 1 teaspoon water and beat only until the egg loses its cohesiveness.

Big Brown Omelettes   *2 servings*

A Big Brown Omelette is different from the classic and basic French omelette. Big Brown Omelettes can be made for from one to eight people. The fillings are usually sautéed right in the pan before the eggs are added, or added at the last minute before the omelette is shoved under the broiler to puff and brown. Large brown omelettes are cut in wedges just like a pie. They can be served with a tangy tomato sauce, mushrooms, or even (God forgive me) catsup. A Big Brown Omelette that has sautéed onions, mushrooms, parsley, chives, and cheese in it needs only a fork and some crunchy toast by its side.

Big Brown Omelettes are wonderful for Sunday dinners or late, late breakfasts after late, late nights. They're great in the morning at a brunch or for lunch. Fixed with stir-fried onions and zucchini and topped with cheese, they make a smashing first course. Very similar to a quiche, but without the calories of the pastry and cream, Big Brown Omelettes are quick, easy, delicious, and nutritious. The many possible combinations of fillings and toppings could fill a book.

Some Basic "Do's" and "Don'ts"

- Always heat the pan before adding any ingredients. Butter should be bubbling.
- Never add ingredients that are watery. Peel and seed tomatoes, salt and drain zucchini, and don't add sauces. Sauces, if used, should top the finished omelette.
- If cheese is to be added, it should be put in last, just before the omelette goes under the broiler.
- Always figure a minimum of 2 eggs per person and never add milk.
- A totally plain Big Brown Omelette needs butter, eggs, and water. The water makes the eggs light and helps them puff up in the final cooking stage.
- Naturally, you'll need a frying pan that will be the right size for the number of people you're serving. A 12-inch pan will do an omelette big enough for eight, and a 5-inch pan will do a single man's dinner. I

have an 8-inch that's fine for three. Use good judgment, and keep in mind how many ingredients you plan to put into your omelettes besides the eggs.

How to Cook a Big Brown Omelette

Beat eggs using at least 2 per person. Add 1 teaspoon water to each egg. Beat again. Melt butter in a frying pan—use approximately ½ teaspoon per egg. If you're sautéing mushrooms, onions, zucchini, or whatever, do it now. When the vegetables are done (don't let them get mushy), or the dehydrated onion you may have used is getting slightly brown, add the eggs by pouring them over and around the ingredients in the pan. Keep the heat medium-high.

As the eggs begin to cook, lift and shove the cooked edges of the egg with a rubber spatula, allowing uncooked egg to flow underneath, as with a French omelette.

When the eggs look two-thirds done, stop lifting or moving the eggs. Add cheese; and when the sides of the eggs are well up the walls of the pan, put the omelette under a broiler. Be sure the omelette is within 4 inches of the heat. Watch the omelette (that's half the fun), and when it's well puffed and golden brown, serve it.

Since a Big Brown Omelette takes only 10 minutes or less to cook, you should have everything else you plan to serve ready and done before you start the actual cooking of the omelette. Push the toast down as the omelette goes under the broiler. To give you a concrete idea of proportions, I will give you a list of ingredients for a Big Brown Omelette for two.

> 1 tablespoon butter
> ¼ cup chopped onion
> ¼ cup thinly sliced celery
> 2 large mushrooms, cut in half and then sliced
> 1 tablespoon chopped parsley
> Coarsely ground pepper
> 5 eggs
> 1½ tablespoons water
> ½ cup grated Cheddar or Jack cheese

Melt the butter in a frying pan; add the onion, celery, and mushrooms. Sauté over medium-high heat until *just done*. Add the pepper. Pour the eggs over all. Pick up the sides as they cook, allowing uncooked egg to flow underneath. When the eggs are two-thirds cooked, stop lifting or stirring and add the cheese. When the sides have cooked up the walls of your pan, put the omelette under the broiler until well puffed and golden brown.

Cold Scrambled Eggs   *4 to 8 servings*

4 eggs
1 tablespoon plus 1 teaspoon water
⅛ teaspoon salt
4 tablespoons (½ stick) butter

Beat the eggs with the water and salt. Melt the butter in a frying pan over low heat. When the butter is good and warm, pour in the eggs. Cook the eggs over low heat, bringing in the cooked edges as soon as they begin to form. The object is to cook the eggs as softly as possible in all that butter. When the eggs look as though they're three-quarters cooked, turn them into a bowl, cover with plastic wrap, and cool.

Cold Scrambled Eggs are wonderful with lox, gravlax, smoked salmon, open-face turkey and shrimp sandwiches, caviar, or even stuffed into paper-thin slices of hard salami rolled into cornucopias. If you dress the side slices of bread on a Danish shrimp sandwich with Cold Scrambled Eggs, try topping the eggs with well-chopped chutney.

Note: If you're worried about that instruction that says to stop cooking the eggs when they look three-quarters done, put aside your fears; you will not be eating uncooked egg. Cold Scrambled Eggs are cooked in so much butter that when they look as though they're only partially cooked, it's really only the still-liquid butter that gives that appearance.

Chilies Rellenos   *6 to 8 servings*

4 eggs
1 cup light cream
2½ cups grated Jack cheese
2 4-ounce cans green chilies, chopped
8 drops Tabasco
½ teaspoon salt

Butter a baking dish of at least 1½-quart capacity. Beat the eggs, add the cream, beat, and stir in all the other ingredients. Pour into a buttered baking dish and bake in a 375° oven for 30 minutes, or until just set.

The recipe may be cut in half.

Dinner Crêpes   *12 to 14 crêpes*

4 large eggs
1 cup milk
Pinch salt
½ cup flour
2 tablespoons butter, melted
1 tablespoon brandy
4 tablespoons (½ stick) butter

Beat the eggs, milk, and salt together. Add the flour and beat. Add the butter and brandy and beat again. (Use a blender or food processor if you like.) Cover and chill the batter for at least 2 hours. When ready to use, whisk with a wire whip. Heat a 7- or 8-inch crêpe pan over a moderately high flame. While it is heating, melt ½ stick butter in another pan, and with a pastry brush, brush the pan with butter. Pick up the pan with your left hand, and add enough crêpe batter so that when you rotate the pan the batter covers the bottom completely. Put the pan back on the burner and cook the crêpe until you see a trace of brown somewhere around the edge. This is the secret. Then turn the crêpe with a flexible spatula or rubber scraper. Count one, two, three, and turn it out onto a piece of waxed paper. Brush the pan with butter again and repeat.

These crêpes make wonderful main courses filled with chicken and mushrooms or any other filling you like.

Entrée Crêpes   *12 to 14 crêpes*

4 large eggs   ⅔ to 1 cup flour
1½ cups water   ¼ teaspoon salt

If you are using a blender or food processor, use 1 cup flour; if you beat the crêpes by hand, use ⅔ cup. These crêpes should be cooked immediately. This batter should *not* stand and work as other crêpe batters must. Since the ingredients are the same as for noodle dough, their taste and texture make them perfect to use with chicken, turkey, or Italian-type fillings. To cook, follow the instructions in the recipe for Dinner Crêpes.

By food processor or blender:
Put the eggs, water, and salt in the work bowl or blender jar. Start the machine. When the liquids are blended, add the flour and blend until the batter is very smooth. Use immediately.

By hand or electric mixer:
Put the eggs, water, and salt in a bowl. Beat until totally combined and smooth. Add ⅔ cup flour and beat again until smooth. Use immediately.

Beer Crêpes

12 to 14 crêpes

4 large eggs
½ cup beer
½ cup light cream
½ cup flour
Pinch salt
2 tablespoons butter
1 tablespoon brandy

Beat the eggs, beer, and cream together. Add the flour and salt, beat again, add the butter and brandy, and beat some more. Chill at least 2 hours. Whisk.

Brush a crêpe pan with melted butter. When the pan is hot, pick it up with the left hand and put enough batter in the pan to coat the bottom. Rotate the pan to distribute the batter, put the pan back on the burner, and cook the first side 1½ minutes, or until a slight trace of brown appears around the rim of the crêpe.

These crêpes are very light and delicate, with a flavor that blends with seafood and fowl.

Fillings for Crêpes

16 crêpes

Here are some things to remember when making crêpes as a main course:

- Always butter or grease the shallow baking dish in which you plan to heat and serve your crêpes.
- Always choose a sauce that will complement the fillings of your crêpes.
- Always add 1 tablespoon of sauce to the filling of each crêpe in order to bind it and to moisten the inside of the crêpe.
- Never overheat the finished crêpes. They should not be allowed to dry out, but should be piping hot, and any cheese within should be melted.

Dinner Crêpes, Series I

1 recipe Dinner or Entrée Crêpes, 7 or 8 inches wide (see Index)
1 recipe White Wine Sauce (see Index)
Any combination you like or one of the fillings listed below

A. 3 cups julienned cooked chicken *or* turkey
1 pound mushrooms, sliced and sautéed

Layer the chicken and mushrooms into 16 crêpes, add 1 tablespoon sauce to each, roll the crêpes up away from you, and put them seam side down in a buttered baking dish. Top with the remaining sauce and heat in a 350° oven for 20 minutes, or until hot.

B. 2 cups julienned cooked chicken *or* turkey
4 large avocados, sliced into 8 wedges each
2 cups grated Jack cheese

Layer chicken, avocado, and cheese into 16 crêpes. Add sauce, roll crêpes away from you, and place the crêpes seam side down in a buttered baking dish. Pour the remaining sauce over the crêpes and heat them in a 350° oven for 20 minutes, or until hot and the cheese is melted.

C. 2 cups julienned cooked chicken *or* turkey
1 pound mushrooms, sliced and sautéed
1 large can peeled seedless green grapes, *or*
2 cups peeled seedless green grapes

Layer chicken, mushrooms, and grapes into 16 crêpes. Add sauce and roll the crêpes away from you. Put the crêpes in a buttered baking dish seam side down. Pour the remaining sauce over the crêpes and heat in a 350° oven for 20 minutes, or until hot.

D. 4 large avocados, sliced into 8 wedges each
3 cups bean sprouts
1½ cups sliced water chestnuts
1 pound mushrooms, sliced and sautéed

Layer avocado, bean sprouts, water chestnuts, and mushrooms with sauce into 16 crêpes, roll them away from you, and put them seam side down in a buttered baking dish. Pour the sauce over the crêpes and heat them in a 350° oven for 20 minutes, or until piping hot.

Dinner Crêpes, Series II

1 recipe Dinner or Entrée Crêpes, 7 or 8 inches wide (see Index)
1 recipe Cream Sauce or White Wine Sauce (see Index)
Any combination you like or one of the fillings listed below

A. 3 cups chopped spinach (see Creamed Spinach but omit cream)
16 strips bacon, cooked until crisp and crumbled
2 cups grated cheese—Jack, Swiss, Gruyère, *or* your choice

Layer spinach, bacon, and cheese into 16 crêpes, add sauce, roll the crêpes away from you, and place them seam side down in a buttered baking dish. Pour the remaining sauce over the crêpes and heat them in a 350° oven for 20 minutes, or until hot and the cheese is melted.

B. 48 spears asparagus, *or* 48 broccoli flowerets, cooked until not quite done
2 cups finely julienned ham
1½ cups grated Jack cheese
1 cup grated Swiss cheese

Layer asparagus, ham, and cheeses into 16 crêpes, add sauce, then roll the crêpes away from you and place them seam side down in a buttered baking dish. Pour the remaining sauce over the crêpes and heat them in a 350° oven for 20 minutes, or until hot and the cheeses are melted.

C. 3 cups finely julienned ham
8 hard-boiled eggs, cut into quarters
1 cup grated Jack cheese
1 cup grated Swiss cheese

Layer ham, 2 wedges of egg, and cheeses into 16 crêpes. Add sauce, roll the crêpes away from you, and put them seam side down in a buttered baking dish. Pour the remaining sauce over the crêpes and heat them in a 350° oven for 20 minutes, or until hot.

D. 2 cups finely julienned ham
2 cups finely julienned cooked turkey
2 cups finely julienned artichoke bottoms (*not* marinated)
1 cup finely julienned green pepper

Toss ham, turkey, artichokes, and pepper together. Divide the filling among 16 crêpes, add sauce in which you've put 1 teaspoon dry mustard, roll the crêpes away from you, and put them seam side down in a buttered baking dish. Pour the remaining sauce over the crêpes and heat them in a 350° oven for 20 minutes, or until hot.

Seafood Crêpes *6 servings*

    2 tablespoons butter
    ¾ pound mushrooms
    ½ cup sherry
    6 ounces scallops, diced into ½-inch pieces
    1 tablespoon butter
    ½ cup white wine
    ⅓ cup crab *or* clam juice
    1 cup bay shrimp
    1 can (1 cup) crab meat
    2 tablespoons butter
    2 shallots, minced, *or* 4 scallions, white part only,
      chopped
    ¼ cup flour
    2 cups liquid from mushrooms and scallops (add water if
      needed)
    ½ cup light cream
    2 pinches cayenne
    ¼ teaspoon paprika
    3 drops Lea & Perrins Worcestershire sauce
      Salt to taste
    1 tablespoon brandy
    1 tablespoon chopped chives
    1 tablespoon chopped parsley
    ½ cup cream
    1 recipe Dinner Crêpes, 7 or 8 inches in diameter (see
      Index)

Melt 2 tablespoons butter in a frying pan, slice clean mushrooms into the pan, add the sherry, cover, and bring to a boil. Lower the heat and simmer for 5 minutes. Put the scallops in a saucepan with 1 tablespoon butter, the white wine, and the crab (from can) or clam broth. Cover and simmer for 5 minutes. Drain both the mushrooms and the scallops in a colander and reserve their liquids.

Melt 2 tablespoons butter in a saucepan. Add the shallots and sauté for 2 minutes; do not brown. Add the flour and whisk with a wire whip. Add the broth from the mushrooms and scallops, and enough water to make a total of 2 cups. Whisk until smooth, then add the cream, cayenne, paprika, Worcestershire, salt, and brandy. Stir after each addition. Allow the sauce to simmer for 3 minutes, then strain and cool it. Combine all seafood, mushrooms, chives, and parsley in a bowl. Add half of the sauce, or just enough to combine.

Divide the mixture among 12 Dinner Crêpes, roll them, and place them seam side down in a buttered oblong casserole. Pour the remaining sauce over the top of the crêpes, sprinkle lightly with grated Parmesan cheese (if desired), and heat in a 350° oven for 20 minutes, or until piping hot.

If you wish to get professional, add ½ cup whipped cream to the sauce that is poured over the crêpes. When crêpes and ingredients are heated through, place the pan under the broiler and brown ever so lightly.

Note: You can use any combination of seafood you have at your disposal.

Spinach Quiche   6 to 8 *servings*

2 tablespoons butter
1 tablespoon flour
1½ cups chopped spinach, or 1 package frozen
1 unbaked pie shell
2 tablespoons grated Parmesan cheese
1 cup grated cheese, half Swiss and half Jack, *or* your choice
Onion salt
4 large eggs
1½ cups milk *or* light cream
Pinch salt

Melt the butter in a small frying pan, add the flour, and stir the *roux* over medium heat for a minute or two. Add the chopped spinach and stir until the mixture is combined and thickened. Taste for salt and pepper. Sprinkle the bottom of the pie shell with the Parmesan. Spoon the spinach all over the Parmesan, connecting the spoonfuls with a knife so that you have a complete layer of spinach. Top the spinach with the cheese and sprinkle lightly with onion salt. Beat the eggs with the milk or cream, add salt, and pour over all. Bake the quiche in a 350° oven for 35 minutes, or until a knife comes out clean.

This is a delicious quiche. You may fancy it up by adding three strips of crisply fried bacon, crumbled, or some julienned ham or sliced hard-boiled eggs. Use your imagination and what happens to be in the refrigerator. Herbs such as chives, parsley, sweet basil, or fennel are wonderful in quiches.

Ham and Cheese Quiche 6 to 8 servings

5 ounces (a healthy ⅔ cup) cooked ham
2 ounces Swiss cheese, grated (½ cup)
2 ounces Jack cheese, grated (½ cup)
1 unbaked pie shell
2 tablespoons grated Parmesan cheese
2 tablespoons finely chopped onion
1½ tablespoons butter
4 large eggs
1½ cups milk *or* light cream
  Pinch salt
  Cayenne

Julienne the ham and grate the cheese. Sprinkle the Parmesan over the bottom of the pie shell, distribute the ham over the Parmesan, and top with the Swiss and Jack cheeses. Sauté the onion in the butter until it starts to take on color. Distribute the butter and onion over the cheese. Beat the eggs with the milk, add salt, and pour over all ingredients in the pie shell. Sprinkle the top of the custard with cayenne pepper. Do so lightly, as cayenne is very hot. Bake in a 350° oven for 35 minutes, or until a knife blade comes out clean. Allow the quiche to sit for 10 minutes before serving.

This makes a beautiful and tasty first course, Sunday brunch, or easy Sunday supper.

Welsh Rabbit
4 to 6 servings

1 pound Cheddar cheese, cut into small cubes
1 tablespoon butter
1 cup beer *or* ale at room temperature
½ teaspoon dry mustard
½ teaspoon paprika

Melt the butter in a chafing dish set over simmering water, or in a double boiler, or in a bowl set in a pan of simmering water. Make sure the top vessel doesn't touch the water. Add the cheese and stir without stopping. When the cheese begins to melt, gradually add the beer. Continue to stir evenly until all the beer has been added and the cheese is completely melted. Add the mustard and paprika. Taste for seasoning. Depending on the cheese used, you may wish to add a pinch of salt. I often add a splash of Worcestershire and a few drops of Tabasco. (Neither is needed if the Cheddar is sharp enough, but really fine aged Cheddar is not always available, so the seasonings are necessary to compensate.) When the sauce is smooth and nicely seasoned, serve over freshly made toast.

Welsh Rabbit makes for a tasty dinner or lunch or brunch. Serve it with a green vegetable and a salad. If you wish, you may top each portion with a poached or fried egg and grace the top or sides with strips of crisp fried bacon. Many people serve Welsh Rabbit with bacon and no egg.

Noodles Romanoff
6 servings

12 ounces fettuccine egg noodles
6 tablespoons butter
2 teaspoons dehydrated onion
1 tablespoon chopped parsley
¼ teaspoon celery salt
⅛ teaspoon coarsely ground pepper
Pinch garlic salt
¾ cup sour cream
⅓ cup grated Parmesan cheese

Boil the noodles until just done; drain in a colander. Melt the butter in a large frying pan. Add the onion and sauté until it starts to turn brown. Add the noodles, followed by all the other ingredients. Toss the noodles continuously with two rubber spatulas or two forks until all is very well combined and thoroughly heated. Serve.

Macaroni and Cheese

6 to 8 *servings*

12 ounces elbow macaroni
3 tablespoons butter
4 tablespoons flour
2 cups milk, *or* 1 cup milk and 1 cup chicken stock
½ teaspoon dry mustard
½ teaspoon salt
   Good pinch cayenne pepper
2 cups grated sharp Cheddar cheese
2 tablespoons grated Parmesan cheese
2 tablespoons fresh bread crumbs

Cook the macaroni according to the package instructions. Meanwhile, melt the butter in a saucepan. Add the flour and cook the *roux* for 2 minutes over moderate heat. Do not allow to brown. Slowly add the liquid, stirring with a wire whisk until well combined and smooth. Add the seasonings and the sharp Cheddar. Cook the cheese sauce over moderate heat. Stir until the cheese is melted and the sauce is smooth. When the macaroni is done, drain it well, then combine it with the sauce. Pour the macaroni and cheese into a well-buttered casserole and top it with the Parmesan and bread crumbs. Bake in a 350° oven for 20 minutes. If you make Macaroni and Cheese ahead of time, add 10 to 15 minutes to the cooking time.

For those who like a sharper taste, add ½ cup white wine to the sauce after all other ingredients have been incorporated.

Macaroni and Cheese is delicious served with "doctored" stewed tomatoes (see Index).

ENTRÉES: FISH AND SHELLFISH

Kim E. Burroughs '81

*F*ish resembles fowl in that the fresh smells *fresh* and the old or bad smells *horrid*. Fish filets cook in a matter of moments, as do most shellfish. When fish loses its translucency, turns opaque, and flakes easily, it's done. When baking or broiling, 10 minutes for each inch of thickness usually does the trick. A combination of 4 tablespoons butter, 2 tablespoons lemon juice, and 1 tablespoon chopped parsley is delicious when spread on broiled fish halfway through the cooking. Always use a quick heat when sautéing fish or shrimp so that the natural juices of the fish will be sealed in and the oil in which it's being cooked will be sealed out.

Any fish filet can be lightly dipped in seasoned flour and sautéed in half butter and half oil. Another quick, easy, and delicious way of cooking fish filets is to dip them in seasoned flour, then into well-beaten egg, and then sauté them.

Seasoning flour for fish frying is usually very simple: flour with added salt and pepper. However, some onion salt, garlic, paprika, celery salt, and even a pinch of chili powder or dry mustard are good additions. Halibut filets are wonderful dipped in fresh bread crumbs or rolled corn flakes mixed with an equal amount of flour and seasoned to taste with salt, pepper, and paprika. The filets should be dipped first in beaten egg and then the coating of your choice. Sauté them over a moderate flame in equal amounts of oil and butter. A good tartar sauce will enhance the taste without blocking it.

Poached fish is very good for your figure but is best served with a calorie-laden sauce such as hollandaise. Fish will poach in almost as short a time as it takes to fry. It's done when it flakes easily with a touch of a fork.

When you dip fish in a batter and deep-fry it, you can be assured that the fish will be done by the time the batter has browned. Never deep-fry large chunks of fish. You should cut the fish into relatively small chunks or medium-sized filets. Be sure the fat is around 370°. When a cube of white bread browns beautifully within 1 minute, the fat is at the perfect temperature.

When making fish chowder, soup, or whatever you call it, add the fish *after* the sauce or basic stock is nearly done. Crab meat can stand up to rather long cooking, but shrimp and lobster will toughen, and other fish will lose its taste and disintegrate.

Abalone, that marvelous muscle, is at its very best when pounded properly, dipped in seasoned flour then in beaten egg, and sautéed over brisk heat for a moment or two per side. Pure heaven.

Halibut, flounder, or any sturdy white-fleshed fish can be placed in a well-buttered baking dish, topped with cheese sauce, sprinkled with Parmesan, and baked for 20 minutes, or until the fish flakes.

Peeled sautéed green grapes go beautifully with sautéed white-fleshed fish, as do sautéed mushrooms or blanched almonds browned in butter. Baby shrimp or bay shrimp tossed in butter, lemon, and parsley are delicious additions to a plain fish filet.

When fish is baked "mission-style," is it topped with peeled sliced tomatoes and onions, salt, pepper, and a sprinkling of white wine.

Whatever way you fix fish, remember: quick heat when sautéing, and not too long. Seafood should never be overcooked.

Halibut au Gratin—Chatam   *4 servings*

For years the Chatam served Halibut au Gratin for lunch on Fridays to the delighted regulars. Since Carl will serve only great northern halibut, which has soared to $5 and $6 a pound at times, Halibut au Gratin is no longer an every-Friday event. *But* . . . with the following recipe you can make it at home on any day of the week.

    4 6- to 8-ounce halibut filets
       Butter, lemon juice, salt, and pepper
    4 tablespoons (½ stick) butter
    3 tablespoons flour
  1¼ cups half-and-half
    2 tablespoons butter
    1 cup fresh bread crumbs
       Freshly grated Parmesan cheese

Thickly butter a baking dish that will just hold the filets in a single layer. Place the filets in the dish and sprinkle them with lemon juice, salt, and pepper. Melt 4 tablespoons butter in a saucepan, add the flour, and cook over moderate heat, stirring constantly. Add one-third of the half-and-half and whisk until smooth and thick. Add the rest of the half-and-half and stir over heat until very thick. Season the cream sauce with salt and pepper to taste. Set aside.

Melt 2 tablespoons butter in a frying pan. Add the bread crumbs and stir over moderate heat until the crumbs take on a light tan color. Remove the crumbs from the heat, measure, and add an equal amount of freshly grated Parmesan cheese. Spoon the cream sauce down the center of each filet. Do not spread the mixture! Top the sauce with the bread-crumb mixture and bake in a 350° oven for 20 minutes, or until the fish tests done.

Scampi

6 servings

1 large onion, finely chopped
½ cup (1 stick) butter
⅓ cup olive oil
¼ cup chopped parsley
3 to 5 cloves garlic, crushed (amount depends on your taste)
2 tablespoons lemon juice
1 teaspoon salt
½ teaspoon freshly ground pepper
2 pounds raw, shelled, and deveined shrimp (as large as you can buy; figure a minimum of ¼ pound per person)

Sauté the onion in butter until just tender but not brown. Add all the other ingredients except the shrimp. Heat until the mixture just begins to bubble. Add the shrimp and cook, stirring all the while, until the shrimp are pink, about 5 minutes.

Things to remember about scampi:

- Have ready everything else you're going to serve.
- Stir the shrimp gently. Chopsticks do a wonderful job.
- If you have some freshly boiled spaghetti waiting, it's delicious tossed with the butter sauce off the scampi and makes a fine side dish.
- Last, but not least, *don't* overcook shrimp. They get tough if you do. They're done when they become pink and opaque.

Collops of Salmon in Casserole—Scandia   *2 servings*

½ pound salmon filet, boned
1 tablespoon butter
½ teaspoon minced shallots, *or* 1 tablespoon minced scallions, white part only
½ cup white wine
Juice of ½ lemon
6 drops Tabasco
6 drops Worcestershire sauce
Pinch salt
Pinch Accent
1 tablespoon flour
1 tablespoon butter
¼ cup cream
20 seedless green grapes
1 teaspoon chopped chives
1 egg yolk
2 tablespoons cream
1 tablespoon whipped cream

Skin the salmon filet and cut it into 1-inch-square pieces (these are collops). In a heavy skillet melt 1 tablespoon butter. Add the salmon pieces and cook, stirring, for 1 minute. Add the shallots and cook for 30 seconds longer. Add the wine, lemon juice, Tabasco, Worcestershire sauce, salt, and Accent. Heat to simmering. Knead the flour into 1 tablespoon butter and add it to the sauce. When smooth, add the cream and simmer for 2 minutes. Transfer the salmon pieces to a casserole or two gratin dishes, using a slotted spoon. Add to each dish 10 seedless grapes. Add to the sauce the chives and the egg yolk beaten with the 2 tablespoons cream. Stir well and heat, but do not boil. Gently fold in the whipped cream and pour the sauce over the salmon and grapes. Garnish the dishes (or casserole) with piped mashed potatoes. Glaze under the broiler to a golden brown.

Scandia's recipe says that this may be made with sea bass, scallops, shrimps, lobster tail pieces, halibut, or albacore. I have found that the whipped cream is not mandatory, but it adds a delicious touch, and you may dispense with the mashed potatoes if you so desire. I know the list of ingredients may seem long, but this is truly an easy, quick meal that will please the most demanding palate. You can double or triple this recipe successfully.

Deviled Crab Casserole à la Carl   *4 to 6 servings*

1 tablespoon vegetable oil
¼ pound mushrooms, sliced
3 shallots, chopped
6 tablespoons butter
4 tablespoons flour
1 teaspoon dry mustard
1 cup half-and-half
½ cup dry white wine
¼ cup dry sherry
   MSG and salt to taste
½ teaspoon Worcestershire sauce
4 drops hot pepper sauce
   Cayenne pepper to taste
1½ tablespoons chopped parsley
2 hard-boiled eggs, chopped
1 pound crab meat
   Bread crumbs
   Paprika
   Butter

Heat the oil in a skillet, add the mushrooms, and sauté lightly. Add the shallots, lower the heat, and sauté 2 minutes longer. Add the butter and heat until melted, then stir in the flour and mustard until smooth. In a separate pan combine the half-and-half and the wines and heat; then stir into the mushroom mixture. Cook and stir until smooth and thickened. Season to taste with MSG and salt. Stir in the Worcestershire and hot pepper sauces. Season to the desired hotness by sprinkling cayenne pepper into the sauce. Add the parsley, eggs, and crab meat and mix gently. Turn the mixture into four or six individual casseroles. Sprinkle each with bread crumbs and paprika and dot with butter. Bake at 375° degrees for 15 to 20 minutes.

Salmon Gravlax—Scandia   24 *servings*

1 *large* fresh salmon—minimum of 10 pounds whole
2 cups sugar
1 cup salt
2 bunches fresh dill
2 tablespoons cracked pepper
Vegetable oil

Filet the raw salmon, thus obtaining two large filets, and pick out any remaining bones with tweezers. Prick the fish all over with the prongs of a fork. Mix the sugar and salt together and rub the mixture into both sides of the salmon filet. Pick the leaves off the dill and crush the stems lightly. Lay the stems in the bottom of a dish that will just fit the fileted fish when laid out flat. Lay the fish on the dill stems and sprinkle with pepper. Chop the dill leaves and sprinkle them over the top of the fish. Add enough oil to cover the fish. Allow the gravlax to sit in a cool place for at least 24 hours. If you don't have a cool place, put the salmon in the refrigerator. At serving time, drain the fish. Slice paper-thin. Serve with Scandia's Dill Sauce.

Scandia's Dill Sauce   *4 cups*

2 cups fresh chopped dill
½ cup sugar
1 cup Dijon mustard
⅓ cup wine vinegar
½ cup mayonnaise (homemade, Best Foods, or Hellmann's)
2 cups vegetable oil

Whisk all the ingredients together in a bowl or blender. The recipe may be cut in half. Both the gravlax and dill sauce will keep well for up to ten days. Wrap the plate with the gravlax on it with plastic wrap, and keep the dill sauce in a glass container.

I have given you Kenneth Hansen's recipe uncut. It is for a large salmon. Usually if you're going to go to the trouble of purchasing a whole salmon with the intention of making gravlax, you have a party in mind, and for a party you'll need to make a considerable amount. If, however, you wish to have some tasty gravlax for your own personal taste treat, cut the recipe in half and use a smaller salmon, or even salmon steaks. Choose either center cuts or a small whole salmon, fileted, which is better yet. If you like lox, you'll love gravlax!

Filet of Trout in Aspic—Scandia 6 *servings*

6 trout, fileted, boned, and skinned
4 cups white wine
1 cup white vinegar
2 cups water
2 teaspoons salt
4 tablespoons sugar
1 teaspoon Accent
4 bay leaves
8 peppercorns, *or* ¼ teaspoon cracked pepper
6 whole allspice
5 sprigs fresh parsley
2 bunches fresh dill, *or* 1 teaspoon dill seed
2 small carrots, scraped and sliced
1 small onion, thinly sliced
3 tablespoons (3 packages) plain gelatin
3 egg whites

Fold the filets in half and place them in a wide-bottomed pan. Cover with all the ingredients except the gelatin and egg whites. Bring to a full boil, remove from the heat, and allow to cool in the broth. When cold, strain the broth into another pot and add to it the gelatin and slightly beaten egg whites. Bring to a boil. The gelatin will dissolve and the egg whites will clarify the broth. Once the broth has boiled, remove it from the heat and allow it to sit while you arrange the filets in individual ramekins. Strain the broth (which will look cloudy) through a sieve lined with a rinsed-out napkin or tea towel. The broth will strain out to a crystal-clear liquid. Cover the filets with the strained aspic, and refrigerate until completely set. Serve in ramekins, or turn out on tender Bibb lettuce leaves. Serve with any of your favorite dressings.

Note: This recipe is a delicious and easy adaptation of a classic. Seafood in aspic is beautiful, healthful, and a joy to the taste buds. If you wish, you can pour a small amount of aspic into the bottoms of the ramekins, chill until set, and then place a sprig of parsley, some chives or cut olives as decoration. Place the filets on top and cover them completely with aspic. Trout filets are wonderful, but you can make this same dish using other fish filets or any seafood of your choosing. Lobster requires a few minutes of simmering before being set to cool in liquid.

Beer Batter for Fish   *1 cup*

¾ cup beer
1 cup flour
½ teaspoon paprika

Cut the fish into cubes or thin strips. Blend all the ingredients. Dip the fish in the batter and deep-fry it in 375° oil. Drain on a rack or paper towels. Any white-fleshed fish does well in this batter.

DESSERTS

Things to Remember About Baking

- Never start a cake or cookie dough with hard butter or fat, except when you use a food processor. Having all ingredients at room temperature helps guarantee success.
- When a recipe calls for sour cream, buttermilk, sour milk, yogurt, bananas, or applesauce, you must add baking soda as the main leavening agent. Remember what needs soda when you create your own recipes.
- Since 1 cup *whipping* cream equals 2 cups *whipped* cream, read recipes carefully to see which is called for.
- When you whip heavy cream, don't add sugar or other flavorings until the cream is quite thick. *Do not* use a food processor to whip cream.
- To get the maximum amount of juice from any type of citrus fruit, roll it on a counter top, pressing as you do so. Then cut the fruit and squeeze.
- Always wash candied fruits before you use them. Put them in a colander and pour boiling water over them. This washes off the preservatives, improving their flavor and protecting your health.
- Grease cake pans heavily with 1 tablespoon pure vegetable shortening per pan. Dust with flour and shake it out if the recipe calls for you to do so. Don't use butter unless the recipe says to; it tends to overbrown cakes.
- Be sure to preheat your oven to the correct temperature before you bake anything in it.

• When you pour a cake batter into a pan, pick the pan up off the counter about 3 or 4 inches and then drop it. Turn the pan a half turn and repeat. This settles the batter evenly and eliminates unwanted air bubbles. Cakes that contain beaten egg whites are the exception.

• Never bake cakes or cookies in the upper half of the oven unless the recipe so states, and always bake on the center of the rack.

• If the size of your oven forces you to crowd cake pans, turn them a half turn when they're halfway through their cooking time. This will help to equalize the baking and the level of the cakes.

• Most baked goods like to bake in private. Constant opening of the oven door will ruin many a masterpiece.

• To determine whether a cake is done, test with a toothpick in the *center* of the cake. A clean toothpick means the item is done.

• Always cool cakes in their pans for 10 minutes before turning them out, and always remove them from the pans when the 10 minutes are up. Removing a cake from its pan too soon or too late can be disastrous.

• Food coloring added to cake frosting or decorating icing darkens as it dries. Always mix colors a shade or two lighter than you really want for the desired effect.

• To ice the top and sides of a cake, run a thin layer of icing around the sides, pushing the icing between the layers so that the cake doesn't droop at the edges. Let the thin layer sit a moment, then frost the cake with a heavier coating. A cake holds together better when it is iced by this method. The same procedure works for whipped cream, which ordinarily doesn't like to stick. If you put on a thin layer first, you can then pile on the whipped cream to your heart's content.

• Cut a hole in the top of rolled Christmas cookies with a straw so that they can be hung from the tree.

• Don't use cookie doughs that contain a lot of leavening for cut-out cookies. The leavening causes them to expand out of shape.

• Drop cookies freeze beautifully, baked or unbaked. Freeze them on a cookie sheet, and when they are totally frozen, store them in plastic bags. Unbaked frozen cookies can go directly from freezer to oven; allow 2 to 4 more minutes' baking time.

• Baked cake layers also freeze well. Wrap them in plastic wrap and foil once they're frozen.

Basic Sponge Cake 3 *layers*

6 eggs, separated
¼ teaspoon cream of tartar
1 cup powdered sugar
1 cup flour

Beat the egg whites stiff, adding the cream of tartar halfway through the beating process.

Beat the egg yolks until they are light in color, add the sugar, and continue to beat until the mixture is smooth. Slowly stir in the flour, blending completely. Fold in the egg whites.

Turn the batter into three 8- or 9-inch cake pans lined with waxed paper and *not* greased. Bake in a 350° oven for 12 minutes, or until the cake tests done. Turn the layers out on a rack to cool. With sponge cake it is sometimes necessary to run a knife around the edge of the pans and to loosen the layers from the bottom by running a limber spatula under the waxed paper.

Sponge cakes can be cut into two layers each and filled with buttercream, whipped cream, or jam (see Summer Fool—Chatam). This Basic Sponge Cake may also be used to make a Danish Layer Cake (see Index).

German Sand Torte 16 *or more servings*

3 cups flour
¼ teaspoon baking powder
1 cup (2 sticks) butter or margarine, softened
3 cups sugar
6 eggs
1 cup sour cream
1½ teaspoons vanilla

Sift the flour and baking powder together; set aside. With an electric mixer, beat the butter and gradually add the sugar. Beat thoroughly. Add the eggs one at a time; beat at least 30 seconds after each addition. Turn the machine to slow speed; add the sour cream and blend well. Add the flour mixture in fifths; I spoon it in with a serving spoon. Scrape the mixing bowl often to make sure that all the flour is incorporated. Add the vanilla last. Pour the batter into a well-greased and floured tube pan, and spread the batter to even it out. Bake in a 350° oven for 1 hour and 15 minutes. Cool 15 minutes. Turn the cake out of the pan and dust it with powdered sugar.

Because of the sour cream, it's fine to use margarine in this cake. It's even better than a pound cake; don't let the 3 cups of sugar throw you. This cake can be cut into 15 to 30 slices, depending on your appetite.

Delicious Pound Cake   *16 or more servings*

1 cup (2 sticks) butter *or* margarine, *or* half butter and half margarine
1⅓ cups sugar
1 teaspoon vanilla
¼ teaspoon almond extract
4 eggs
2¼ cups flour
½ teaspoon baking powder
½ teaspoon salt
¼ cup milk

Cream the butter and sugar well. Add the vanilla and almond extract. Beat in the eggs one at a time; beat *well* after each addition. Sift the dry ingredients together. Add half the dry ingredients and beat 30 seconds; add the milk and beat 30 seconds more. Add the remaining half of the dry ingredients and beat well. Pour the batter into a well-greased tube pan and bake it in a 325° oven for 70 to 90 minutes, or until a toothpick comes out clean. Cool 15 minutes and turn the cake out of the pan. You may dust it with powdered sugar.

Lemon Frosting   *frosts 2 layers*

2 tablespoons butter *or* margarine, softened
2 cups powdered sugar
1 tablespoon lemon juice
2 teaspoons grated lemon rind
2 tablespoons milk

Beat the butter and sugar together, add the lemon juice and rind, then the milk. Beat until smooth and spreadable.

Orange Frosting

frosts 2 layers

Combine the same ingredients as for Lemon Frosting, substituting orange juice and orange rind for the lemon.

Chocolate Fudge Icing

frosts 2 layers

3 squares baking chocolate
3 tablespoons butter
3 cups powdered sugar
6 tablespoons brewed coffee
1 teaspoon vanilla
1 teaspoon brandy or Kahlúa (optional)

Melt the chocolate and butter in small bowl in a 225° oven. *Do not stir.* Put the sugar in a mixing bowl and add the melted chocolate and butter along with the coffee and flavorings. Beat until completely smooth.

For a three-layer cake, increase the amount of sugar to 4 cups and the coffee to ½ cup.

Vanilla Frosting

frosts two layers

4 tablespoons (½ stick) butter *or* margarine
3⅓ cups powdered sugar
3 tablespoons milk
2 teaspoons vanilla

Combine all the ingredients until smooth, adding more milk if the frosting is too stiff and more sugar if it's too runny. Remember that powdered-sugar frostings thicken as they cool, so the consistency can be a bit runnier than you might think. If the frosting is *just* spreadable when you frost the cake, you'll end up with a hard, rather stiff, frosting. Keep it creamy.

Summer Fool—Chatam

12 servings

This delicious confection is made of layers of sponge cake brimming with fresh peaches, strawberries, and whipped cream. The secret (which imitators rarely detect) is the currant jelly, which is to fruit what salt is to a steak.

2 cups whipping cream
2 tablespoons sugar
1 Basic Sponge Cake, 8 inches round, 2 inches high (see Index)
1 cup currant jelly, whipped thin for spreading
4 cups fresh peaches, peeled and thinly sliced
4 cups fresh strawberries, washed and thinly sliced
Additional whipped cream

Slice the sponge cake into four layers, each ½ inch thick. Place one layer in the bottom of a glass bowl. Spread it with one-quarter of the whipped currant jelly. Arrange a layer of peaches on top of the jelly, followed by a layer of strawberries and a layer of whipped cream. Continue layering until all the ingredients have been used, ending with fruit. Using a pastry bag, decorate the top of the dessert with additional whipped cream.

Carole's Dessert Crêpes   6 *servings*

4 large eggs
1 cup milk
1 tablespoon sugar
Pinch salt
½ cup flour
2 tablespoons butter, melted
1 tablespoon brandy
¼ cup (½ stick) butter

Beat the eggs, milk, sugar, and salt together. Add the flour; beat again. Stir in the butter and brandy. (You can do all this in a blender or food processor pronto!) Refrigerate for at least 2 hours.

Heat a crêpe pan (a 5-inch Teflon pan is great for dessert crêpes) over a moderately high flame. While the pan is heating, melt ¼ cup butter in another small pan. With a pastry brush, brush the crêpe pan with melted butter (pick the pan up in your left hand), and add enough crêpe batter to the pan so that when you rotate it, the batter just covers the bottom completely. Put the pan back on the burner and cook the crêpe until you can see a trace of brown somewhere around the edge. (This is a secret. The beginning crêpe maker always wants to turn the crêpe long before it's done.) When the top looks dry, it's an indication it's almost ready; but if you wait until you can see the tinge of brown, you'll have winning crêpes every single time. When you do finally see the brown (it seems to take forever), turn the crêpe with a flexible plastic spatula or a rubber scraper. Ninety-nine percent of a crêpe's cooking is done on the first side, so count one, two, three; then turn the crêpe out onto the counter or onto a piece of waxed paper. Brush the pan again with butter and repeat until all the crêpe batter has been cooked.

If your first crêpe looks like a failure, don't despair—your pan may not yet be hot enough or is uneven in temperature. Again, brush the pan with butter and proceed with the next one. While you're waiting for the brown to show on that second crêpe, eat the first "mistake" with some butter and sugar. (It is sometimes necessary to call a perfectly beautiful crêpe a "mistake.") When all crêpes are made, proceed with the filling and finishing of your crêpe recipe.

If you like to spoil your family on Sundays, make some crêpe batter on Saturday afternoon; cover and refrigerate it until the next morning. Let your family fill the crêpes with their favorite jam and sour cream or butter and powdered sugar as they come out of the pan.

I work with two pans at once. Since the crêpes must cook for a minute or more on that first side, it's easy to time two pans so that you're done in half the time. I've walked into the kitchen of the Chatam restaurant on a Sunday when we're closed, only to find my father busy with six 8-inch crêpe pans going at once. Surely you and I can handle two!

Easy Suzette   6 servings

    Rind of 1 orange
¼ cup (½ stick) butter
2 tablespoons orange juice
1 tablespoon Grand Marnier
½ cup powdered sugar
1 recipe Carole's Dessert Crêpes (preceding recipe)
    Juice of 1 orange
⅓ cup brandy

Cut the rind from the orange with a very sharp knife, taking no white with each strip cut. You should be able to see the tiny holes in the skin of the orange on the back of each strip. Put the rind and all the other ingredients in a food processor or blender, and process until smooth. If you have neither food processor nor blender, chop the orange rind fine and blend all the ingredients by hand.

Spread a small amount of crêpe filling onto the center of each crêpe. Fold each crêpe in quarters as you would a hankie and arrange them decoratively on a buttered flameproof serving dish. (When I do them in my rectangular baking dish, I overlap them in two parallel lines; I overlap them in a circle around the edge of my round baking plate. Make it pretty!) Put the crêpes aside if you're going to serve them within an hour or two. Cover and refrigerate them if it'll be many hours before you serve them. When you get ready to serve your guests' dinner, take the crêpes out of the refrigerator and place them by the stove so that they'll reach room temperature.

When dinner is over, squeeze the juice of 1 orange over the crêpes and warm them in a 300° oven for 5 or 10 minutes. Warm ⅓ cup brandy in a small saucepan. The brandy should get to body temperature or around 100°. Don't put the brandy on the stove and walk away; keep testing and let the brandy get warm, *not* hot. While the crêpes were getting warm in the oven, you should have gotten coffee to your guests, so you can now present your crêpes. Light the warm brandy and pour the blue-flaming liquid over the crêpes. *Voilà!* Crêpes Suzette you made in the morning.

Crêpes Suzette are delicious, but there's no end to the other variations you can make out of crêpes. Fill them with blueberry preserves and sour cream, or fresh blueberries thickened with sugar, cornstarch, and lemon juice. Fresh peaches, peeled and sugared, along with some custard cream or sour cream make a dream of a dessert. Try sliced and sweetened strawberries and Cointreau, or butter, ground walnuts, and bourbon, mixed with some powdered sugar.

Peaches and Cream   6 servings

¾ cup sugar
1 tablespoon cornstarch
3 to 4 cups sliced peaches, fresh or frozen
Juice of ½ lemon, at least 1½ tablespoons
1 recipe Carole's Dessert Crêpes, baked in a 5-inch pan (see Index)

Stir the sugar and cornstarch together until they are completely combined. Put the peaches in a large (preferably nonstick) frying pan, and add the sugar and cornstarch mixture and the lemon juice. Stir the peaches with a rubber spatula over high heat until their juice has thickened slightly and is clear, about 4 to 5 minutes. Spoon a few peach slices onto a crêpe, fold the side nearest you over the peaches, then fold both sides over the middle, and finally roll up the crêpe, rolling it away from you. Place the crêpe, seam side down, in a buttered baking dish. Repeat the process with the other crêpes until all crêpes and peaches are used. Pour the remaining sauce over the crêpes and heat in a 350° oven for 10 minutes, or until hot. Serve with whipped cream or softened vanilla ice cream that has been whipped with a beater or food processor.

If you wish to make these ahead of time, follow the recipe to the point where you are ready to pour the sauce over the crêpes; instead, set the sauce aside in a small saucepan and cover the crêpes until ready to use. Just before serving, heat the sauce, pour it over the crêpes, and heat them in the oven.

Note: You may add 1 ounce Grand Marnier to the sauce before you pour it over the crêpes.

Pâte à Chou   *3 cups*

Pâte à chou is the paste from which cream puffs, chocolate eclairs, Chocolate Eclair Torte, and Paris-Brest are made. It is also used to make small hors d'oeuvres and smooth heavy dumplings that are wonderful smothered in a sour cream and paprika sauce. As much as I love my food processor, I truly believe that *pâte à chou* is better beaten by hand. Besides, it's great exercise.

    1 cup water
    ½ cup (1 stick) butter
    1 cup flour
    4 large eggs

Put the water in a fair-sized saucepan that will be good to beat by hand in. Add the butter, cut into chunks. Bring the water to a boil, and when the butter has melted, add the flour all at once. Remove the pan from the heat and beat in the flour with a wooden spoon. When the flour has been absorbed into the water-and-butter mixture, return the pan to the stove and beat the mixture over moderate heat for approximately 1 minute, or until all is combined and of a very smooth consistency. Remove the pan from the heat and allow it to cool for about 2 minutes. The mixture should still be hot.

Break in an egg and beat with a wooden spoon until all is combined. The basic *roux* will break into scallop-type pieces before taking in all the egg. Just keep beating until the mixture is smooth and has lost its shine. Repeat with the remaining eggs, beating them in one at a time. Bake the dough on a very lightly greased cookie sheet in a 400° oven for 15 minutes. Reduce the heat to 350° and continue baking for 30 minutes, or until the paste is golden brown and dry. You can shape it as for a Paris-Brest or a Chocolate Eclair

Torte–Chatam (see Index). It's best to check baking times and temperatures with the recipe in which you'll be using the *pâte à chou,* for these vary according to the size and shape of the *pâte.*

Quick Custard

3 cups

¾ cup sugar
4 tablespoons cornstarch
2½ cups milk
3 large eggs
1 teaspoon vanilla
1 tablespoon Grand Marnier

Whisk the sugar and cornstarch together in a saucepan *(not* aluminum). Gradually whisk in the milk, making sure the mixture is smooth. Beat in the eggs and whisk until completely combined. Cook over medium heat, whisking constantly, until the mixture reaches the boiling point and thickens. This is easily done *if* you scrape the bottom of the pan with the wire whip *constantly!* Be sure to use a heavy saucepan. When the mixture begins to thicken and boil, lift the pan from the heat with one hand and continue whisking with the other. If the custard isn't thick, put the pan back on the heat, whisk, and cook until the proper consistency is reached. Remove from the heat, cool slightly, then stir in the vanilla and Grand Marnier. Place a piece of buttered waxed paper on top of the custard and cool it completely.

This custard can be used as is or folded into 1 cup whipping cream, stiffly whipped. It can also be folded into a mixture of 6 tablespoons butter beaten with ⅔ cup powdered sugar to produce a buttercream that is excellent used between cake layers, in chocolate eclairs, Paris-Brest (following recipe), and other desserts.

Paris-Brest

12 servings

Paris-Brest got its name from the famous thousand-kilometer bike race from Brest, France, to Paris. Even though the facts aren't very scintillating, the name still brings smiles to those who don't know the spelling or the story. The gynecologist who frequents our restaurants usually wants to know if we're serving the right or the left.

1 recipe *pâte à chou* (see Index)
1 recipe Quick Custard, cooled (preceding recipe)
4 tablespoons (½ stick) butter
6 tablespoons powdered sugar
1 recipe Danish Apples, cooled, liquid jelled (see Index)
Powdered sugar

Lightly grease and flour a large cookie sheet. Make an oval of the *pâte à chou* either by pressing it through a large plain pastry tube or by spooning mounds of it onto the cookie sheet in an oval. With a dinner knife connect the mounds and spread the *pâte à chou* until an even oval 1½ inches high is formed. Bake the oval in a 425° oven for 15 minutes. Lower the heat to 350° and bake another 30 to 40 minutes, or until the oval is golden and dry.

Cool the oval and then carefully slit it in half horizontally with a sharp knife (a boning knife does this job neatly). Spreading your hands wide, work them under the top of the oval and carefully set it aside. Place four pieces of waxed paper on your most beautiful platter, leaving a hole in the center, but making sure that the edges are covered. Place the bottom of the oval on the waxed paper. Center it on the platter.

Make Quick Custard; cool it. Beat the butter and sugar together, add the custard in small amounts, and continue beating until all is combined. Spoon the buttercream into the bottom of the oval. Make Danish Apples, drain well, and cook their liquid down to a jelly over high heat. Chill both apples and jelly. Arrange the apples over the buttercream, spoon the jelly over the apples, and carefully replace the top of the Paris-Brest. Dust top with powdered sugar. Carefully remove the waxed paper. *Voilà!* A dessert fit for a king.

The original Paris-Brest was made more simply. It contained nothing but custard on the inside and powdered sugar on top. Variations now abound; slivered almonds can be baked into the top of the oval, as can a combination of sugar and ground nuts. Whole strawberries or your favorite poached fruit is delicious, and, if you are in a hurry, whipped cream topped with raspberry jam will fill the bill and your guests. Again, use your imagination and what you have on hand.

Cut the pastry with a very sharp knife using an up-and-down sawing motion.

Chocolate Eclair Torte—Chatam   10 to 12 *servings*

1 recipe *pâte à chou* (see Index)
2 tablespoons sugar
½ cup finely chopped walnuts
1 recipe Quick Custard (see Index)
4 tablespoons (½ stick) butter
6 tablespoons powdered sugar
4 squares semisweet chocolate
2 tablespoons butter

Lightly grease three 9-inch cake pans. Make *pâte à chou* and divide it equally among the pans. With a rubber spatula spread the paste evenly. Sprinkle the paste with the sugar and nuts. Bake in a 400° oven for 15 minutes, lower the heat to 350°, and continue baking for another 20 minutes, or until the paste is well puffed, golden brown, and light in weight. Remove the layers from the oven and cool them on racks. The cake layers will be uneven, puffed more in some places than in others, but don't worry.

While the layers are baking, make Quick Custard and cool the pan in a sink of cold water, stirring occasionally to prevent a crust from forming. Beat the butter with the powdered sugar until smooth and add the custard a spoonful at a time, beating all the while. When the custard cream is smooth and the cake layers are cooled completely, melt the chocolate and butter over very low heat. Don't stir the chocolate-butter mixture while it's melting. When completely melted, stir it with a rubber spatula and drizzle it over the three cake layers. The object is *not* to cover the cake layer completely, but to grace the tops of all the puffed areas and drizzle chocolate in between. If you allow the chocolate-butter mixture simply to run off the end of your spatula, you can do a beautiful job. Allow the chocolate to cool and set. Place a layer on a cake plate and spoon half the custard cream onto it. Most of it should go in the middle; don't spoon any custard around the edges. Top with the second layer of cake and spoon the other half of the custard cream mostly onto the middle of it, as you did on the first. Place the third and last layer of cake over the second layer of custard and gently settle it on. If any custard oozes out, scoop it cleanly off with a knife. Chill the cake for at least 2 hours. Cut it with a sharp knife in an up-and-down sawing motion.

Note: You can omit the sugar and nuts from the *pâte à chou* cake layers. You may also cheat by making a package of instant vanilla pudding and using it in place of the custard cream, but this whole beautiful creation is really quick and easy to make, so you might as well go all the way. At the restaurant they pipe whipped cream up the sides of the finished torte; you may do so if you wish, but it's not at all necessary.

ひらひらひらひらひらひらひらひらひらひらひら

CHEESECAKE

Some years ago, as I was working the evening shift at the restaurant, Peter Ustinov strolled in, chatting in French to a petite and very attractive young French woman.

I took them to a quiet booth and made sure they knew of our specialties. I also made sure their order was properly taken.

When it came time for the great actor to have dessert, I suggested our cheesecake. Mr. Ustinov laughed. "My dear, I am possibly the world's best judge of cheesecake, and I doubt that you could produce one to my liking." I looked at him and he added, "No offense meant; cheesecake is simply a passion with me."

I laughed and said that I was so positive that he would love our cheesecake that I would give him a piece on the house. One bite and he was hooked. He quickly ordered another piece!

After that, Mr. Ustinov kept coming back with friends, eager for cheesecake. Then about a month after Mr. Ustinov's first appearance, he said he was going to Mexico to make a film. He asked if we could send him one of our cheesecakes, adding that he was leaving the next morning.

The following morning I glued the phone to my ear and finally reached someone who could give me the information I needed. I was informed:

"Yes," they would take a cheesecake on one of the planes that flew to location twice a week.

"No," it probably wouldn't get to Mr. Ustinov.

"Yes," the box would get to Mr. Ustinov, but not the cake.

"No," the cake would be replaced by a note much like the ones Elizabeth Taylor received in chili cartons from Chasens.

"Yes," the note would read, "you have very good taste."

No, we didn't send the cheesecake, and yes, I'm going to give you the recipe.

ひらひらひらひらひらひらひらひらひらひらひら

Carl Andersen's Chatam Cheesecake   *12 to 16 servings*

Before I give you the recipe, here are some tips on what makes the cheesecake so good. They apply to any baked cheesecake recipe, so perhaps you can improve the recipe you already have simply by handling the ingredients correctly.

- Butter the spring-form pan before you press the graham-cracker crust into it.
- After pressing in the crust, put the pan in the freezer for 5 minutes.
- Remove the pan from the freezer and bake the crust for 5 minutes in a 350° oven.
- Be sure the cream cheese is at room temperature.
- Beat and beat and scrape and scrape. Cream cheese demands a lot of beating, and if you don't scrape the bowl, much of the cream cheese will cling there and cause lumps in your cake.
- Don't overbake! You should remove the cake from the oven when the cake has risen and the middle is barely set. Because of the cream cheese, it *will* set in the refrigerator within 24 hours. Cheesecake is always better the next day.

Carl Andersen's Chatam Cheesecake is best when it's one day old. It will keep for a week and be just as good as on the second day.

Graham-Cracker Crust

2 cups graham crackers crumbs
¼ cup sugar
⅓ cup plus 1 tablespoon butter *or* margarine, melted

Mix the graham crackers and sugar together. Stir in the butter and press the mixture into a buttered 10-inch spring-form pan. Put the pan in the freezer for 5 minutes, then in a 350° oven for 5 minutes.

Cheesecake

4 8-ounce packages cream cheese
5 eggs
1 cup plus 2 tablespoons sugar
Pinch salt
¾ cup sour cream
2 tablespoons vanilla

Topping

1 pint sour cream
½ cup sugar
1 teaspoon vanilla

In a large bowl, using an electric mixer, beat the cream cheese for 2 minutes, or until it is very smooth. Add 3 eggs, one at a time, and beat *well* after *every* addition. Scrape the bowl often! Add the sugar and salt and beat some more. Add 2 more eggs, one at a time, and beat well after each addition. Add the sour cream and beat. Then add the vanilla and beat again. Pour into a crust-lined pan and bake in a 350° oven for 45 to 55 minutes, depending on the altitude and the size of the eggs used. When the cake has risen to the top of the crust, remove it from the oven and cool it. With a wire whip, beat together the sour cream, sugar, and vanilla for the topping. When it is smooth and runny, pour it on top of the cake and put the cake back into a 350° oven for 5 more minutes. Cool and refrigerate the cake in the pan and keep your hands off until it is chilled and set.

On the day you plan to serve the cake, unmold it by running a very sharp, thin-bladed knife around the pan, pressing the blade to the side so as not to cut into the crust. Unlatch the spring form and carefully remove it. Slip the knife horizontally under the cake until you think the point of it is at dead center. Now press the blade against the bottom of the pan and slowly rotate the pan one complete turn. Now slip a wide-bladed knife, such as a good French chef's knife, completely under the cake. Lift the pan and cake up, hold it just above and to the side of the plate on which you wish to set the cake, then with one magnificent lifting and turning motion, slide the cheese-cake onto the plate.

Carl's Pecan Torte

8 servings

About fifteen years ago my father began presenting his restaurant public with some truly exceptional desserts. If you were to visit his establishment you would be confronted with a refrigerated case of six to ten different mousses, creams, tortes, and pastries that were prepared fresh in his kitchen every day.

Carl gave me permission to adapt one of his special dessert recipes for home kitchen use, and I present it here with love.

½ cup (1 stick) butter *or* margarine
½ cup powdered sugar
1 cup flour

2 eggs
1 cup brown sugar
3 tablespoons flour
1 teaspoon baking powder
1 to 1½ cups chopped pecans

3 tablespoons red currant jelly

1 cup whipping cream
1 tablespoon powdered sugar

Beat the butter until soft and fluffy. Add the powdered sugar and beat well. Add the flour and beat only until combined.

Divide the dough between two well-greased 9-inch cake pans. With your fingers spread the dough out in the pans and press it to make the tops of the layers even. Bake in a 350° oven for 12 minutes. The layers should not brown, but a very light tan can be tolerated.

While the bottom layers of the torte are baking, whip the eggs with a wire whip. Add the brown sugar and beat until well combined. Add the 3 table-spoons flour and the baking powder. Mix well, then stir in the pecans.

When the bottom layers of the torte are done, remove them from the oven and divide the pecan mixture between the two pans. With a dinner knife spread the pecan mixture to within ¼ inch of the edge of the pans. Return the pans to the oven and bake for another 20 minutes. The top of the torte should be a chocolate brown and the sides should start to pull away from the pans.

Remove the pans from the oven. Cool for 5 minutes. Run a sharp knife around edges and turn the torte layers out. Turn them once more so that the pecan layer is on top. Cool completely.

Using a large knife, cut each layer into eight equal pie-shaped wedges. Do this by cutting the layers in half, then each half in half, and then each quarter in half.

Whip the jelly with a fork until it is semi-runny. Fold a large piece of waxed paper in half, then roll it into a cone, keeping the folded edge at the narrow tip. Tape the cone's outer edge to hold it in shape.

Holding the cone point down, pour in the beaten jelly. With scissors cut the tip of the cone to create a small opening not exceeding ⅛ inch in diameter. Folding the top of the cone, gently press the jelly out onto each wedge of torte in a zigzag fashion. You should end up with a very thin zigzag line of jelly running the length of each wedge.

Beat the whipping cream. When it is fairly stiff, add 1 tablespoon powdered sugar and continue beating until very stiff. Pipe the cream in a zigzag pattern onto the wedges of torte through a large fluted pastry tube. Since you are going to place one piece of torte on top of another, so that every piece of torte has two layers, you can make the top zigzags very pretty and the bottoms a simpler and straighter line. When all wedges of torte have been decorated, stack them up double-decker fashion and place them on a pretty plate or pedestaled cake stand.

Though you may find the directions lengthy, the torte is quite simple to make and oh's and ah's always greet this beautiful dessert.

Since this torte has a chewy, nutty texture, don't expect your dessert fork to glide through it. Get in there and wrangle yourself a bite. After one bite your fork will seem to glide on through.

You can put toothpicks in some of the pieces and then cover the whole thing with plastic wrap. Covered and refrigerated, the torte will keep for three days . . . as long as no one goes into the refrigerator.

Carl's Lemon Torte   *10 servings*

Dough

>   2 cups flour
>   1 cup (2 sticks) margarine
>   ½ cup powdered sugar

Custard Topping

>   4 eggs
>   2 cups sugar
>   4 tablespoons lemon juice
>   4 tablespoons lemon rind
>   4 tablespoons flour
>   1 teaspoon baking powder

Cream Filling

>   2 cups whipping cream
>   2 tablespoons powdered sugar

Sauce

>   ½ cup sugar
>   2 tablespoons cornstarch
>   Juice of 1 lemon plus enough water to make ½ cup
>   Rind of 1 lemon
>   1 egg
>   1 tablespoon butter

Combine the flour, margarine, and powdered sugar and work them together until a dough is formed. This can be done in a food processor if care is taken not to overwork the dough. Divide the dough in half, pat it into two well-greased 9-inch cake pans, and bake in a 350° oven for 15 minutes.

Meanwhile, beat the 4 eggs until light. Add 2 cups sugar, the lemon juice, and the rind. Beat until smooth. Stir in the flour and baking powder. When the dough has baked for 15 minutes, pour the custard topping over it, dividing it equally between the two pans. Bake another 25 minutes, or until the custard is set. Cool the torte layers for 10 minutes in their pans. Very carefully invert one layer onto a cooling rack, then turn again onto another cooling rack so that the layer is right side up. Turn the other layer onto a cooling rack and then onto a serving plate. Cool completely.

Whip the whipping cream. When it is stiff, add the 2 tablespoons powdered sugar and beat until very stiff. Set aside 1 cup of the whipped cream, covered. Refrigerate.

As soon as the cake layers are completely cooled, assemble the torte. Spread some of the rest of the whipped cream on the cake on the serving plate, place the other layer on top, and frost the sides of the torte with whipped cream coming up over the sides onto the top, leaving a 4-inch circle of exposed torte in the center. Dust the open circle of torte with powdered sugar. Refrigerate.

To make the sauce, combine the sugar with the cornstarch. Stir in the lemon juice, water, and rind. Cook over medium-high heat until the mixture boils. Lower the heat and stir for 2 more minutes. Remove from heat. Beat the egg in a small bowl, add 1 tablespoon hot lemon custard, stir, and then add the egg to the sauce. Whisk. Add the butter and whisk again until the butter melts. Strain it into a bowl and cover it with plastic wrap to prevent a skin from forming. Chill. Before serving, fold the reserved cup of whipped cream into the lemon sauce. Cut the torte with a sharp knife, using a jabbing up-and-down motion. Place a cut slice on a plate and spoon some lemon sauce over it, or serve the cut slices and pass the sauce, allowing each guest to spoon on as much as he or she desires.

Carl's Danish Fruitcake
9 to 12 servings

In December 1970 two readers wrote the SOS column of the *Los Angeles Times* for the recipe for Danish fruitcake from Carl Andersen's Chatam restaurant. SOS contacted Carl, who gave the recipe along with the fact that "a Dane wouldn't recognize the cake, but that's what I call it." It's an extremely easy cake to make and it keeps well, especially if covered and refrigerated. You'll find it a great snack for the kids just in from school and an easy dessert for short-notice company.

1¼ cups unsifted flour
1 teaspoon baking soda
1 cup sugar

1 egg

2 cups fruit cocktail plus juice from can

1 teaspoon vanilla

¼ cup slivered almonds

¼ cup sugar

¼ cup (½ stick) butter, melted

3 tablespoons currant jelly

1 cup whipping cream (optional)

Put the flour, soda, and sugar in a bowl. Whisk with a wire whip. Make a well in the center of the flour mixture and put in the egg, fruit cocktail, and vanilla. Beat with a wire whip until all is well combined. Don't overbeat. Pour the batter into a well-greased 9-inch square pan and sprinkle with the slivered almonds and ¼ cup sugar. Drizzle the melted butter over the cake. Use a pastry brush to do this; simply dip the brush in the butter and let it run off the end of the brush onto the cake. Bake in a 350° oven for 40 minutes, or until the cake is browned and shrinks away from the sides of the pan. Allow the cake to cool in the pan for 15 minutes, then turn it out of the pan and invert it onto a serving plate so that the sugar-and-nut side is up. Whip the currant jelly with a wire whip and spread it on top of the cake. Whip the cream until stiff and serve it on top of the cake. At the restaurant they pipe the cream through a fluted pastry tube in fancy squiggles until the entire top of the cake is covered with sweet whipped cream.

For a picnic dessert, forgo the whipped cream and leave jelly-frosted cake right in the pan as an easy carry-along.

🦡🦡🦡🦡🦡🦡🦡🦡🦡🦡🦡🦡🦡🦡🦡🦡🦡🦡🦡🦡

BIRTHDAY CAKES

The old Scandia, which was situated on the north side of Sunset Boulevard about a block west of the present-day Scandia, was small and extremely cozy. It was a great place to watch starlets being seduced by producers (or were the starlets seducing the producers?), and as a teenager I was enthralled and always looked forward to Saturday nights at Scandia.

From the age of twelve on, my birthday parties were held there. One that was special was when my future husband, Bob Burroughs, Alan Ladd, Jr., his date and my best friend, Janet Frank, and my parents all went to celebrate my big sixteen. We had a lovely time and a marvelous dinner. Suddenly I realized that everyone in the room was grinning at me and beginning to sing. A Danish apple cake, complete with candles, was set before me, and Bob Crosby stood up on the other side of the small dining room and sang a truly rousing rendition of "Happy Birthday." I got so embarrassed that I don't remember the rest of the evening very well. I do remember the cake, though. It was delicious.

🐛🐛🐛🐛🐛🐛🐛🐛🐛🐛🐛🐛🐛🐛🐛🐛🐛🐛🐛🐛🐛

Apple Cake—Scandia   *12 or more servings*

    6 tablespoons (¾ stick) butter
    5 cups fresh bread crumbs
    ½ cup sugar

    10 large green apples (about 7 pounds)
    ¾ cup sugar
    ½ cup water
    ½ cup white wine
       Rind and juice of 1 lemon

    ½ cup toasted slivered almonds
    ½ cup currant jelly
    12 macaroons
    1 cup whipping cream

Melt the butter in a large heavy skillet. Mix the bread crumbs and ½ cup sugar together and add them to the pan. Brown the crumbs over moderately high heat, turning constantly, until all the crumbs are a dark golden brown. Remove the pan from the heat, but allow the crumbs to sit in the pan to dry out. Peel the apples, cut them into quarters, and cut out the cores. Place the apples in a very large pot with a cover. Add the water, wine, ¾ cup sugar, and the lemon juice and rind. (Cut the rind carefully from the lemon, just as you would cut the peel from an apple—be sure to cut only the outer yellow portion. If you get good at this, you'll be able to cut the rind from the lemon in one continuous peel.) Cover the pot and bring the apples to a boil. Lower the heat to medium and cook for 5 minutes, or until the apples are just done. Drain the apples in a colander. Butter an 8- or 10-inch spring-form pan well and place one-third of the toasted bread crumbs in the bottom. Over the crumbs arrange half the apples. On top of the apples sprinkle the almonds, then the currant jelly, and then arrange the macaroons over the jelly, followed by another third of the bread crumbs. On top of the second layer of bread crumbs arrange the other half of the apples and top with the remaining third of the bread crumbs. Bake the cake in a 425° oven for 25 minutes. Do not allow the top to brown too much. If it starts to get too brown, place a loose piece of foil over the pan, but allow room for steam to escape. When time is up, take the cake out of oven, cool it, and refrigerate it. Undo the spring form, remove it, and decorate the cake with whipped cream and a sprinkling of toasted almonds.

Danish Apples   3 cups

> 5 large apples, green or yellow preferred
> ½ cup sugar
> ⅓ cup dry sherry
> 2 teaspoons vanilla

Pare the apples, quarter them, and slice each quarter into ⅓-inch wedges. Put the apples in a 2-quart saucepan. Sprinkle sugar over the apples, followed by the sherry and vanilla. Put a tight lid on the pan and bring to a rapid boil over high heat. When the apples reach a full boil, mark the time and boil for 2 minutes. Remove the pan from the heat and pour the apples into a large strainer or colander. Drain the juice into a small saucepan or frying pan. Reduce the juice over high heat until it is thick or to the jelly state, depending on the planned use.

The apples can be eaten as is or used in a traditional Danish layer cake, in Aeble Skivers, German pancakes, crêpes, or Paris-Brest (see Index). The jelly or thickened sauce can be used to embellish any of the dishes mentioned.

Danish Layer Cake à la Carole   12 or more servings

I have named my Danish Layer Cake "à la Carole" as it is my own creation, though based on ideas and techniques used in other layer cakes. The apples come from the traditional apple cake the Danes love so much. The custard cream (as opposed to whipped cream) comes from a Danish cake submitted by a Danish lady in the Midwest who gave her recipe to a Lutheran cookbook. I've changed the composition of the custard cream, but the idea is the same. The nuts and chocolate are my additions.

In fancy restaurants you'll find that cakes called Danish layer cakes usually consist of six different layers in which apricot and chocolate, sandwiched between whipped cream or custard cream, alternate as fillings. Scandia's has a marvelous blanket of marzipan wrapped around it, whereas the Chatam's has a thick layer of whipped cream.

Though layer cakes are not put together in a matter of minutes, they are well worth the effort it takes. They don't dry out rapidly, and if you keep them covered in the refrigerator you can enjoy them for a day or two. Try one, then add your own ideas, using the ingredients that please your palate the most.

The Layers

5 large eggs, separated
¾ cup sugar
4 tablespoons water
1 cup flour
1 teaspoon baking powder
1 teaspoon vanilla

Line the bottom of three 8- or 9-inch cake pans with waxed paper; *do not* grease them. Separate the eggs and beat the whites until stiff. In another bowl beat the egg yolks until they are lemon-colored. Slowly add the sugar in a fine stream while continuing to beat. Add the water and beat until the sugar is dissolved. Add the flour and baking powder, which have been sifted together, and beat on low speed until just combined. Stir in the vanilla, then gently fold in the beaten egg whites with a spatula. Divide the batter among the three pans and bake in a 325° oven for 20 minutes, or until the tops of the cakes are golden. Allow the cakes to cool for 10 minutes. Run a knife around the edges of the pan and then ease the layers from the pans by running the knife under the waxed paper. Cool the cakes completely on a rack, then peel off the waxed paper.

Fillings and Put-Togethers

1 recipe Quick Custard (see Index)
4 tablespoons (½ stick) butter, softened
6 tablespoons powdered sugar

1 recipe Danish Apples (see Index)
1 cup chopped nut meats
1 cup grated semisweet chocolate
1 cup whipping cream

To build this fantastic dessert, start by getting the cakes in the oven. Then make some Quick Custard and set it to cool in a sinkful of cold water. Make

Danish Apples, drain, and cook the juice to a jelly. Chop the nuts and grate the chocolate. Since this cake is really better a day old, you can wait to ice the outside with the whipped cream the next day if you wish.

Cream the 4 tablespoons butter with the powdered sugar until light. Add the Quick Custard a tablespoonful at a time, beating continuously.

When the cake is cool, cut each layer in half with a long, thin knife (a boning knife is good)—stick it into the center of the cake and use a sawing motion as you turn the cake around. The layers should be thin.

You should now have ready: 6 layers of cake, custard cream, Danish Apples, apple jelly, chopped nuts, grated chocolate, and whipped cream (if you plan to serve the cake that day). Place a layer of cake on a cake plate, spread with custard, put a layer of apples over the custard, and sprinkle with nuts. Add another layer of cake, spread with custard cream, sprinkle heavily with chocolate. Repeat these two layers until all the ingredients are used, ending with a chocolate layer.

If you have any apples left, and you should, put them in the center of the top in a pretty circular pattern. Surround the apples with whatever chocolate you have left. Spoon the apple jelly over the apples to glaze.

When the cake has been built, ice the sides with the whipped cream and bring the cream up over the top about an inch. If you plan to serve the cake the next day, put toothpicks in the top layer and cover and surround the cake with plastic wrap so that it's airtight. Ice with whipped cream the following day.

I won't try to kid you that this is an easy cake to make, and I won't lie to you and tell you that you can whip it up in no time, but I will tell you that each step is really quite easy and I feel the 2 or 3 hours spent are worth it, especially for my daughter's birthday. She wouldn't settle for anything less, and after tasting this cake you might not either.

Grand Marnier Soufflé
6 to 8 *servings*

2 tablespoons butter
2 tablespoons flour
½ cup hot milk
1 teaspoon vanilla
2 tablespoons Grand Marnier
6 egg whites
1 tablespoon sugar
5 egg yolks
4 tablespoons sugar

Preheat the oven to 400°. Butter a 1½-quart soufflé dish, dust it with granulated sugar, and set it aside. Melt the butter in a saucepan. Add the flour and cook the *roux* for 2 minutes, stirring continuously. Do not allow the *roux* to brown. Add the hot milk and stir over moderate heat until well blended, smooth, and thick. Remove from the heat and stir in the vanilla and Grand Marnier. Beat the egg whites with an electric mixer until almost stiff. Sprinkle in 1 tablespoon sugar and continue beating until the whites hold their shape. With the same mixer, move to the bowl containing the 5 egg yolks and beat them until they are light in color. Add 4 tablespoons sugar and beat until thick. Remove the beaters; with a wire whisk, gently combine the cream sauce with the egg-yolk mixture. Add 2 tablespoons beaten egg white and blend. With a rubber spatula, gently add all the egg-white mixture to the egg-yolk mixture. *Fold* the mixtures together by going down one side of the bowl and up the other, using a rubber spatula. As the spatula is on the upswing, give the bowl a quarter turn; repeat until all is combined and light. *Don't stir* and don't overfold. Gently pour the batter into the soufflé dish. Run your thumb around the dish to form a moat near the edge. Put the dish in the center of a 400° oven and bake it for 18 to 20 minutes. Serve immediately with Grand Marnier Sauce (see Index). *Do not overcook.*

Grand Marnier Sauce   *2 cups*

½ cup sugar
2 tablespoons flour
2 cups milk
1 teaspoon vanilla
2 tablespoons Grand Marnier

Mix the sugar and flour together in a saucepan. Slowly add the milk, stirring constantly with a wire whip. Cook over medium-high heat. When the mixture starts to bubble, lower the heat and simmer 5 minutes. Stir throughout the procedure. When the cooking time has ended, cool the sauce. Add the vanilla and Grand Marnier. Stir and strain. Cover with a lightly buttered piece of waxed paper; chill.

This sauce may be served cold over ice cream, poached pears, fruit, or cake, or reheated and served in its traditional form either poured into an individual Grand Marnier Soufflé or over a serving of Grand Marnier Soufflé. This sauce is also excellent with a chocolate soufflé or vanilla soufflé. I've also served it over a cold chocolate mousse.

Cold Chocolate Soufflé *12 servings*

4 ounces semisweet chocolate
2 ounces unsweetened chocolate
¼ cup strong coffee
2 envelopes gelatin
½ cup cold water
1½ cups scalded milk
6 egg yolks
½ cup sugar
½ cup water
½ cup sugar
¼ cup triple sec
7 egg whites
2 cups whipping cream
1 teaspoon vanilla
2 teaspoons crème de cacao or Kahlúa

Melt the chocolates with the coffee over very low heat. When the chocolate is melted, remove from the heat and stir to combine. Pour the gelatin into the cold water; allow it to sit while you scald the milk. In the top of a double boiler or in a bowl that will fit over a pot of hot water, beat the egg yolks with ½ cup sugar with an electric mixer until it is very light in color and doubled in bulk. Slowly add the scalded milk, continuing to beat. Turn the heat up and beat over boiling water until very hot. Add the gelatin and beat until the gelatin is completely dissolved. Remove from the heat and cool to warm. While the egg mixture is still hot, whisk in the chocolate mixture until all is smooth. Cool. Set the bowl into a cold-water bath in order to hasten the cooling process. If you've used a Pyrex top boiler, turn the mixture into a stainless-steel bowl to cool.

While the chocolate mixture is cooling, boil the ½ cup water with ½ cup sugar and the triple sec until the syrup spins a thread. While the sugar syrup cooks, beat the egg whites until they are stiff and hold their shape. When the sugar syrup reaches the thread stage, pour it into the egg whites in a fine, thin stream. Beat the egg whites at high speed during the entire process, then continue to beat for 4 or 5 minutes longer, or until the mixture is cool and will hold its own ridges. Beat the whipping cream. Add the vanilla and crème de cacao to the chocolate mixture. Whisk in one-third of the egg-white mixture, then very carefully fold in the rest of the egg whites with a rubber spatula. Once the whites are incorporated, fold in the whipped cream, taking care to cut and fold the mixture gently.

Make a stand-up collar out of double foil to fit around a 2-quart soufflé dish. Have it extend at least 4 inches above the rim of the dish. Tape and tie the collar in place. Lightly butter or oil the dish and collar. (The buttering can be done to both the bowl and the collar before the collar is tied on.) Sprinkle the entire works with sugar. Pour the soufflé mixture into the dish. Smooth the top or leave it in swirls. Refrigerate it for a minimum of 4 hours. To serve, carefully remove the collar; spoon into dishes with two serving spoons and top with Grand Marnier Sauce, Cold Chocolate Sauce (see Index), or whipped cream and chocolate curls. This soufflé is velvety smooth and takes only an hour to make.

🌿🌿🌿🌿🌿🌿🌿🌿🌿🌿🌿🌿🌿🌿🌿🌿🌿🌿🌿

IN APPRECIATION OF AN APRICOT

The tree *Prunus armeniaca* produces a yellowish fruit that often blushes with a pink or rose tinge. When the fruit is cut in half, the large, dark brown seed is easily extracted. When the fruit is fully ripe, the seed will fall out of its own accord. The fruit is known to us all as the apricot, and I'm sure many of you, like me, can remember as a child the fun of sitting in your aunt's apricot tree and gorging yourself on its sun-ripened treasures.

You can find apricots measuring only 1 inch in diameter and a few with a diameter of five inches. Neiman-Marcus sells dried apricots from Australia that are over two inches in diameter—after drying! They are a good half-inch thick, and two constitute a small meal.

You can buy tiny, shriveled-up, dried apricots at your local markets in six-ounce packages. Don't weep; they can be forced to give you pleasure.

🌿🌿🌿🌿🌿🌿🌿🌿🌿🌿🌿🌿🌿🌿🌿🌿🌿🌿🌿

Apricot Mousse   *10 to 12 servings*

6 ounces dried apricots
Water
¾ cup sugar
½ cup water
1 package or 1 tablespoon plain gelatin

2 tablespoons Grand Marnier, *or* ½ teaspoon orange extract, *or* ½ teaspoon almond extract, *or* 2 tablespoons brandy *or* rum
2 cups whipping cream
2 tablespoons sugar

Soak the apricots in water to cover overnight. In the morning place them in a saucepan and add water (if needed) so that the fruit is completely covered. Cover the pan and simmer the apricots over moderate heat for 20 to 30 minutes, or until the fruit is very soft. Cool slightly, then puree the apricots and their liquid in a blender or food processor. If neither is available, push the fruit through a food mill or strainer. Measure the apricot puree; you should have 4 cups. If the puree measures less than that, add enough water to bring the measure to 4 cups. Return the puree to the saucepan, add ¾ cup sugar, and bring it to a slow boil. Meanwhile, soften the gelatin in ½ cup water. Stir the apricot puree, and when it reaches the boiling point add the gelatin and cook until completely dissolved. Remove the pan from the heat and allow to cool. This process can be greatly hastened by placing the pan in a sink filled with cold water. Add the Grand Marnier or other flavoring of your choice. Place a piece of plastic wrap directly on the surface of the puree and set it in the refrigerator until the puree is cold and begins to set. Whip the cream until thickened. Add 2 tablespoons sugar and continue beating until the cream is very stiff. Fold one-third of the cream into the puree. You may stir this first third in with a stirring motion, making sure that it is totally incorporated. Now gently fold in the other two-thirds of the whipped cream with a rubber spatula, so that the cream doesn't lose the air you have beaten into it. Pour the Apricot Mousse into an attractive serving bowl or individual cups or glasses. The mousse can be served as is or decorated with whipped cream, chocolate curls or shavings, whole poached dried apricots, or apricot jam. Keep it in the refrigerator covered with plastic wrap until served.

Note: If you wish a stronger apricot flavor and fewer calories, reduce the whipped cream to 1 cup. The dessert will then serve 6 to 8.

Danish Rice Pudding   *10 servings*

When Christmas time rolls around, different customs are followed in different countries. We in America have Santa Claus, the Christmas tree, mince pies, and steamed puddings. In Denmark they have Nisse Men, the Christ-

mas tree decked with Danish flags as opposed to popcorn, and rice pudding. One whole blanched almond is added to Danish Rice Pudding, and the child who finds it is guaranteed an extra present.

As one of five children, my father figured the odds were against him, so he'd wait until the coast was clear and then seek out the pudding that was cooling in the pantry. After climbing up onto a stool, he'd carefully probe it with his index finger. When he located the single blanched almond, he'd quickly move it to a particular corner, which he would ask for when serving time arrived.

It was some years later that he realized that all his brothers and sisters did the same thing and that even so, somehow *every* child received a whole almond and an extra gift. Could it be that his father slipped a whole blanched almond to each child? Did Mother Andersen make two puddings—one to eat and one to probe? If there are no answers to these questions, there is still the mouth-watering dessert itself.

Danish Rice Pudding differs from its French cousins, Riz à l'Aimant and Riz à l'Impératrice, in that it contains no gelatin and is served from a lovely crystal bowl (or other serving dish) rather than being poured into a mold and later unmolded onto a serving platter. The consistency is so marvelous that nothing else in its field can match it, to my way of thinking.

When making this pudding, please don't try to speed up the cooking time. The long, slow cooking is mandatory. Also, be sure to add the almond paste while the rice is still warm. The rest is easy.

2 cups milk
2 cups light cream
¼ cup sugar
Pinch salt
½ cup long-grain white rice
2 ounces almond paste
1 teaspoon vanilla
3½ ounces (1 cup) blanched, slivered almonds
1 cup whipping cream, stiffly whipped
2 tablespoons sugar

Butter a 1½-quart casserole. Put the milk, cream, sugar, salt, and rice in the casserole, cover it, and bake it in a 300° oven for 1 hour. Remove the lid, stir the rice, and bake for another hour in a 300° oven, uncovered. Remove the dish from the oven, and remove and discard the milk skin that has formed on top. Pour the rice into a bowl and add the almond paste, crumbled or processed in a food processor until crumbly. Add the vanilla and mix thoroughly. Place a piece of plastic wrap over the pudding so that another skin can't form. Cool it, then chill it in the refrigerator. Whip the cream until stiff, add 2 tablespoons sugar, and whip until the cream is quite stiff (but don't let it turn into butter). Fold the whipped cream and almonds into the pudding, pour it into a crystal, glass, or lovely pottery bowl, and cover it once again until serving time. One whole blanched almond may be hidden in the corner of your choice.

Danish Rice Pudding can be decorated with more whipped cream piped through a fluted pastry tube, or served in the traditional manner with a fruit sauce. The most common fruit sauce served in Denmark is raspberry (see below), but any berry sauce can be used, and even a good chocolate sauce will make your guests very happy.

Note: If there is any excess milk floating around after the cooked rice mixture has cooled, pour it off, then proceed.

Raspberry Sauce I
1½ cups

1 cup raspberry jam
¼ cup water
¼ cup Kirsch

Put the jam and water in a blender jar or food processor bowl and blend until smooth. Heat the mixture in a saucepan over moderate heat until it nears the boiling point. Remove from the heat and cool it slightly. Add the Kirsch and pour the sauce into a serving pitcher. Allow it to cool completely.

Raspberry Sauce II
3 cups

2 cups fresh raspberries
½ cup water
1 cup sugar
3 tablespoons Grand Marnier

Put the raspberries, water, and sugar in a saucepan. Bring the mixture to a boil and boil for 3 minutes, stirring constantly. Remove the pan from the heat, cool slightly, and add the Grand Marnier. Cool the sauce in a serving pitcher.

Bread Pudding à la Faunce
8 to 12 servings

1 quart milk	1 teaspoon vanilla
4 large eggs	4 or 5 slices toast
½ cup sugar	Butter
Pinch salt	Cinnamon

Heat the milk, but don't let it boil. In a bowl beat the eggs with the sugar and salt. Slowly add the hot milk, whisking the mixture all the while. Add the vanilla. Butter the toast heavily the minute it comes from the toaster.

Butter a 9-by-9-inch Pyrex or French porcelain baking dish. Pour the custard into it and gently place the toast on top of the custard; you may cut the toast in half or in fancy shapes if you like. Sprinkle the pudding with cinnamon. Allow it to sit for 10 minutes, then bake it in a 325° oven for 45 minutes, or until a knife comes out clean. Whether those who sit at your table are nine months or ninety years old, they'll all ask for more.

Bread Pudding is usually made with white or egg bread, but it is marvelous made with raisin bread.

Ethyle's Use Your Noodle Kugel *12 servings*

8 ounces broad noodles
4 tablespoons (½ stick) butter
½ cup sugar
3 large eggs
¾ cup milk
¾ cup sour cream
½ teaspoon cinnamon
¼ cup raisins, white preferred

1 cup crushed (not too fine) corn flakes
2 tablespoons butter, melted
½ teaspoon cinnamon

Cook the noodles as directed on the package. Mix the butter and sugar together. Beat in the eggs. Add the milk, sour cream, cinnamon, and raisins, and combine the mixture with the noodles. Pour into a well-buttered 8-by-8-inch baking dish. Mix the corn flakes, butter, and cinnamon and sprinkle the topping over the kugel. Bake in a 325° oven for 1 hour and 15 minutes, or until a knife comes out clean (test after 1 hour).

Christmas Persimmon Pudding *8 servings*

2 tablespoons butter
1 cup sugar
2 cups flour
1 teaspoon salt
2 teaspoons baking soda
½ teaspoon cinnamon
½ cup raisins, plumped in hot water
½ cup chopped nut meats, walnuts *or* pecans preferred
⅓ cup chopped citron
1 cup persimmon pulp
½ cup milk
1 teaspoon vanilla

Cream the butter and sugar together. Sift the flour, salt, soda, and cinnamon together. Add the sifted ingredients to the butter-and-sugar mixture. Stir the raisins, nuts, and citron into the mixture and then the persimmon, milk, and vanilla. Blend well. Put the batter in a well-greased casserole with a lid. The pudding shouldn't exceed a depth of 4 inches. If the casserole has no lid, tie two sheets of foil over the top. Set the casserole in a larger pan, pour boiling water up to the level of the pudding, and bake it in a 350° oven for 1½ hours. Check the pudding; if the center is still wet, bake it longer. According to the size and shape of the casserole, the pudding could take as long as 3 hours, but check it after the first 1½ hours. Serve *hot* with Hard Sauce (see Index) or whipped cream.

Like all other steamed puddings, this can be reheated. Put the leftover pudding in a flameproof dish, cover it with a lid or foil, and put it in a pan of water just as you did to bake it. Half an hour usually does it, and it's just as good the second time around.

Steamed Carrot Pudding   8 servings

1½ cups flour
½ teaspoon salt
½ teaspoon baking soda
¾ teaspoon baking powder
½ teaspoon cinnamon
¼ teaspoon ground cloves
¼ teaspoon ground allspice
½ cup (1 stick) margarine
½ cup packed brown sugar
1 egg
1 tablespoon water
1 cup grated carrots
2 teaspoons grated orange rind
½ cup raisins

Sift together the dry ingredients, seasonings, and spices. Cream the margarine with the sugar; add the egg and water. Beat well. Stir in the carrots, orange rind, and raisins, then gradually stir in the sifted flour mixture. Turn into a well-greased 1½-quart mold or flameproof bowl. Cover with a lid or a double thickness of foil. Place the mold in a deep pot, add hot water halfway up the mold, cover, and simmer for 1 hour and 15 minutes. Serve with Orange Sauce (see below).

Orange Sauce   2 *cups*

½ cup sugar
3 tablespoons cornstarch
1 cup water
¼ teaspoon salt
¼ cup grated orange rind
2 cups orange juice

Whisk the sugar and cornstarch together; slowly add the water and whisk until smooth. Add the remaining ingredients and cook until thick and clear.

Aeble Skivers or Apple Dumpling Doughnuts   *12 servings*

3 eggs
1 tablespoon sugar
½ teaspoon salt
2 cups buttermilk
2 cups flour
1 teaspoon baking powder
1 teaspoon baking soda
Butter
Applesauce, homemade preferred, *or* Danish Apples (see Index)

Separate the eggs and beat the whites until stiff. Beat the yolks until they are light; add the sugar, then the salt and buttermilk. Sift the flour and leavenings together and add them to the egg-yolk mixture. Fold in the beaten egg whites.

For Aeble Skivers you need the special Aeble Skiver pan you see hanging in Danish bakeries and restaurants. It looks like a high-rimmed frying pan with half-round cups in it. I find the cast-iron ones best.

Heat the Aeble Skiver pan; put ½ teaspoon butter in each depression, running it around the rim so that it melts down all sides. Fill the depressions two-thirds full of batter. When all the depressions have batter in them, put 1 teaspoon applesauce or apples in the center of each. When the batter starts baking up over the rims of the cups and surrounding the applesauce, it's time to turn the dumpling doughnuts. A knitting needle or skewer works well. The underside of the Aeble Skiver should be brown and stable. Stick your knitting needle into an edge and turn the dumpling over in its cup. This is all easier than it sounds, and you will see how to do it when the time comes. Don't worry if the batter hasn't covered the applesauce completely. It will as you turn the Aeble Skiver. Allow the Aeble Skivers to brown on the other side; then jab right through the center and transfer to a warm plate. Repeat the process until the batter is gone. Dust the Aeble Skivers with powdered sugar and enjoy.

Lorraine's Strawberry Ice Cream   *2 quarts*

1 quart ripe strawberries, hulled and mashed
½ cup sugar
⅓ cup flour
¼ teaspoon salt
2 cups sugar
2 cups half-and-half
6 eggs
3 teaspoons vanilla
4 cups heavy whipping cream

Mix the mashed strawberries with the ½ cup sugar and let the mixture stand while you combine the flour, salt, and 2 cups sugar in a medium-sized saucepan. Whisk with a wire whip, then gradually whisk in the half-and-half. Put the pan over moderate heat and cook, stirring constantly, until the mixture has thickened. Remove the pan from the heat; beat in the 6 eggs, which have been beaten together in another bowl, and return the pan to the stove to cook for 1 more minute. Stir constantly. Cool the custard in a cold-water bath; when it is cool, add the vanilla, strawberries, and the 4 cups of cream. Put the mixture into the can of your ice cream machine and process according to the machine's directions.

Frozen berries may be used if you drain off some of their juice.
Fantastic ice cream!

Fresh Fruit Sherbet
1 pint

4 medium peaches, *or* 2 pints strawberries
1 cup sour cream
¾ cup sugar
¼ teaspoon almond extract (for peaches)
1 teaspoon lemon juice

Wash and peel or stem the fruit. Chop it fine, or process it in a food processor. Mix all the ingredients together and beat with an electric mixer for at least 3 full minutes. Freeze for 1 or 2 hours, or until the substance is almost frozen solid. Remove from the freezer and beat again for 3 minutes. Return to the freezer for at least 3 hours. Serve.

This is really delicious, but it should be eaten within one or two weeks of being made. Don't worry; there's rarely any left.

Note: You can freeze and beat all in the same container. This saves a lot of time, trouble, and loss of sherbet.

Points About Pies

•   The less you work and stir a pie crust, the more tender it will be. Don't knead pie dough!

•   When rolling out pie dough, flatten it with the palm of your hand so that it is about 6 inches across and circular. With a rolling pin start in the center and roll the dough outward. By repeatedly rolling from the center you can shape the dough easily and reduce toughness. When you roll back and forth, you work the dough twice as much.

•   To make pie dough in a food processor, you must use a fat that hardens when cold, like butter or lard. A processor blends, rather than cuts in, any fat that is soft, thus producing a cookie-type dough rather than the pie pastry you want.

•   Pie dough always tends to shrink while baking. Correct for this by pushing the dough into the pie pan, making it loose. Pull the overhanging dough up onto the rim to form a scalloped edge. Never pull dough from within the pie pan. If you are baking a pie shell with no filling in it, put a piece of waxed paper in the bottom and add 1 cup uncooked rice (or beans). Two-thirds of the way through the baking time, remove the paper and rice (save it for your next pie shell; it can be used for years). The weight of the rice will keep the dough from pulling up off the bottom of the pan.

· Always cut a vent in the top crust of any covered pie to allow steam to escape. This helps decrease any overflow and also keeps the top crust dry and flaky.

· Put fruit pies on a cookie sheet before popping them into the oven to catch the runover.

🍃🍃🍃🍃🍃🍃🍃🍃🍃🍃🍃🍃🍃🍃🍃🍃🍃🍃🍃🍃🍃

PIE PROBLEMS

When my father, Carl, first began cooking for a multimillionaire in Hartford, Connecticut, the lady of the house asked him to make an apple pie. What was a pie? Had the master chefs of Copenhagen neglected to teach him something? (Danish cuisine does not include pies.) Carl looked into every cookbook he could find and soon discovered what a pie was. As his first apple pie was baking, he kept peeking at it and soon noticed that it was going to run over; the juices were oozing out near the rim of the pie. Carl removed the pie from the oven, cut a neat little vent near the rim, and through it drained about ⅔ cup of the juices that had become too ample for the pie shell. Back into the oven went the pie. He then reduced the juices over high heat until they thickened and added some brandy and a lump of butter. When the pie was done and golden brown, Carl removed it from the oven and through another vent he'd already cut in the center of the pie he poured the brandied buttered juices, which were now of syrup consistency. The lady of the house said she'd never eaten an apple pie to equal it. (See Apple Pie in Index.)

Most fruit pies like to run around. They're a loose group. However, you can put them back together in the delicious manner described above.

🍃🍃🍃🍃🍃🍃🍃🍃🍃🍃🍃🍃🍃🍃🍃🍃🍃🍃🍃🍃🍃

Infallible Pie Crust I   *2 crusts*

This pie dough is aptly named. It not only works every time, but creates the flakiest pie dough imaginable. The recipe should be done by hand since it uses vegetable shortening; however, I've made this same recipe using lard and butter, and butter only. These changes allowed me to use the food processor; the results were excellent.

1½ cups flour
1 teaspoon salt
⅔ cup vegetable shortening
¼ cup water

Put 1 cup flour and the salt into a bowl. Cut the shortening into the flour mixture. In another small bowl stir the remaining ½ cup flour into a paste with the water. Add the paste to the first mixture, blend, and form a ball. Divide the dough and roll it out thin on a lightly floured board.

Infallible Pie Crust with Lard and Butter II   *2 crusts*

1½ cups flour
¼ cup water
1 teaspoon salt
⅓ cup cold lard
⅓ cup cold butter

In a small bowl mix ½ cup flour into a paste with the water. In the work bowl of the food processor, put 1 cup flour, the salt, lard, and butter. Process until the mixture resembles fine meal. Pour the processed mixture into the bowl with the paste and blend with a wooden spoon or your hands until it forms a ball. Proceed as for Infallible Pie Crust I.

Infallible Pie Crust III   *2 crusts*

1½ cups flour
⅔ cup butter
1 teaspoon salt
¼ cup water

Proceed as for Infallible Pie Crust II.

Note: You may add 1 tablespoon sugar to the flour and shortening mixture in all three of these recipes if you desire.

Caroline's Crust   *2 crusts*

⅔ cup Spry *or* other solid vegetable shortening
2 cups flour
1 teaspoon salt
Up to 5 tablespoons cold water

Work the shortening into the flour with a pastry blender or two knives. Add the salt and blend until the mixture resembles fine meal. Add the water a little at a time. Toss the dough with a fork or your hands as you mix in the water. As soon as the dough starts to hold together, push it together with your hands and form it into a ball. You may use the pie dough immediately or chill it for 30 minutes or so for an even flakier pie crust.

Grandmom's Pie Crust   *2 crusts*

> 2 cups flour
> 1¼ teaspoons salt
> 3 tablespoons sugar
> 1 cup Crisco *or* other vegetable shortening of your choice
> 3 tablespoons cold water

Put all the dry ingredients in a bowl. Cut in the Crisco with a pastry blender or two knives until the mixture resembles coarse meal. Stir in the water with a fork, tossing the dough in the bowl until the dough starts to hold together. With your hands push the dough into a ball. Wrap in plastic wrap and chill in the refrigerator for 30 minutes. (This is not mandatory, but it helps produce an even flakier pie crust.)

Note: If shells only are needed, line two pie shells with dough and prick the entire surface with a fork. Bake in a 425° oven for 15 minutes.

Strawberry Pie—Chatam   *8 servings*

Use a 10-inch pie plate lined with pie pastry and baked to a golden brown. When you bake the crust, be sure to place a piece of waxed paper in the bottom, plus 1 cup beans or rice. This keeps the crust from puffing up off the bottom of the pan, and with this pie you'll need all the space provided in a 10-inch pie plate.

> 4 pints fresh strawberries
> 2 cups sugar
> ¼ cup cornstarch
> ¼ cup lemon juice
> 2 cups whipping cream
> 2 tablespoons powdered sugar

Wash and hull the strawberries. Using the largest ones, line the bottom of the baked pie shell, placing the berries with their points up. Crush the rest of the berries; they should measure about 4 cups. Place the crushed berries in a large Teflon or enameled frying pan. Add the sugar, which has been well blended with the cornstarch. Add the lemon juice. Stir well and bring to a boil over medium-high heat. Scrape the pan with a rubber spatula all the while. When the mixture comes to a boil, lower the heat slightly and cook for 2 more minutes. The mixture should be thick and clear. If you are using early or late berries, you might not get the deep red color that comes with midseason berries. In this case add 3 drops red food coloring and stir until combined. Allow the cooked berries to cool slightly, then pour them over the berries in the shell. Chill until set. Whip the cream until stiff, add the powdered sugar, and spread the cream on top of the pie.

Note: The Chatam strawberry torte is built up on a puff paste (*pâte à chou*) shell. You can simulate the torte by spreading the bottom of your baked pie shell with whipped currant jelly and then sprinkling the jelly with toasted slivered almonds. Once you've dolled up the bottom of your pie shell, proceed to make the pie as described above.

Black-Bottom Cream Pie   *2 9-inch pies*

> 3 ounces baking chocolate
> 1 tablespoon butter
> 1 envelope gelatin
> 3 tablespoons water
> 1 cup sugar
> 3 tablespoons cornstarch
> 3½ cups milk
> 6 egg yolks
> Pinch salt
> 2 tablespoons rum
> 1 teaspoon vanilla
> 2 baked 9-inch pie shells
> 6 egg whites
> ½ cup sugar

Set the chocolate and butter in a small bowl in a warm oven to melt them. Sprinkle the gelatin over cold water and allow it to sit for 5 minutes. Combine 1 cup sugar with cornstarch and whisk them together in a saucepan.

Slowly add the milk; whisk until smooth. Whisk in the egg yolks. When all is smoothly blended, cook over medium heat, whisking with a wire whip continuously until the mixture is hot, slightly thickened, and coats a spoon. Remove the custard from the heat and transfer one-third of it to another bowl. To the custard remaining in the saucepan add the gelatin and stir until it is completely dissolved. You may have to put it back on the heat to do so. When the gelatin in the pan is dissolved, stir in the rum and vanilla. Set it aside to cool, or put it into a cold-water bath to hasten the entire operation. Add the melted chocolate and butter to the custard in the bowl. Blend well and divide the mixture between the two pie shells. Set the pie shells in the refrigerator to cool and set.

Beat the egg whites until stiff but still wet. Add ½ cup sugar and beat until the whites are stiff enough to hold ridges. When the rum-flavored custard is completely cool and has started to set, carefully fold in the egg whites. Be sure you *fold* them; don't stir. Divide the rum custard meringue between the two pie shells and allow the pies to set in the refrigerator for a minimum of 3 hours.

These pies are beautiful as is, but if you wish to get more festive, you can decorate them with chocolate curls or a ring of grated semisweet chocolate.

Apple Pie   *8 servings*

    1 cup white sugar
    ½ cup packed brown sugar
    ¼ cup flour
    2 teaspoons cinnamon
      Dough for double-crust pie
    6 large tart apples
    1 tablespoon lemon juice
    1 tablespoon butter

Combine the sugars, flour, and cinnamon in a small bowl; set aside. Make the pie dough and line a pie pan with the bottom crust.

Pare, core, and slice the apples. (I like mine sliced at least ½ inch thick.) Sprinkle the lemon juice over the apples as you cut them into a bowl, and toss each apple with the lemon juice to prevent discoloration.

When all the apples are cut, toss them with the sugar mixture and pack into the pie shell. Dot with butter and cover with the top crust. Crimp the edges well to seal in the juice. Cut a triangular vent in the top of the pie. Sprinkle the top crust with 1 teaspoon sugar, or brush with milk. Bake the pie on a cookie sheet in a 400° oven for 1 hour, or until golden brown.

The cookie sheet is for the spillover. Peek at your pie after 30 minutes has elapsed, and if it is running over, remove it from the oven, on the cookie sheet, and cut a side vent right next to the rim of the pie shell. Using a pot holder carefully drain off ½ cup or more of the juice from the pie into a small saucepan. Return the pie to the oven on a clean cookie sheet. Take the juice you've drained from the pie plus any juice you can get off of the cookie sheet and reduce the syrup over high heat until thick. Remove from the heat and stir in 1 tablespoon brandy. When the pie is done, pour the thick brandied syrup back into the pie through the center vent.

Pie in a Bag
8 servings

    4 or 5 large green apples
    ½ cup sugar
    2 tablespoons flour
    2 tablespoons lemon juice
    ½ teaspoon nutmeg
    1 unbaked pie shell
    ½ cup sugar
    ½ cup flour
    ½ cup (1 stick) butter

Peel, core, and cut the apples into eighths or twelfths. The slices should be at least ½ inch thick. Toss the apples with the sugar, flour, lemon juice, and nutmeg. Pile snugly into the pie shell. Mix the sugar, flour, and butter together in a food processor or with a pastry blender. Pat the mixture over the apples. Put the pie on a cookie sheet; put the cookie sheet in a large brown shopping bag and paper-clip it closed. Place the bag on another cookie sheet. Bake in a 425° oven on the middle shelf for 1 hour.

I know this sounds silly, but you won't think so when you taste it.

Mince Pie
2 9-inch pies

    Dough for 2 9-inch double-crust pies
    1 quart Green Tomato Mincemeat (see Index) or your
      choice
    4 green apples, pared, cored, and sliced
    2 tablespoons sugar
    1 cup nut meats, walnut *or* pecans preferred
    ¼ cup brandy
    2 tablespoons butter

Line two 9-inch pie shells with the pie dough of your choice. Put the mincemeat in a bowl. Add the apples, sugar, nuts, and brandy. Mix well and divide the mixture between the pie shells. Dot each pie with 1 tablespoon butter cut into bits and cover each pie with a top crust. Cut a vent in the center of each pie and bake them in a 375° oven for 1 hour, or until the crusts are golden brown.

This pie is best served with whipped cream, Hard Sauce (see Index), or vanilla ice cream.

Chocolate Cream Pie   *8 servings*

     3 squares unsweetened chocolate
     3 tablespoons butter
     1 cup sugar
     3 tablespoons cornstarch
    2½ cups milk
     3 eggs
       Pinch salt
     1 teaspoon vanilla
     1 baked 10-inch pie shell
     2 cups whipping cream
     1 tablespoon sugar
     1 or 2 ounces shaved semisweet chocolate

Melt the chocolate and butter together over very low heat or in a low oven. Do not stir the mixture while it's melting. In a saucepan whisk the sugar and cornstarch together. Slowly add the milk and whisk until smooth. Beat in the eggs *well.* Add salt and put the pan over medium heat. Whisk the mixture with a wire whip the entire time it takes to cook. (I often read while I'm doing this, but whatever you do, don't stop whisking.) In about 5 minutes the mixture will begin to thicken. Now, *beat* the mixture until it almost boils. Remove the pan from the heat. Put the pan in a sinkful of cold water and whisk until slightly cooled. Add the vanilla and chocolate-butter mixture. Whisk the entire concoction until smooth and totally blended. Pour it into the pie shell and set the pie in the refrigerator. Whip the cream until stiff, sweeten it with sugar, and spread it on top of the chocolate mixture. Shave or grate the chocolate and decorate the top of the pie with a ring of chocolate.

Half a Ghirardelli Eagle bar (2 ounces), shaved with a large knife, is an added touch of heaven on this pie. With or without shaved chocolate, your family will demand this one often.

Mic's Lemon Meringue Pie

Juice of 3 lemons, plus water to equal 1¾ cups liquid
3 tablespoons cornstarch
1½ cups sugar
2 tablespoons butter
3 egg yolks
4 egg whites
2 tablespoons sugar
1 baked pie shell

Boil the lemon juice and water. Thoroughly mix the cornstarch and sugar. Slowly pour the sugar mixture into the boiling liquid, stirring all the while. Cook the mixture over medium heat until it is thick and clear. Stir constantly throughout the cooking process.

When the mixture is very thick, remove it from the heat and whisk in the butter. When the butter has melted, add the egg yolks and beat the mixture until it is completely combined and smooth. Pour it into the pie shell.

Beat the egg whites until they start to hold their shape. Add the sugar and continue beating until stiff. Spoon the meringue onto the lemon custard and spread it with a dinner knife. Make swirls and peaks if you like and then bake in a 375° oven for 10 minutes, or until the meringue takes on a light tan color. Cool the pie completely and then refrigerate it.

A TIME FOR BAKING COOKIES

In late April I sat on the wooden slats of the front walk planting onion sets. They're very hardy, so I thought I might get away with an early planting. If they didn't survive the almost inevitable freezes of the next month and a half, it wouldn't be any huge loss, as I'd purchased more than 400 sets.

The cat was pretending that the bag of onions was catnip and was rolling on his back up against it, and the dogs were trying to get in my way, when suddenly the wind came up. The day before, the wind had produced some wild moments in the late afternoon. Long before dawn it had awakened me with its violence, and it had denuded the ground of most of its snow cover.

Now the wind hit my back with gust after gust—each one stronger than the one before. Soon my hat left me, racing across the snow-patched lawn and coming to rest against the small corral's fence. I looked behind me to see the gray-black storm front racing toward me like a lion after its prey.

My hands trembled as I quickly covered the exposed sets I'd been planting. The rain started to hit, so I grabbed the onion bag and ran to fetch my hat. By the time I'd covered forty feet of lawn at full speed, the rain had turned to hail and was coming at me horizontally with piercing force.

The dogs and cat were with me as we bounded onto the porch. It took me more time than anticipated to grab the kindling box and make it to the door. The wind pushed with immense force as the hail turned to snow and blew in under the porch with a vengeance.

The black heart of the storm was coming fast as I dashed out to retrieve two logs from the diminishing stack of wood. This time it was difficult to get back to the front door, and I noticed that the temperature had fallen fifteen degrees as I pushed past the thermometer.

I had no sooner made it to the fireplace when my husband, Dick, burst through the door saying the storm was too much, even in the safety of the enclosed backhoe.

It had now been three or four minutes since the first gust of wind had hit my back. As Dick and I stood for a moment or two before the front windows, the snow fell and blew so fast that it completely covered the border bed I'd been planting. It was a good day to bake some cookies rather than plant onion sets.

Almond Macaroons   3 dozen

8 ounces (1 cup) almond paste (found in the fancy food section)
1 cup sugar
3 egg whites or less

Crumble the almond paste in a blender or food processor. Mix the almond paste with the sugar and work them together with your hands or a beater. Slowly work in the egg whites, one at a time. Depending on the size of the eggs you're using, you will need 2½ to 3 egg whites to make the mixture workable, but not too soft. It should be of a consistency that you can push through a pastry tube. The batter should hold its shape (just barely) when dropped from a teaspoon. Pipe small dollops of macaroon batter onto a cookie sheet lined with waxed paper, or drop by teaspoonfuls onto waxed paper. Sprinkle with a little sugar and bake in a 325° oven for 25 to 30 minutes. The macaroons should not get brown, but a very light tan is all right. Remove from the oven, pull the waxed paper onto a wrung-out damp tea towel, and remove the macaroons to a cooling rack.

Oatmeal Cookies *10 dozen*

1 cup (2 sticks) margarine *or* vegetable shortening
1 cup white sugar
1 cup packed brown sugar
2 large eggs
2 teaspoons vanilla
2 tablespoons brandy
1¾ cups flour
1 teaspoon salt
1 teaspoon baking soda
3 cups quick-cooking oatmeal
⅓ cup wheat germ
1 cup chopped nuts, your preference
1 cup raisins, steeped in hot water for 5 minutes and drained

Cream the shortening and sugars until light; add the eggs, vanilla, and brandy. Combine the flour, salt, and soda; add them to the batter and beat. Stir in the oatmeal, wheat germ, nuts, and raisins. Drop by spoonfuls onto lightly greased cookie sheets. Bake in a 350° oven for 10 to 12 minutes. Remove the cookies from the sheet while they are still warm.

At Christmas time, add your favorite dried or candied fruits, coconut, or even chocolate chips.

If you don't wish to freeze some, or don't wish to make so many, cut the recipe in half.

Peanut Butter Cookies   *4 dozen*

2 eggs
1 cup packed brown sugar
1 cup white sugar
¾ cup (1½ sticks) margarine *or* vegetable shortening
¾ cup peanut butter (creamy or crunchy)
2 teaspoons vanilla
2 cups flour
¾ teaspoon salt
1 teaspoon baking soda

With an electric beater, beat the eggs in a small bowl. Beat the sugars, shortening, and peanut butter together in a large bowl until well blended and smooth. Add the eggs and vanilla; beat. Add the flour which has been sifted together with the salt and soda. Stir until well combined. Roll the dough into balls and mark them with a fork, or drop the dough by spoonfuls onto a lightly greased cookie sheet. Bake in a 350° oven for 8 to 10 minutes. Remove to a rack to cool.

Cherry Nut Centers   *2½ to 3 dozen*

2 tablespoons sugar
½ cup ground nuts

1 cup flour
½ cup sugar
    Pinch salt
½ cup (1 stick) butter
1 egg
1 teaspoon vanilla
2 teaspoons Grand Marnier
2 teaspoons finely grated orange rind
    Candied red cherries
    Peach jam

Grind the sugar and nuts in the work bowl of a food processor until fine. Set aside. Put the flour, sugar, salt, and butter in the processor bowl. Turn the machine on and off four or five times. Add the egg, vanilla, Grand Marnier, and orange rind. Turn the processor on and off until the mixture is just smooth and combined.

Roll teaspoonfuls of dough in the nut mixture, forming the dough into balls. Place the cookies on a greased cookie sheet and push half a cherry into the center of each. Bake in a 350° oven for 12 minutes, or until the cookies are a very light tan. While they are still warm, spoon ½ teaspoon peach jam over the cherry of each.

These are very fancy, easy, and delightful.

Mexican Wedding Cakes   *4 dozen*

> 1 cup (2 sticks) butter, *or* half butter and half margarine, softened
> ½ cup powdered sugar
> 2 cups flour
> ¼ teaspoon salt
> 1 teaspoon vanilla

Cream the butter and sugar together. Add all the other ingredients in order and mix until well blended. Pinch off small pieces of dough and roll them into finger shapes. Bake on lightly buttered cookie sheets in a 375° oven for 10 or 12 minutes. Do not let them brown. Remove them from the oven and roll them in powdered sugar. If the dough becomes too soft to handle, chill it in the refrigerator until you can handle it.

Just Right Brownies   *1½ dozen*

> ½ cup (1 stick) butter *or* margarine
> 2 squares baking chocolate
> 1 cup sugar
> 2 eggs
> 1 teaspoon vanilla
> 1 scant cup flour

Grease a 9-by-9-inch baking dish and preheat the oven to 350°. In a 2- or 3-quart saucepan melt the butter and chocolate over low heat. Remove the pan from the heat and stir in the sugar. Add the eggs and vanilla and beat by hand until smooth. Stir in the flour and pour the batter into the baking dish. Bake in a 350° oven for 20 minutes, or until a toothpick comes out clean. One cup of nuts may be added if you like.

Note: This is one recipe in which I always use margarine. These are so moist and fudgy that I never frost them. It would seem a sin.

Lemon Torte Cookie Bars   *2 dozen*

2 cups flour
1 cup (2 sticks) margarine
½ cup powdered sugar
4 eggs
2 cups sugar
4 tablespoons lemon juice
4 tablespoons lemon rind
4 tablespoons flour
1 teaspoon baking powder

Mix the flour, margarine, and powdered sugar until thoroughly blended. Press into a 9-by-13-inch pan. Bake in a 350° oven for 20 minutes. Beat the eggs until light and add the 2 cups sugar, lemon juice, and lemon rind, and stir until blended. Fold in the 4 tablespoons flour and the baking powder. Pour the egg-lemon batter over the hot crust. Return the pan to the oven and bake another 25 minutes. Dust with powdered sugar while still warm. When cool, cut into desired shapes.

Springerle   *4 dozen*

Springerle are rectangular, whitish-tan cookies with embossed designs baked into their tops. Aniseed is baked into their bottoms, and the best ones are chewy on the bottom and crunchy on the top. There should be an air space between the embossed design and the chewy bottom.

The Germans, who created this incredible cookie, love to dunk them in white wine, as one would dunk a doughnut into coffee. Wine dunking is almost a necessity if the Springerle are served in their natural hard state, but the cookies are more delicious if kept for two days in an airtight container with half an apple for company. The moisture given off by the apple makes the bottoms of the Springerle soften while the crusty top remains firm.

3¼ cups flour
1 teaspoon baking powder
2 tablespoons clarified butter
4 large eggs
2 cups sugar, superfine preferred
2 tablespoons aniseed

Sift the flour with the baking powder. Clarify the butter, measure 2 table-spoons, and keep it warm enough to stay liquid. Beat the eggs with an electric beater for 10 minutes. They should be light in color and several times greater in volume. Slowly add the sugar in a fine stream, beating throughout the process. Continue beating until the total beating time equals 20 minutes.

Remove the beaters from the egg-sugar batter and proceed with a rubber spatula. *Fold* the flour in alternately with the clarified butter. Do not stir at any time. The last addition should be flour, and the dough should show signs of resistance to it. Stop folding the minute you think the flour has been incorporated.

Put a quarter of the dough on a well-floured pastry board or cloth. With your hands push the dough together into a rectangular mound the approximate size of your Springerle mold. The dough should be close to 1 inch in depth. Flour the Springerle board well, dust the top of the dough with flour, and press the mold onto the top of the dough. Nestle it into the dough until you feel that the design cavities have been filled, then gently lift the Springerle board from the dough.

If you are using a Springerle rolling pin, shape the dough into a rectangle the width of the pin. Dust the dough with flour and flour the rolling pin well. Roll the pin across the dough evenly and smoothly.

After the designs have been pressed or rolled into the dough, trim the edges with a large sharp knife. Cut the cookies apart along the design lines and place them 1 inch apart on cookie sheets that have been buttered and liberally strewn with aniseed. *Do not* try to brush the flour from the tops of the cookies. This must be done *after* they are baked.

Cover the Springerle with clean tea towels and allow them to dry in a cool place overnight or for up to 24 hours. Bake them in a preheated 350° oven for 5 minutes. Lower the heat to 300° and bake 20 minutes more, or until the tops are raised and dry-looking. Do not allow the cookies to brown.

After the cookies have cooled on the cookie sheets, brush all excess flour from the tops. Store them in an airtight container.

Springerle will keep for a month or more. Two days before you're ready to eat them, add half an apple to the container, or dip the hard cookies in white wine.

Lebkuchen   *5 dozen*

These are great traditional Christmas cookies. Since you make them far in advance, they're ready, with no mess at the last minute.

1¼ cups honey
¼ cup white sugar
¼ cup packed brown sugar
2 tablespoons butter
1 tablespoon lemon juice
   Grated rind of 1 lemon
½ cup finely chopped citron
½ cup finely chopped almonds
1 teaspoon baking soda
1 teaspoon cinnamon
½ teaspoon nutmeg
½ teaspoon cardamom
¼ teaspoon cloves
4 cups flour
   Juice of ½ lemon
   Powdered sugar

Melt the honey, sugars, and butter in a small saucepan. Cool somewhat and add the lemon juice and rind, citron, and almonds. Sift the soda and spices with 2 cups of flour. Stir the flour-spice mixture into the honey mixture. Gradually add the rest of the flour until a somewhat stiff, sticky dough is formed. In some instances this may take more than 4 cups flour and in others, less. The dough needs to be a bit hard to stir. Refrigerate it overnight.

The next day allow the dough to warm to room temperature. Divide the dough in half. With your hands, spread and push the dough out into a thin layer on a lightly greased cookie sheet. Try for a rectangular shape. You'll have to push hard and work the dough to get it thin; keep at it. Bake in a 350° oven for 15 minutes, or until the dough looks slightly puffed and dry. It shouldn't brown but attain a tan. As soon as the Lebkuchen are out of the oven, cut them into squares or rectangles with a sharp knife.

To make the glaze, incorporate enough powdered sugar into the lemon juice to create a thin, runny frosting. With a pastry brush or a broad knife, brush a thin cover of glaze over the cut Lebkuchen. When cool and dry, store the cookies in an airtight container for at least two weeks. A month is better; and if you can wait two months, you'll have an even better cookie. When ready to use, insert a slice of apple in the container. Wait two days and then go wild.

Note: If you're wondering about the long aging process, it's because these are thin honey cakes, and honey works with flour very differently from most substances. The aging not only enhances the flavor, but makes the cookies more chewy and tender.

Snowballs I   *4 dozen*

    1 cup (2 sticks) butter
    ½ cup powdered sugar
    2 cups flour
    1 cup ground nuts

Have the butter soft and work all the other ingredients into it. When the dough is well blended, pinch off small amounts and roll them into balls the size of small walnuts. Place on lightly greased cookie sheets, put them in the refrigerator for 10 minutes (so the cookies will hold their shape), and bake in a 375° oven for 10 minutes. Roll in powdered sugar.

Snowballs II   *2 dozen*

    ⅔ cup butter
    2 tablespoons sugar
    1 cup flour
    1 cup ground nuts
    1 teaspoon vanilla

Follow the directions for Snow Balls I, adding the vanilla last.

Both Snowball recipes are delicious. The first makes a larger batch; they melt in your mouth and are lovingly sweet. The second has more substance to it and the butter-nut flavor dominates.

Mor Morsens   *4 to 5 dozen*

    1 cup (2 sticks) butter
    1 cup sugar
    5 large eggs
    2 cups flour
    ½ cup coarsely chopped almonds
    1 cup currants

Cream the butter with the sugar until light and fluffy. Add the eggs, one at a time, beating after each addition. Add the flour in small amounts, stirring just enough to blend. Spread the batter in a well-greased cookie sheet with a high lip. Sprinkle the almonds and currants evenly over the batter. Bake in a 325° oven for 25 to 30 minutes. Do not allow the cookies to brown. Cool and cut into diamond shapes.

Kolacky (Polish Christmas Cookies) *2 dozen*

3 ounces cream cheese
4 ounces (1 stick) butter
1 cup *sifted* flour
Apricot *or* peach *or* raspberry jam

Have the cream cheese and butter (margarine won't do) at room temperature; blend. Add the flour to the cream cheese–butter mixture and work with a wooden spoon until the flour is totally absorbed. Chill the dough for 15 minutes, or until it's manageable. Roll out the dough on a lightly floured board to a thickness of ¼ inch. With a 2-inch round cutter, cut circles. Place the circles on an ungreased cookie sheet. Place ½ teaspoon jam in the center of each cookie. Bake in a 350° oven for 20 minutes, or until the cookies are a very light tan. Don't allow the Kolacky to brown.

By food processor: Use cold cream cheese and butter. Put the flour in the bowl of a food processor fitted with the steel blade. Cut the cheese and butter into chunks and distribute them on top of the flour. Run the machine until the mixture is blended and forms a ball. Chill and continue as above.

Candy

We try to stay away from too much candy in our household (except for my husband, Richard, who is a Ghirardelli Eagle bar freak). But at Christmas time the fudge, penoche, and divinity simply must be made or it wouldn't be Christmas.

Candy is probably the hardest of the culinary skills to master. Just when you think you can expertly whip up a batch of fudge, one fails on you. Don't be too hard on yourself. You probably forgot and made candy on a rainy day. That's a no-no—too much moisture in the air, and candy won't set.

Another thing to remember is that sugar must always be completely dissolved *before* you bring the mass to a boil. If you don't stir the candy over low heat until the sugar is completely dissolved, it will form sugar crystals as it starts to boil, and there goes your creamy fudge.

As candy boils, it forms very large bubbles, thus increasing its bulk several times. Therefore, always cook candy in a pot at least four times larger than the amount of the ingredients.

Once you've dissolved the sugar over low heat and allowed the candy to boil, put a lid on the pot for about 1 full minute. The steam will wash down and dissolve the sugar crystals that have probably formed along the sides of the pot. I usually stir candy with a rubber spatula to scrape the bottom of the pan and clean the sides of the pot as I stir.

You should stir most candies over low heat until all the sugar is dissolved; once the boiling stage has begun, let the candy cook undisturbed, dipping in with a spoon only to check its progress.

If you don't have a candy thermometer, you must learn to test candy by using the old cold-water method. Candy is cooked to stages ranging from the soft-ball stage to the hard-crack stage. Drop a few drops of candy from a spoon into cold water. If it simply disintegrates, it has a way to go. Once it can be formed into a ball with your fingers (you must work down in the water) and holds its shape, you're at the beginning of the soft-ball stage—which I think is the most difficult to determine. There is a variance of several degrees in which the candy will test to the soft-ball stage. I test about once every minute or two, and when I start getting a nice little soft ball, I usually cook the candy 2 or 3 minutes longer. Remove the pot from the stove and test again. If all has gone properly, you should again get a soft ball but one that seems to have substance to it. If you work the little ball between your fingers and find no difference, cook the candy a bit longer and test again.

Fudge   *2 to 3 dozen pieces*

This is what I call *real* fudge! The recipe is the old cook, cool, and beat method, which has been used and passed around so much because the fudge it makes is dark, rich, and creamy. There's no marshmallowy gooeyness to it—just pure, smooth chocolate goodness.

To have this fudge turn out properly, it's important to remember the most important candy rule: stir over low heat until *all* of the sugar is dissolved before you allow the fudge to boil.

　　2 cups sugar
　　2 squares unsweetened baking chocolate
　　⅔ cup canned milk *or* light cream *or* milk
　　2 tablespoons light corn syrup
　　2 tablespoons butter
　　1 teaspoon vanilla

Place all the ingredients except the vanilla in a pot and heat slowly, stirring constantly until the sugar is dissolved. Once the boiling point is reached, cook undisturbed until the candy thermometer reaches 240° F. (110° C.), or until a soft ball is formed when a few drops of candy are dropped into a small cup of very cold water. When the proper temperature or soft-ball stage has been reached, remove from the heat; stir in the vanilla and allow the fudge to cool undisturbed until lukewarm (this means 110° F. or around 40° C., or when you can stand to hold your hand on the bottom of the pot). Beat until the fudge is creamy and loses its shine. Pour into a buttered pan, cool, and cut it into squares. If you like nuts in your fudge, add them halfway through the beating process.

D and C's Easy Dark Fudge

4 dozen pieces

My husband and I are both very partial to semisweet chocolate, and most easy fudges are too sweet and light for our taste—but this one fills the bill.

    1 12-ounce bag chocolate chips
    4 ounces baking chocolate, shaved, chopped, or grated
    1 can evaporated milk
 3½ cups sugar
    4 ounces marshmallow cream (over half of a large jar)
    4 tablespoons (½ stick) butter *or* margarine
      Pinch salt
    2 teaspoons vanilla
    1 cup nut meats (optional)

Put the chocolate chips and shaved baking chocolate into a large bowl. In a 3- or 4-quart saucepan put the milk, sugar, marshmallow cream, butter, and salt. Bring to a boil and continue cooking at a full boil for 7 minutes. You *must* stir the concoction continuously throughout the boiling process. I use a wooden spoon that has a flat end, or a rubber spatula. Both scrape the pan bottom with a wide swath and prevent the sugar from burning. (I also read while stirring; but of course it depends on how you like to use your time.) Pour the boiling sugar mixture over the chocolate and beat until all the chocolate pieces are melted. Add the vanilla and beat some more. Add nut meats, if desired. Pour the still-warm mixture into a buttered pan, cool, and refrigerate. Cut when cold and set.

Penoche

2 to 3 dozen pieces

3 cups packed brown sugar, *or* 2 cups brown sugar and 1
cup white sugar
1 cup milk, canned *or* whole
2 tablespoons butter
1½ teaspoons vanilla

Combine all the ingredients except the vanilla in a saucepan. Stir over low
heat until the sugars have completely dissolved. (This is sometimes hard to
tell when dealing with brown sugar, as its appearance changes very little from
one stage to another. Tasting is a good way to tell when the sugar has
melted.) Once the sugars have melted, stop stirring and boil until the candy
thermometer reads 240° F. (110° C.), or to the soft-ball stage. Remove the
pan from the heat, stir in the vanilla, and allow to cool to lukewarm. Do not
disturb the candy while it is cooling. When the candy is lukewarm, the candy
thermometer should read 104° F. (40° C.). If you can stand to hold your
hand on the bottom of the pot, it's time to beat the candy. With a wooden
spoon, beat it until it is thickened, smooth, and has lost its sheen. Pour it
into a buttered pan. Cut when cooled.

Divinity

4 dozen pieces

3 egg whites   ¾ cup white Karo syrup
3 cups sugar   1 cup walnuts
¾ cup water   1 teaspoon vanilla
Pinch salt

Put the egg whites into the large bowl of an electric mixer. Put the sugar,
water, salt, and Karo into a 3- or 4-quart saucepan and stir over low heat
until the sugar has dissolved. Once the sugar has dissolved, allow the mixture
to come to a boil. While the sugar mixture is boiling, beat the egg whites
until they're very stiff and slightly dry. Boil the sugar mixture until a fine
thread comes off a wooden spoon after being dipped into it. Turn the electric mixer to a high setting, and very slowly pour the boiling sugar syrup into
the beaten egg whites. Continue beating at high speed until ridges begin to
form and hold their shape. Remove the bowl from the mixer and by hand
stir in the walnuts and vanilla. Continue stirring by hand until the spoonfuls
or "kisses" you drop from a spoon stand and hold their shape. Drop the
Divinity kisses onto waxed paper, or spoon the entire concoction into a very
lightly buttered pan and cut when cooled. (I prefer the latter method.)

SAUCES AND CONDIMENTS

FLYING SAUCES

In the forties Henry Fonda's wife would often call my father, Carl, to come over and barbecue for a weekend party. The Fondas gave parties in a lodge that had been built between their swimming pool and tennis court. It measured approximately 30 by 85 feet, and my father referred to it as the whoopee room.

On one particular Sunday, Carl found the whoopee room full of visiting Russian actors and performers who were enjoying glass after glass of Black Velvets—that wonderful blend of dark Guinness stout and champagne.

At one end of the whoopee room was a huge built-in barbecue pit. At the other was an immense round table in the middle of which was a giant lazy susan, itself double the size of a standard round table. The lazy susan offered a large variety of condiments and sauce bottles—catsup, A-1 sauce, Lea & Perrins, mustards, horse-radish, and the like—for barbecue.

The Black Velvets inspired the Russians to start doing the Ka-zatsky, that strenuous Russian leg-kicking dance. The other guests were trying to join in when Carl sounded the dinner gong. Everyone grabbed another Black Velvet and seated himself at the immense round table.

The barbecue was served; as the guests began, one Russian asked another Russian on the other side of the table to swing around to him a particular mustard. Whether inspired by the dancing or the barbecue, that Russian was in high gear, and when he swung the lazy susan around, he *swung* it. Bottles and jars went flying in every direction, hitting wall, floor, head, and plate. There wasn't a person or thing in the room that didn't look and smell like a spice cabinet.

Luckily the whoopee room was disaster-proof. Some cold wet cloths for bumped heads and messy floors, plus a few more Black Velvets, saved the party.

Brad's Barbecue Sauce 2 cups

½ cup sugar
3 tablespoons flour
¾ cup water
2 teaspoons salt
¾ cup catsup
2 tablespoons vinegar (your choice)
2 tablespoons Worcestershire sauce
4 tablespoons soy sauce
½ cup chopped onion (optional)

In a saucepan whisk the sugar and flour together; slowly add the water and whisk until smooth. Add all the other ingredients and cook over moderate heat until thick and smooth.

The sauce may be stored in the refrigerator. It's great on any meat or fowl.

Light Barbecue Sauce 1⅓ cups

Juice of ½ lemon
⅓ cup catsup
½ cup white wine
1 clove garlic, crushed
½ teaspoon salt
¼ teaspoon pepper
½ cup olive oil
3 tablespoons soy sauce

Mix all the ingredients together. The sauce is best on chicken or fish. If you omit the salt, you can use it as a marinade.

Richard's Hot, Hot Mustard 2 cups

1 cup Colman's dry mustard
1 cup packed brown sugar
1 teaspoon salt
3 teaspoons white vinegar
1 jigger brandy
Boiling water

Mix all the ingredients except the boiling water. Stir well and add boiling water until the mixture is the consistency of regular mustard—not thick, but not too runny either. Beat 2 minutes, then let sit until gas bubbles rise to the surface. Put the mustard into sterilized jars and screw the lids on loosely. Store in a cool cupboard, but *do not* refrigerate. This is truly a great mustard, but it's *very* hot. I use it sparingly on sandwiches while heartier souls slather it on. Since this mustard is so hot, a little goes a long way, so you may wish to cut the recipe in half.

Chinese Hot Mustard ⅓ *cup*

¼ cup Colman's dry mustard
Hot water

Put the mustard in a small bowl and add enough hot water to make a thin paste. This is the mustard you get in Chinese restaurants with your fried shrimp and egg rolls.

Mustard Sauce (for Cold Cracked Crab) 1 *cup*

1 teaspoon Colman's dry mustard
2 teaspoons white vinegar
½ cup mayonnaise (homemade, Best Foods, or Hellmann's)
½ cup sour cream
1 teaspoon sugar
1 teaspoon lemon juice

Make a paste of the mustard and vinegar; add the rest of the ingredients and blend well.

Tartare Sauce 1 *cup*

1 cup mayonnaise (homemade, Best Foods, or Hellmann's)
1 tablespoon finely chopped sweet gherkins
2 teaspoons finely chopped parsley
1 teaspoon prepared mustard, Poupon preferred
1 tablespoon lemon juice
1 teaspoon finely minced onion, *or* ¼ teaspoon onion juice

Mix all the ingredients together. Serve with fried or sautéed fish.

Cocktail Sauce   *1 cup*

1 cup prepared chili sauce
1 teaspoon prepared horseradish
1 tablespoon lemon juice

Mix all the ingredients together and taste. If you want the sauce to have more zip, add more horseradish. This sauce is traditionally served with cold shrimp.

ɮɮɮɮɮɮɮɮɮɮɮɮɮɮɮɮɮɮɮɮɮɮ

THE GREAT AMERICAN DISASTER—GRAVIES AND SAUCES

When you were a kid, did your mother ever show you how to mix some white flour with some water to a smooth paste? Glue—the cheapest and most available in any house.

Gravies and sauces are made of flour and water plus fat of some sort, seasonings, and flavorings. But if you put all those ingredients together and stir only until just smooth and hot, you will have hot, watered-down paste.

The only thing that'll change your *paste* into a gravy or sauce is *cooking* the flour in it. It takes 5 *minutes* to cook the flour in your pot.

If there are ingredients that should be added at the last moment, such as sour cream, whipped cream, or booze, cook the gravy or sauce for at least 5 minutes; *then* add that last ingredient.

ɮɮɮɮɮɮɮɮɮɮɮɮɮɮɮɮɮɮɮɮɮɮ

Sauce Sampler

Many great cookbooks list sauces by their French names. That's wonderful if you speak French, if you've had formal chef's training, or if you've done a lot of homework and reading. I've had many fine cooks come to my cooking classes and lament that though they consider themselves to be better than fair when it comes to whipping up a good meal, they hesitate in using what everyone calls "the best cookbooks" because they have trouble with the instructions and the French throws them. If that sounds familiar, don't feel bad. If the best French cookbooks were filled with English names and titles there would be many a French housewife who would find herself staring blankly at a page entitled "Mushroom Wine Sauce." Here is a short list that may help.

Béchamel Sauce	White Sauce, often referred to as a cream sauce
Velouté	White Sauce made with stock, usually chicken, veal, or fish
Mornay Sauce	White Sauce made with the addition of cheese, usually Gruyère and Parmesan. Our cheese sauces are usually made with Cheddar, which is much harsher but lovely too
Bordelaise	Brown Sauce made with rich beef stock, flavored with red wine, shallots, and sometimes beef marrow

These four sauces are the most common, and many other sauces are simply take-offs on these major themes. Don't let foreign names throw you. Do some reading and testing. Be sure to use a wire whip when making sauce. No other stirring tool will produce such a smooth sauce.

In the Thick of Things

Roux: The most common sauces start with a *roux*, a thickening mixture of fat and flour. The fat can be (and usually is) butter, but any type of fat that will not overpower the flavor of the sauce will do. To make a *roux*, melt the fat in a saucepan until it is hot. Never let it brown. When the fat is hot, add flour and stir until well combined. The *roux* should be cooked a moment or two in order to cook the flour; however, care must be taken not to let the *roux* brown, unless the recipe calls for it. Once the *roux* is blended and cooked, liquids are added and whisked with a wire whip until smooth. The greater the proportion of *roux* to liquid, the thicker the sauce.

Beurre Manié: *Beurre manié* also thickens sauces. It is used to thicken sauces that have already been simmering and put together, such as the broth from a pot roast or the sauce surrounding your beef stew. Two or three parts butter are kneaded with one part flour until a smooth paste is formed. The *beurre manié* is added to the hot liquids a small bit at a time until the sauce is smooth and thickened to the proper consistency. You can use *beurre manié* when you find that you've added too much liquid to a soup or sauce. *Never* add straight flour to any hot sauce, broth, or liquid; you will end up with lumps and a very poor sauce.

Other Notes on Sauce-Making

- When adding egg yolks to a hot sauce in order to thicken it, remove the pan from the heat, stir 2 tablespoons hot sauce into the yolks, then whip in the egg yolk with a wire whip, place the sauce back on very low heat, and whisk until thickened. *Do not* allow the mixture to boil after adding egg yolks.
- Sour cream thins a sauce or gravy. Always plan on its thinning property and compensate for it by making the sauce quite thick before adding the sour cream.
- Never allow a sauce to which sour cream has been added to boil.

White Wine Sauce   *2 cups*

½ stick (¼ cup) butter
1 teaspoon dehydrated shallots, *or* 1 fresh shallot, minced
¼ cup flour
1½ cups chicken stock
½ cup milk *or* light cream
1 tablespoon finely chopped parsley
⅛ teaspoon pepper
1 teaspoon chicken base, *or* 1 bouillon cube
½ cup white wine
2 tablespoons brandy

Melt the butter in a saucepan. If using a fresh shallot, add it to the butter and sauté for 1 minute. Do not allow the butter to brown. Add the flour, blending with a wire whip until smooth. Add chicken stock a little at a time, stirring to make a smooth consistency with each addition. Add all the other ingredients in order. Stir the sauce after each addition and taste for salt when all has been added and simmered for 5 minutes. Because of the saltiness of the chicken stock and the chicken base, it is impossible to say the exact amount of salt that you will need. It is factors such as this that create the common "salt and pepper to taste" you see so often. This sauce is marvelous with chicken, seafood, chicken, or turkey combined with mushrooms and noodles.

Mushroom Wine Sauce

3 cups

While the White Wine Sauce is simmering for its customary 5 minutes, sauté ½ pound washed and sliced mushrooms in 2 tablespoons butter and 2 teaspoons lemon juice. When the mushrooms begin to take on color, add ¼ cup white wine. Toss the mushrooms over high heat and cook them until the liquid in the pan is slightly reduced. Add the mushrooms and the liquid to the White Wine Sauce and stir to combine.

Cream Sauce

2 cups

   ¼ cup (½ stick) butter
   ¼ cup flour
   1 teaspoon dehydrated shallots *or* onions
   1 cup chicken stock
 1½ cups milk
   1 tablespoon chopped parsley
     Salt and pepper to taste

Melt the butter in a saucepan. Add the flour, and cook the *roux* for 2 minutes over medium heat. Do not allow the *roux* to burn or take on color. Add the shallots or onions and then whisk in the stock with a wire whip until smooth. Add the milk and whisk again until smooth. Add parsley and correct the seasoning for salt and pepper. Simmer the sauce for 5 minutes, stirring occasionally. When ready to use, *strain* the sauce.

If you like a thinner sauce, add more chicken stock. Grated cheese of your choice may be added when the sauce has been completed, but before the 5-minute simmering time. Don't forget to strain the sauce before you use it.

Cheese Sauce   *2 cups*

    3 tablespoons butter
    4 tablespoons flour
    1¾ cups milk
    ½ teaspoon salt
    ⅛ teaspoon pepper, white preferred
    1 teaspoon dry mustard
    1 cup grated Cheddar *or* Longhorn cheese

Melt the butter in a saucepan, add the flour, and stir the *roux* over moderate heat for 2 minutes. Slowly add the milk, whisking with a wire whip the entire time. Add all the other ingredients and continue to stir until all is combined and smooth. Check for salt and simmer 3 more minutes. This is a great sauce over cauliflower, broccoli, or with macaroni.

Blender Hollandaise   *1¼ cups*

    1 cup (2 sticks) butter
    4 egg yolks (3 will do if you use large eggs)
    2 tablespoons lemon juice
    ¼ teaspoon salt
    Good pinch cayenne pepper *or* white pepper *or*
    Tabasco

In a small saucepan heat the butter until very hot and bubbling. Do not allow it to brown. Put into the blender jar the egg yolks, lemon juice, salt, and seasoning of your choice. Put the lid on the blender jar, start the machine on low, immediately remove the lid, and pour in the hot butter in a steady stream. When all the butter has been added, stop the machine. Serve the sauce immediately, or put it into a small bowl and set it into a larger bowl. Add *hot* water to the larger bowl to a depth of 2 inches. *Don't* keep the sauce warm over direct heat.

Blender Béarnaise   1¼ *cups*

½ cup white wine
2 tablespoons tarragon vinegar
1 tablespoon chopped fresh tarragon, *or* 1½ teaspoons dried tarragon
2 teaspoons chopped fresh chervil, *or* 1 teaspoon dried chervil
1 tablespoon chopped shallots *or* minced onion if you must
¼ teaspoon coarsely ground pepper
1 recipe Blender Hollandaise (preceding recipe)

Put the wine, vinegar, and all seasonings in a small pan and cook over high heat until the liquid has been reduced to about 1½ tablespoons. In the meantime make Blender Hollandaise. The two procedures should come out at about the same time, or you can make the Béarnaise essence ahead of time and warm it when ready. As soon as the Blender Hollandaise is done, pour the Béarnaise liquid and seasonings into the Hollandaise and blend on high speed for 8 seconds. Serve immediately, or keep warm in a bowl of *hot* water, just as for plain Hollandaise.

Brown Butter Sauce

Melt any desired amount of butter over moderate heat until it turns a golden brown. Watch the butter carefully and shake the pan to ensure even cooking of the butter. Brown Butter Sauce is delicious on fish and seafood.

Meunière Sauce

Meunière Sauce is Brown Butter Sauce with lemon juice squeezed into it. Start the sauce as you would Brown Butter Sauce. As soon as the butter begins to turn brown, add the juice of ½ lemon. If you're using more than ½ cup butter, add the juice of a whole lemon. This sauce is excellent on sautéed fish.

Hard Sauce
¾ cup

½ cup (1 stick) butter
1½ cups powdered sugar
2 tablespoons brandy

Beat the butter until light, add the sugar, then the brandy. Beat well. Pack into a small bowl and chill until firm. Spoon out or cut out with a knife, and use as a topping for steamed puddings, hot mince or apple pie, or hot baked apples. Hard Sauce freezes and keeps very nicely as long as it's well wrapped.

Cold Chocolate Sauce
1½ cups

3 ounces baking chocolate
1½ cups milk
1 cup sugar
Pinch salt
1 teaspoon vanilla
2 tablespoons brandy (optional)

Put the chocolate in a saucepan, add the milk, and warm the mixture over low heat without stirring for 3 minutes, or until the chocolate melts. Stir the mixture and add the sugar and salt. Increase the heat and stir until the sugar is melted and the mixture is smooth. Allow the mixture to come to a boil and cook for 3 minutes. Remove the pan from the heat, and when somewhat cooled, add the vanilla and brandy. The brandy is optional, but if the sauce is going over chocolate soufflé or mousse, you'll love it.

Hot Fudge Sauce
1⅓ cups

2 squares unsweetened chocolate
⅔ cup canned milk *or* half-and-half
1 cup sugar
1 teaspoon vanilla

Break the chocolate squares into pieces and combine them with all the ingredients but the vanilla. Bring slowly to a boil over medium heat and boil for 4 minutes. Stir often. Remove from the heat and add the vanilla.

CANNING AND JAMMING

GREEN TOMATOES

It had been one of those hectic days. We were over in Jackson for the night, did a bunch of chores in the morning, and then came over the pass to the ranch after lunch.

In the afternoon I made green tomato pickles (which I had salted down the day before), Green Tomato Chutney, and Green Tomato Mincemeat. By ten o'clock there were five quarts of dill pickles in the canner and four quarts waiting to get in.

But around 4:20 in the afternoon, after I'd gotten the chutney to a slow simmer, I said, "To hell with it!" I threw my saddle in the back of the jeep, drove up to where the horses were pasturing, and took a little ride on my horse, Bourbon. I felt a whole lot better afterward.

That's the kind of day you can expect when the night air dips to 21° F. and the greenhouse says, "That's all, folks!"

I've got green tomatoes coming out my ears. We had a delivery of logs for the potato cellar this evening and the fellow's wife came along to help.

"Do you can?" I asked—dumb question to ask any woman around these parts! So she took a big bag of green tomatoes and a pickle recipe.

Sheriff Rogers and his wife, Monika, were coming over for dinner the next night, and she said she'd love to have some green tomatoes. I decided if I made some Salsa Verde for my Mexican food and some more mincemeat, I could give the rest to Monika.

Wonderful things can be made from green tomatoes. If you have no garden, your produce market is the most likely source. Smile at the owner and promise him a jar of whatever you plan to make. Or try a friendly neighbor who has some loaded vines that need thinning. Exchange a recipe for some tomatoes.

Or look in the yellow pages for a nearby hydroponics grower and call to see if you can put in an order. When all else fails and you live in a big city, try to make a real occasion of it and run down to the big wholesale produce mart in the center of your town around 4:30 or 5:00 A.M. (If you're a female, take a man along. In most big cities the produce marts aren't in the best sections of town.) Oh, and call a few days in advance to be sure they've got green tomatoes so that your trip won't be in vain.

Once you have your green tomatoes, get your kitchen spotless, buy new lids for your jars, scrub them, get them ready to be sterilized, and then go to town making chutney, mincemeat, pickles, and green salsa. They're all delicious and great to give as gifts, not to mention saving you money and stocking your shelves for the winter.

What You Should Know about Canning

• Never start to can or jam until you've thoroughly cleaned and scoured your sink and kitchen.

• Wash both jars and lids in *hot* soapy water or in a dishwasher.

• Washed jars can be readied for canning by placing them on a cookie sheet in a 275° oven for 20 minutes, or by boiling them for 10 minutes.

• Canning lids must always be boiled for at least 20 minutes.

• You can reuse canning jars that are in excellent condition, but you must *never* reuse a canning lid. Rings, yes; lids, no.

• After filling a jar, wipe the rim with a *clean* cloth that has been dipped into boiling water. Then put on the lid and ring.

• Always use uniodized salt when pickling. It is also known as kosher, pickling, or pure granulated salt.

• Botulism, a sometimes deadly type of food poisoning, is a toxin that grows in foods that have been improperly canned, left out uncovered in warm weather or in containers where fresh products are added to old. Botulism is rare and easily avoided if the simple rules of good food preparation and cleanliness are followed.

• When the jars you canned this morning are cool, test the seal by pressing the lid. It should be rigid and slightly depressed. If you can push the lid and move it, redo it or put it in the refrigerator for immediate use—it didn't seal.

• When canning fruits, vegetables, pickles, etc., *always* run a knife down all four sides of your jars before cleaning the jar rims and sealing. This allows trapped air, which can cause spoilage, to escape, thus saving you from ruining your canned goods.

- Never try to can overripe fruits or vegetables. The fruit should go into cobblers or puddings and the vegetables should be tossed.
- Store *all* canned goods in a cool, dark place.
- *Never* use a can or jar of canned goods that oozes or squirts liquid or blows up and out upon opening.
- If you open canned goods and the contents smell or look bad, throw both contents and container away, but not where animals or small children can get at them.
- A good jelly bag can be made from an old pillowcase. Boil the pillowcase in water to which you've added 1 tablespoon baking soda. Rinse thoroughly.
- When pickling or canning cucumbers or tomatoes, cut off the blossom ends of the fruit, as they contain enzymes that can spoil the jars.
- To test a jam or jelly, place a plate in the freezer until it is cold to touch. Drop one or two drops of jelly on the plate. If the drop stands up, the jelly is done. If it flattens out, the jelly must boil some more. Frequent testing is advisable.
- Processing canned goods means to place filled and capped jars on a rack in a kettle of boiling water. The water should cover the jars by 2 inches.

Green Tomato Chutney   *4 pints*

    4½ pounds green tomatoes
    2 large or 3 medium green apples
    ½ lemon, rind and all
    2 cups cider vinegar
    2½ cups packed brown sugar
    1 large clove garlic, *or* 1 teaspoon garlic powder
    ⅛ teaspoon cayenne pepper
    1 teaspoon chili powder
    4 tablespoons finely slivered candied ginger
    ½ teaspoon celery salt
    1 teaspoon salt
    2 teaspoons ground ginger
    ½ teaspoon ground allspice
    ½ teaspoon ground cinnamon
    ½ teaspoon ground cloves
    1 teaspoon dehydrated shallots, *or* 3 fresh shallots
    ¼ cup sherry
    1 cup raisins, golden preferred

Wash and core the tomatoes, peel and core the apples, and wash the lemon. Chop the tomatoes, apples, and lemon. Put them in pot of at least 3-quart capacity; add the rest of the ingredients. If using fresh garlic, mince or press it. Bring the mixture to a boil, lower the heat, and simmer for 45 minutes, stirring occasionally. The mixture should be thick and dark. Cook longer if the color and consistency are not right at 45 minutes. Put into sterilized jars, run a knife down the sides to release air, seal the jars, and let them cool. Store in a dark, cool place.

Green Tomato Mincemeat   *4 to 5 quarts*

If you love mincemeat, scurry up some green tomatoes and make the following recipe. If you have a food processor, it's a snap.

The best thing about this particular mincemeat is that it contains no suet, just fruits and vegetables, plus seasonings and sugar. Suet itself has little or no taste. It's a binder, a stretcher, and with the addition of meat, a pseudo-tenderizer. My mincemeat doesn't contain any meat, and so I omit suet with its excess calories without losing mincemeat's good taste.

    20 small to medium green tomatoes
     2 large oranges, rind and all
    ½ lemon, rind and all
     1 pound raisins
     5 large green apples
    3½ cups packed brown sugar
    ½ cup cider vinegar
       Juice of 1 lemon
     1 cup water
     1 tablespoon cinnamon
    ½ teaspoon ground cloves
    ½ teaspoon ground ginger
    ½ teaspoon ground nutmeg
    ½ teaspoon ground allspice
    ½ teaspoon salt
    ½ teaspoon mace
    ½ cup brandy

Wash, core, and chop the green tomatoes; cover with boiling water and let stand 5 minutes. Pare and core the apples, wash the oranges and lemon, and chop or grind all. Drain the tomatoes. In the meantime put the sugar, vinegar, lemon juice, and water in a large pot—at least 4-quart capacity—and bring to a boil. Add all the ingredients but the brandy. Simmer for 30 minutes, stirring occasionally. Add the brandy; stir well; pack into hot sterilized jars. Seal and process for 30 minutes.

Red Pepper Jam   *2 pints*

The Red Pepper Jam recipe that Carl Andersen traded to Kenneth Hansen of Scandia for his Caesar Salad Dressing had originally been given to Carl by a friend from Boston. Her family always made it for the holidays. When they entertained they would pile whipped cream cheese into a large circular mound in the middle of a round platter. Around the edge of the cream cheese they would spoon a nice thick ring of Red Pepper Jam, and around the jam they'd place a ring of fresh mint leaves. Hors d'oeuvre–sized bread was always served alongside the beautiful white, red, and green platter, and each guest helped himself to cream cheese and Red Pepper Jam.

Today, both restaurants serve Red Pepper Jam with an assortment of Danish open-face sandwiches, and of course in cream cheese and Red Pepper Jam sandwiches on pumpernickel.

Care must be taken in making Red Pepper Jam, as it has to be cooked over very low heat for a long time to ensure the retention of its beautiful red color. Other than watching the degree of heat, it's as simple to make as any other jam.

    12 large red sweet peppers
    1½ tablespoons salt
     3 cups sugar
     2 cups cider vinegar

Wash, trim, and clean the peppers, removing all seeds and membranes. Chop the peppers fine in a food processor or by hand. They must be finely chopped. Put the chopped pepper in a colander, mix in the salt, and let stand 3 to 4 hours over a bowl to drain. Lightly rinse the peppers; put them in a wide-bottomed pan or pot, add the sugar and vinegar, and stir over low heat until the sugar is melted. Simmer the jam for 4 hours. *Do not boil.* Stir occasionally and keep at a bare simmer. This long, slow cooking will produce a fine, bright red jam that is fantastic with cold meat, fowl, and fish. When simmering is done, pour the jam into hot, sterilized jars and seal. Don't forget to put some into a pretty container for immediate use; keep it refrigerated.

Salsa Verde

4½ pints

20 small green tomatoes (4 pounds)
2 large onions
1 large clove garlic, *or* ½ teaspoon garlic powder
2 tablespoons chopped parsley
1 teaspoon salt
2 tablespoons sugar
2 tablespoons dehydrated sweet pepper flakes
3 to 6 dehydrated small hot chilies, crumbled (6 makes it *hot*)
1 teaspoon coriander
¼ teaspoon oregano
½ teaspoon cumin
2 cans (4 ounces) green chilies, diced
1 cup water

Wash, core, and chop the green tomatoes. Cover them with boiling water and let stand 5 minutes. Chop the onions and garlic. Drain the tomatoes and combine all the ingredients. Bring to a boil, then simmer for 20 minutes. Ladle into hot, sterilized jars, leaving at least 1 inch head room; cap, cool, and freeze. Or ladle into hot, sterilized jars, leaving ½ inch head room; seal and process for 20 minutes.

Salsa Roja

2 quarts

8 cups peeled, cored, and chopped ripe tomatoes (about 15 to 20)
4 cups chopped onions (about 4 medium to large)
2 teaspoons salt
¼ teaspoon pepper
2 cloves garlic, *or* 1 teaspoon garlic powder
6 dehydrated small hot chilies, crumbled (4 if you don't like it *hot*)
1 teaspoon chervil
½ teaspoon turmeric
1 teaspoon cumin
1 tablespoon chopped parsley
1 tablespoon sugar
Juice of 1 lime

Combine all the ingredients in a 4-quart pot; bring to a boil, reduce the heat, and simmer for 30 minutes, stirring occasionally. Skim if necessary. Ladle into hot, sterilized jars, leaving at least 1 inch head room; seal and process for 20 minutes.

This is the type of salsa served with tortilla chips in Mexican restaurants. It's excellent added to all sorts of Mexican foods or spooned into tacos.

Pickled Watermelon Rind
4 quarts

1 watermelon with the thickest rind you can find
¼ cup salt (pickling, without iodine)
  Water and ice
5 cups sugar
2 cups white vinegar
1½ tablespoons whole cloves
1 tablespoon whole allspice
1 tablespoon stick cinnamon, broken into pieces
1 thinly sliced lemon, rind and all

Cut the watermelon into eight lengthwise pieces. Cut out the flesh and reserve to serve later. Cut the rind into 1-inch pieces. Trim every bit of the green skin from the rind, and also trim any pink left on the inside. Put the rind cubes in a crock or stainless-steel pot. Dissolve the salt in 1 quart water, pour it over the rind, and fill the crock with crushed ice. Allow to stand overnight. In the morning drain the rind, put it in a large cooking vessel, and cover with fresh water. Bring to a boil, reduce the heat, and simmer until just tender, about 10 minutes. The rind should still have a little crunch to it. Drain again. Combine the sugar, vinegar, and spices which you've tied up in a cheesecloth bag. Bring to a boil, then pour over the drained rind. Boil the rind in the syrup for 45 minutes, or until the rind looks transparent. The cooking time may be much less if the rind is thin, so watch it carefully. Pack the pickled watermelon rind in hot, sterilized jars, run a knife down the sides, clean the rim, and seal. Each jar should "click" as it cools, signifying a good seal.

Caroline's Real Fig Jam   *2 quarts*

        8 cups fresh black mission figs
        6 cups sugar
        1 lemon, sliced paper-thin

Peel and dice the figs into a pot; add the sugar and lemon. Stir over low heat until the sugar has melted. Keep the heat on medium-low and allow the jam to simmer slowly. The jam shouldn't be left. Stir and watch it, and be sure to scrape the bottom of the pot often. The jam shouldn't darken. When the jam has thickened, pour it into hot, sterilized jars and seal. This is a light, slightly thickened jam that makes your mouth hunger for more and more and more, especially if you love fresh figs.

Peach Jam   *1 quart*

        5 cups diced peaches (about 10 peaches, depending on size)
        3 cups sugar
        Juice of ½ lemon

Pour boiling water over the peaches; let them sit for 1 minute, drain, peel, and cut the flesh into dice, measuring the fruit as you do so. Save three stones. Put all the ingredients, including the stones, in a 12-inch frying pan, preferably Teflon. Bring slowly to a boil, stirring occasionally. Once the boiling point has been reached, turn the heat to medium-high and boil briskly. Stir the jam often with a rubber spatula, which allows you to scrape the bottom of the pan completely and keep the jam from scorching. Cook for 20 minutes, or until it reaches jam consistency. The time needed to reach this point depends largely on the juice content of the peaches. Test the consistency by putting a few drops of jam on a very cold plate; if it's jam, it will sit up on the plate. Pour it into hot, sterilized jars.

Orange Marmalade   *4 to 5 quarts*

        9 oranges
        6 lemons
        4 quarts water
        8 pounds (16 cups) sugar

Wash the fruit and trim the ends. Cut in half from top to bottom, and slice as thin as possible. You're finished in 5 minutes if you have a food processor. Put the fruit in a large pot, not aluminum or cast-iron, and preferably heavy. Cover with water and let sit until the next day. The original recipe called for a wait of 36 hours, but anything over 24 will do the trick. After the fruit has sat for the allotted time, bring the mixture to a boil; lower the heat and simmer for 2 hours. Add the sugar, stir until it dissolves, and simmer 1 more hour. Ladle into hot, sterilized jars and seal.

This marmalade stays light in color and is not bitter as so many commercial brands are. It has many fans. It makes a great Christmas gift and is cheap to make when winter oranges are available at a good price.

Orange-Peach Marmalade   *2 quarts*

        12 medium to large peaches
         4 large oranges
            Sugar
         2 tablespoons lemon juice
         3 drops almond extract

Pour boiling water over the peaches and allow them to stand for 3 minutes. Wash the oranges, trim ends, and slice them as thin as possible. (A food processor makes this a snap.) Peel the peaches and dice the fruit off their stones. Reserve 4 stones. Measure the fruit; for each cupful of fruit add ¼ cup sugar. Put all fruit, the 4 stones, and the sugar into a large pot and stir over medium heat until the sugar has melted. Bring to a boil, add the lemon juice, and cook over medium-low heat until thick, usually 1 hour or more. You must stir this delicious mass frequently or it'll burn. When the marmalade has thickened and is ready for your hot, sterilized jars, add the almond extract and stir well.

HOME BREWS

ﷲﷲﷲﷲﷲﷲﷲﷲﷲﷲﷲﷲﷲﷲﷲﷲﷲﷲﷲﷲﷲﷲﷲ

HOMEMADE BREWS

One day in the early sixties, while I was living in Mill Valley, a friend called and asked: "Carole, do you think we could make a cordial like the one you make from blackberries using cherry plums?"

"If we can get them free, it's sure worth a try," I replied.

So off went four of us with baskets, boxes, kids, and dogs to a house somewhere north of Tiburon.

In the yard stood twelve cherry plum trees so decked with fruit that we had to laugh. We picked twelve lugs, and the trees still looked the same as when we'd arrived.

Back home we all gathered at my house with our dark bottles (necessary for aging homemade brews), our pots, our kids, and our sugar and spice. On went every burner I had. Plums were washed, stemmed, and chopped. They were then covered with water and set to simmer until they were mushy soft, when the pulp was poured into old preboiled pillowcases, tied with stout string and hung from kitchen cupboards to drip into pots and bowls.

We collected the juice, measured it, and added two cups of sugar to each quart of liquid, then put the pots on the stove, each one with a spice bag. Twenty minutes later we set the fluids to cool and took a coffee break.

When the syrup was cool, we added liquor, stirred, funneled the liquid into bottles, corked them, dipped their necks in wax, and put on labels. The job had taken all day.

Six months later, in the midst of a divorce that didn't go through, I'd moved from Mill Valley back to Los Angeles and in unpacking came across the aging plum cordial and opened a bottle. Life was pretty miserable at that moment, but the taste of the cordial made it worse.

After the horrid taste disappeared, another, different one remained. Awful though the cordial was, something told me not to throw the rest of the eighteen bottles out.

The next years of my life were hectic and full of moves. By the time 1970 rolled around, and we'd finally purchased a home of our own, only nine of the bottles were left. The rest had gone at different times to the trash bin.

In early 1973 the divorce that hadn't taken place before took. Sometime later in 1973 I had company for dinner. After the meal I brought out one of the last bottles of blackberry cordial from our Mill Valley days. My guests were very taken with its delightful taste, and the conversation turned to homemade brews. I suddenly remembered the awful cherry plum cordial. Excusing myself from the table, I ran to the back bath, crawled in under the sink, and extracted a dusty nine-year-old bottle.

Back at the table I wiped the bottle clean and laughed as I told how horrid the stuff was. I cut the wax and extracted the cork. I sniffed incredulously. I sniffed again. No one said a word, as my face must have been conveying it all. I poured and took a sip; then another. Grinning, I said, "Well, I'll be damned!" Time had transformed the horrid brew into a heavenly delight.

The moral to the story is: Don't give up on homemade cordials. My family has never forgiven me for tossing nine bottles of heaven away. Most cordials are ready for consumption six months after the making, but all of them improve with age.

Homemade Cordials

Fruit, blackberries, boysenberries, loganberries, blueber-
ries, elderberries, raspberries, cranberries preferred
Water
Sugar
Whole allspice
Cloves
Cinnamon stick
Whiskey, brandy, or vodka

Peaches and apricots are delicious, but it's very difficult to get a clear liquid from them unless you have a juicer.

Have ready dark wine, cordial, or brandy bottles. If you have or can get some empty liquor bottles that contained such lovely things as Grand Marnier, Courvoisier, or Rémy Martin, *don't* wash the bottles because that little bit of liquor that's always left in the bottle will add to your cordial.

Whether you pick or buy your berries, try to have at least 2 quarts or as much as 8 quarts. Wash and pick over the fruit. If you're using a solid fruit such as peaches or plums, chop it or put it through a food processor.

Put the washed berries in a large pot (not aluminum) and add water *just* to cover. Simmer the fruit until it can be mashed into a pulp with a potato masher; this usually takes 15 to 20 minutes, depending on the ripeness of the fruit. Pour the fruit into a jelly bag and hang it over a pot. I do this in the afternoon and allow the juice to drip overnight so that I can get every drop. Don't squeeze the bag to extract the juice, as this will cloud the mixture. In the morning, or when the bag stops dripping, measure the liquid collected and to each quart add 2 cups sugar. Boil the juice and sugar along with a spice bag for 20 minutes. Figure approximately 1 teaspoon of each spice for each quart of liquid. If you're doing a large amount, you can cut down on the spice to 1 tablespoon of each spice for the entire batch.

After boiling the mixture for 20 minutes, remove the spice bag and cool. Measure again, and to each quart of syrup add 2 cups whiskey, brandy, or vodka. If you are using dark berries, whiskey works fine; if you are using a light fruit, brandy or vodka is better.

Bottle and cork the cordial. Store in cool, dark place for at least six months—the older it is, the better.

On the ranch we have wild blueberries, chokecherries and serviceberries. The kids made up a cordial from a mixed collection of these, and the results are now being thoroughly enjoyed. Experiment and try to be patient.

Coffee Liqueur (Phony Kahlúa)   *2½ quarts*

    2 cups water
    4 cups sugar
    ½ cup instant coffee
    1 cup boiling water
    2 tablespoons vanilla
    2 teaspoons glycerin (not absolutely necessary)
      Fifth of vodka (cheap)
    2 cups brandy (cheap)

Boil 2 cups water with the sugar for 5 minutes. Dissolve the instant coffee in 1 cup boiling water. Add the coffee mixture to the sugar mixture; cool. Stir in the vanilla, glycerin, and booze. Funnel into dark bottles, preferably old brandy, cognac, or liquor bottles. Store at least six months in cool, dark place.

Glögg   *2 quarts*

    2 cups water
    1½ cups sugar
    ½ cup raisins
    ½ lemon, sliced thin
    1 orange, sliced thin
    1 teaspoon whole cloves
    2 sticks cinnamon
    ¼ cup blanched slivered almonds (optional)
    1 quart red wine
    1 cup port
    ½ cup brandy

Boil the water, sugar, raisins, fruit, spices, and almonds together for 5 minutes. Add the liquor and heat over a low flame until hot. Do not allow it to boil.

This warms cold skiers and snow shovelers, but don't let them drive after three or more glasses.

Lemon Syrup for Lemonade   *1 quart*

Grated rind of 4 lemons
Juice of 7 lemons
4 cups water
4½ cups sugar

Combine the grated rind and the juice; refrigerate the mixture overnight. The next day boil the water and sugar together for 5 minutes. Cool the mixture and strain the lemon mixture into it. Store the syrup in the refrigerator.

For truly delicious lemonade, put 1 tablespoon lemon syrup in an 8-ounce glass; fill with water and ice and enjoy some truly incredible lemonade.

SUPER SANDWICHES

Sundays are special. Sunday is the day on which the daily routine is often changed. The office or place of work is put aside, and you are free to sit in front of the tube, pack up a picnic, or maybe visit a museum. Perhaps you're a sailor or a hiking freak or a sun worshipper. You may be one of those who hold mini open house on Sundays. Whatever your pleasure happens to be, super sandwiches can liven up the day.

Chatam Special

The Chatam Special is an immense Dagwood of a sandwich that has been sold in the family's restaurant for forty years. Well over a million Chatams have been sold from that one small restaurant, and I'm sure the tally is a good double that if I'd just bother to get out the calculator. People take Chatams to New York, Hawaii, and Europe. People take Chatams to the Hollywood Bowl and out on their yachts. People take them from the restaurant because to make a Chatam at home would be very time-consuming and rather expensive if you used the finest of all ingredients, which is of great importance.

Not everyone lives in Los Angeles, even though sometimes it seems that way. So in case you're having the gang over to watch the Super Bowl, here's how to make them super Chatam sandwiches yourself.

>Large light rye bread, no seeds
>Thinly sliced turkey, breast meat preferred
>Thinly sliced Swiss cheese, imported preferred
>Chatam Coleslaw (see Index)
>Russian Dressing (see Index)
>Thinly sliced ham, Hormel Cure '81 preferred
>Whipped butter

For each sandwich, butter two slices of rye bread. On one of the slices put a layer of turkey. Make sure the layer is even and completely covers the bread. On top of the turkey put an even and complete cover of Swiss cheese. Squeeze the juice from a good handful of marinated slaw and mound it on the Swiss cheese. The slaw should be a minimum of ½ inch in height. Don't spread the slaw out to the edges; we'll take care of that in a minute. Over the slaw spoon a goodly amount of Russian Dressing in a line down the center of the slaw; do not spread it. Now cover all with a complete layer of ham, top with the second piece of bread, and get ready to settle the sandwich. With the broad, flat side of a large butcher knife, tap the sandwich up and down its length. This will distribute the slaw and the dressing and create a sandwich that can be cut even though it's 2 inches high. With the biggest and the *sharpest* knife you have, cut the Chatam into three pieces with strong, smooth, clean, and quick strokes. If the bread is rather small, you may cut the sandwich in two.

You can build a Chatam with twice the amount of meat and no slaw and really have yourself a protein-rich meal. Don't forget the Russian Dressing.

Chutney Special

Another favorite of mine from the long list of sandwiches served by Mom and Dad is the Chutney Special. It's a unique and wonderful treat to the taste buds.

> Two slices bread, pumpernickel preferred
> Butter and mayonnaise
> 1 tablespoon chopped chutney, your choice, *or* Green Tomato Chutney (see Index)
> Thinly sliced rare roast beef
> Thinly sliced Swiss cheese

Whip the butter and chop the chutney. Spread butter on both slices of bread. Also spread with mayonnaise, if desired. Place a good layer of beef on one slice of bread. Spread the beef with chutney. Cover with a layer of Swiss cheese, top with the second piece of bread, cut, and enjoy.

Lettuce may be added.

Meal-in-One Dagwoods

What you put into your super sandwiches usually depends on what's obtainable and what ingredients your wallet can afford. Keeping all this in mind, I make the following suggestions for meal-in-one Dagwoods. The bread is up to you, though I have found the vegetarian sandwiches go best on whole-grain breads and sandwiches made with meats go best on ryes or pumpernickels. The ingredients are listed in the order in which they go into the sandwich. If you find a combination you particularly like, name it after someone you love.

Mayonnaise, mustard, tomato, thinly sliced onion, bean sprouts, Jack cheese; add avocado if available

Mayonnaise, mustard, liverwurst, dill pickle, Swiss cheese, lettuce, tomato if desired

Toasted bread, mayonnaise, scrambled eggs, salt, and pepper

Liver pâté, Swiss cheese

Cream cheese, Red Pepper Jam (see Index)

Mayonnaise, fried bacon, avocado, tomato, lettuce

Mayonnaise, turkey, bacon, ham, tomato, lettuce

Mayonnaise, turkey, avocado, salt, pepper, lettuce

Mayonnaise, mustard, bologna, American cheese, tomato, lettuce

Mayonnaise, paper-thin hard salami, Swiss cheese, tomato, lettuce

Crab salad, avocado

Tuna salad, avocado or tomato

Egg salad, lettuce

Roast beef, tomato, lettuce

Mayonnaise, mustard, bologna, Swiss cheese, paper-thin hard salami or thick soft salami, tomato, American cheese, lettuce

Butter, baby shrimp, Russian dressing, avocado

Chicken salad, lettuce

Roast pork, salt, pepper, tomato, lettuce; mayonnaise if desired

The list is endless. Any leftover meat can be sliced thin and made into an excellent sandwich. Whether you're a mayonnaise lover or not, sandwiches need some lubricant, and a good mayonnaise does wonders in adding moisture and accent to the other foods layered upon it. Try not to use a sweet mayonnaise; it detracts from the other things that go between slices of bread.

Open-Face Sandwiches

Some of the best sandwiches are open-face. These are eaten with a knife and fork, and many are just right for a luncheon or easy supper; they are full of vitamins as well.

Knockwurst Special

> 1 large or 2 medium slices bread (try Sourdough French Bread, see Index)
> Russian Dressing (see Index)
> Layer of sliced tomato
> 2 boiled knockwurst, split lengthwise
> ½ cup grated sharp Cheddar cheese

Assemble and put under the broiler until the cheese melts.

Italian Avocado

> Toasted bread
> Mayonnaise
> Sliced avocado
> Salt and pepper
> Sliced or grated mozzarella cheese

Assemble and put under the broiler until the cheese melts.

Salad Melt

> Toasted bread
> Tuna or chicken salad
> Thinly sliced tomato
> Sliced or grated Jack cheese, enough to cover all

Assemble and put under the broiler until the cheese melts.

Open Reuben

Toasted bread
Sliced corned beef preheated in the oven, radar oven,
or its own broth
Heated sauerkraut
Russian Dressing (optional, see Index)
Swiss cheese to cover

Assemble and put under the broiler until the cheese melts.

Mexican Special

Fried tortilla
Leftover refried beans, refried
Sliced leftover enchiladas, warmed in foil in the oven
Thinly sliced tomato
Sliced avocado
Jack cheese to cover

Assemble and put under the broiler until the cheese melts. Serve with
Salsa Roja or Verde (see Index) and a salad. Maybe a beer?

Danish Duck Sandwich

Butter two trimmed pieces of bread. Cut one on the diagonal, forming two
triangles. Put the whole piece on the lower half of a plate and butt the two
longer sides of the triangles against the opposing sides of the center piece.
Cut the breast from half a roast duck and place it on the center slice of
bread. You may slice it first if you wish. Garnish the sandwich with applesauce, Red Pepper Jam (see Index), quartered tomatoes, and sliced cucumbers, and place pickled beets in small lettuce cups above the bread. Add
carrot and celery sticks on both sides.

Note: This sandwich can also be made with roast chicken breast. Red
Pepper Jam goes well with it, but you may substitute chutney and Curry
Dressing (see Index).

Try slipping a thin slice of raw onion into any of the above. Onion is great
for high blood pressure, as is garlic. Try peanut butter and fried crisp bacon
put under the broiler until the peanut butter has a high sheen to it, or cook
up some Italian sausage and start building. Don't forget the great all-Amer-
ican open-face burger. With a little time and some imagination you can feed
a crowd in a hurry and have very satisfied customers.

In hot weather, try the following ideas for a late-night supper.

Danish Turkey

Butter two trimmed pieces of bread. Cut one, corner to corner, forming two triangles. Put the whole piece of bread in the center of a plate. Butt the two longest sides of the triangles against the center piece on opposing sides.

Cover the center slice of bread with thinly sliced white meat of turkey. Pile a line of shrimp diagonally across the turkey. Mound Cold Scrambled Eggs (see Index) on the triangles. Spoon a band of chopped chutney over the eggs and serve a side dish of Curry Dressing (see Index). You may garnish the plate with tomato wedges nestled in a lettuce cup.

Shrimp or Lobster Special

Butter and arrange bread on a plate as directed for Danish Turkey. Place five jumbo poached, shelled, and deveined shrimp on the center piece of bread, or half of a cooked and shelled lobster. On the side triangles of bread place two halves of hard-boiled eggs. Decorate the plate with tomatoes, cucumbers, and pickles. Serve Russian Dressing (see Index) on the side.

If you wish to go all the way, spoon caviar onto the yolks of the hard-boiled eggs. You can either slice the half lobster or allow your guest to cut at will.

Tea Sandwiches

Butter and watercress on trimmed bread can be made in any kitchen, as can cream cheese and Red Pepper Jam or cream cheese and chutney. But professional tea sandwiches demand a food processor or a high-quality blender. For beautiful tea sandwiches, combine 1 cup cooked turkey with 1 cup soft butter, add salt and pepper to taste, and blend until smooth. Spread on a variety of breads, close with another piece of bread, trim, and cut into fancy shapes.

Another beautiful filling is 1 cup cooked ham, 1 cup soft butter, and 1 teaspoon Poupon or dry mustard. Blend in the food processor until smooth. Leftover roast pork makes a marvelous spread. Blend and season just as you would for turkey spread.

Chicken liver pâté on pumpernickel is one of my favorite tea sandwiches or regular sandwiches. Chicken liver pâté and Swiss cheese is also a great combination. If you use chicken liver pâté and Swiss for tea sandwiches, you should put them together by spreading a thin layer of pâté on each slice of bread; top one with the Swiss and glue it all together with the other slice of bread. With the Swiss cheese encased with pâté, the sandwich won't fall apart on your guests or the floor.

ENTERTAINING

Giving Parties

Parties are always a treat, especially when a bit of elegance, fun, or old-fashioned ingenuity is thrown into the planning. Some basic rules that I always follow are:

•   Know your guests. If it's a small dinner party, make sure your guests won't clash. If you're throwing a large cocktail party, the reverse is true—variety is truly the spice of life.

•   Plan your menu well. Don't plan on more than you're capable of doing. Don't try out new dishes on your guests. Stick with your best and most beautiful recipes. Make ahead of time all the foods that can be frozen, thus saving yourself time and energy on the big day.

•   Be creative. Whether it's six for dinner or fifty for hors d'oeuvres, try to create an atmosphere in the decor of your table and surroundings.

•   If you're planning a big party but can't afford to hire help, either ask friends to help tend bar and serve, or make very sure that your guests can help themselves easily.

•   If you give an elegant dinner party using your finest crystal, china, and silver, don't allow the guests to help with the dishes. Crystal is best done on a clear-headed morning rather than late at night after a big day.

•   People are getting back to elegance, and it is gratifying to entertain in the finest manner possible, but if you're not set up for elegance, give your guests the best you have. A colorful table, greens from the garden, candles galore, an ethnic meal, or a party to which guests bring their very finest dish, all make for delightful, fun evenings—and after all, that's the name of the game.

Recently, I cooked a Mexican dinner for a party of eight. After decorating my table with colorful candles and gay napkins, I called my guests and told them that since we were having a totally Mexican dinner, I thought we should "dress" for the occasion. They didn't have time to think and took to the idea without a fuss. My costumed guests decorated our home and a wonderful time was had by all.

• Lighting and music are very important mood setters. They should be considered when setting the tone of your party. Bright lights don't mix with soft music and an intimate evening.

• Use what you have. Use Aunt Sonia's crystal, the hand-painted dessert dishes you got for a wedding present, and Grandma's cut-crystal decanter. If you can't take the time and trouble to share all that's at your disposal in order to entertain your guests, my attitude is—don't bother. Entertaining in your home is a sharing, giving experience. What you have to share isn't important; it's how you share it. I had a friend who at one point in her life was extremely low on funds. She needed china, so off she went to rummage sales, Goodwill, and garage sales. Soon she had twelve place settings of china, all of different patterns. Her table was one of the most delightful I've ever sat at, and her chili, homemade bread, and cheap wine were always enjoyed.

• If something should go wrong (God forbid), laugh it off. Push the party forward and don't dwell on the incident. If your guests are enjoying themselves, they'll forget.

Some rules are made to be broken, but not those time-honored ones governing the menu. The first thing to think of when planning a dinner party is the main course. It is the pivot of any meal.

If it is to be steak or roast beef, you'll be safe with a wide variety of foods. On the other hand, crêpes stuffed with chicken, mushrooms, and wine sauce need to be treated with respect and softness. To start with a heavily seasoned Caesar salad would make it impossible for your guests to taste the delicacy of the wine sauce. A smooth cream of asparagus soup, an avocado with baby shrimp salad, or even a lightly dressed watercress salad would be a better first course before the upcoming crêpes.

With the crêpes you could serve wild rice tossed with sautéed onions, celery, and water chestnuts, some fresh green beans, or some pea pods and julienned celery.

For dessert you can go wild; the meal has been soft, seductive, and delicious. The palate hasn't been bruised, just soothed; so now you can present any dessert you wish.

Hors d'oeuvres are a part of the meal, just as much as the salad, side dish, or dessert. You don't want your hors d'oeuvres to clash with your dinner any more than you want your first course to clash with your second course.

A bean dip with its wonderfully sharp seasonings won't bother a beef,

Mexican or pasta dinner, but it would be all wrong for the crêpes or your favorite curry. Though the curry is also highly seasoned, its seasonings would clash with the bean dip.

The idea is that a delicate main course should not be overshadowed. Strive for contrast in texture and color, keeping in mind that too much spice just before a delicate-tasting course won't work.

I'd like to put in a word for first courses. It's become an American tradition to serve a salad, the main course, and dessert. I love salads, but there are wonderful things to do for a first course other than salad. If you serve a soup or fish course first, you'll find your guests applauding and begging for more.

I often serve two courses before the main course. Sound like too much food? It isn't if the portions are small and delicious; and each taste treat leads to the next. Serving many courses lengthens the time at table, enhances conversation, and actually aids digestion since there is usually some time between them.

The Other Side of the Party

Parties are fun to give, but it is just as much fun to be a guest. The Danes have very strict rules about being a guest, as do most people of European extraction. Most Europeans come to the door with some small gift in hand. Flowers usually signify a first visit, but a bottle of wine, candy, or something homemade is often the offering. When visiting Europeans come to this country, they usually carry in their suitcases small gifts from their homeland to give to the hosts of homes into which they're welcomed.

The late world-renowned opera singer Lauritz Melchior was born in Copenhagen in 1890 and died in Los Angeles in the late 1970s. Though he lived in the America he loved so much through a good portion of his life, he maintained many customs of his native Denmark. The Danes have a lovely custom which says that once past the age of sixty-five, you may give yourself your own birthday parties. Fearing he might not see his eightieth year, Lauritz began giving himself fabulous birthday parties, starting with his seventy-ninth. His parties were always sit-down dinner affairs with the finest of wines and the best of foods, served by numerous servants.

At one of Lauritz's last birthday parties a prominent Hollywood couple was late and still hadn't arrived when the scheduled time for dinner came. Lauritz seemed to take no notice; the dinner gong was sounded and the guests sat down to begin the feast. Two chairs stood obviously empty. When the late arrivals slipped into their seats, Lauritz was holding forth in conversation—he never even glanced their way.

I have known Danes so eager to be prompt that they arrive early at their destination and sit in their cars until the proper time. It is also a time-honored Danish tradition that everyone leaves a party at the same time. As the evening wears on and the hour gets late, someone instinctively says, "*Nu skall ve gaa hjem?*"—in other words, "Now, shall we go home?" As though an alarm has gone off, guests rise, kiss, hug, shake hands, give thanks, and depart. No 3:00 A.M. stragglers!

A few years back I had the pleasure of being a dinner guest in the home of Vivian and Tommy Thomsen. It was an elaborate evening, and Lauritz Melchior was seated down the table to my right, his immense height towering over us. The hour had grown very late and we still sat at table. Someone glanced at his watch, and "*Nu skall ve gaa hjem?*" was heard above the various small conversations. As we all rose, I heard Lauritz say in his thick Danish accent, "This has been a special and beautiful evening, full of love and friendship. Before we all leave, I'd like to close with a song." He then sang the Lord's Prayer. It was a moving end to a memorable evening.

INDEX

EQUIVALENTS

Liquids

1 teaspoon	=	60 drops
1 tablespoon	=	½ ounce
2 tablespoons	=	1 ounce
¼ cup	=	2 ounces
⅓ cup	=	2⅔ ounces
½ cup	=	4 ounces
⅔ cup	=	5⅓ ounces
¾ cup	=	6 ounces
1 cup	=	8 ounces
2 cups	=	16 ounces = 1 pint
4 cups	=	32 ounces = 1 quart
16 cups	=	128 ounces = 4 quarts = 1 gallon
dash	=	1/16 teaspoon

Dry Measure

1 tablespoon	=	3 teaspoons
4 tablespoons	=	¼ cup
8 tablespoons	=	½ cup
12 tablespoons	=	¾ cup
16 tablespoons	=	1 cup
pinch	=	1/16 teaspoon

Butter or Margarine

1 pound (4 sticks)	=	2 cups
¾ pound (3 sticks)	=	1½ cups
½ pound (2 sticks)	=	1 cup
¼ pound (1 stick)	=	½ cup or 8 tablespoons
⅛ pound (½ stick)	=	¼ cup or 4 tablespoons

All-Purpose Flour (Sifted)

1 cup	=	4 ounces
4 cups	=	1 pound

All-Purpose Flour (Unsifted)

1 cup	=	5 ounces
3½ cups	=	1 pound

Sugar

1 cup	=	8 ounces
2 cups	=	1 pound

Confectioner's Sugar

1 cup	=	4½ ounces

Brown Sugar (Lightly Packed)

1 cup	=	6 ounces
2⅔ cups	=	1 pound

Eggs

1 cup	=	5 large eggs
	=	6 to 6½ medium eggs

Rice

1 cup uncooked	=	3 cups cooked

Wild Rice

1 cup uncooked	=	4½ cups cooked

Equivalents and Equations

thin sauce	=	1 tablespoon butter plus 1 tablespoon flour to each cup liquid
medium sauce	=	2 tablespoons butter plus 2 tablespoons flour to each cup of liquid
thick sauce	=	3 tablespoons butter plus 3 tablespoons flour to each cup of liquid
rich sauce	=	1 or 2 egg yolks beaten into each cup sauce and reheated, but never boiled

Oven Temperatures (Fahrenheit)

250° to 300°	=	very slow
300° to 325°	=	slow
325° to 350°	=	moderate
400° to 425°	=	hot
450° to 500°	=	very hot

When baking in high altitudes, increase the amount of heat needed by 25°. When baking a cake, increase the amount of flour slightly and decrease the amount of leavening as well. Sponge cakes, however, are not affected by altitude, nor is *pâte à chou*.

Proportions

2 teaspoons of baking powder to 1 cup flour
1 tablespoon gelatin (1 envelope) to 2 cups liquid
½ teaspoon baking soda to 1 cup sour milk or buttermilk
½ teaspoon baking soda to 1 cup applesauce or 2 bananas
½ teaspoon baking soda to 1 cup molasses
Baking soda is used only along *with* baking powder
1 teaspoon salt to 1 quart finished soup or sauce
1 teaspoon salt to 3 or 4 cups flour

Substitutions

1 teaspoon baking powder	=	¼ teaspoon baking soda plus ⅜ teaspoon cream of tartar
buttermilk	=	yogurt
1 cup sour milk	=	1 tablespoon vinegar added to 1 cup whole milk
1 ounce chocolate	=	3 tablespoons carob powder plus 2 tablespoons water
1 cup cracker crumbs	=	1 cup less 2 tablespoons fresh bread crumbs
1 medium clove garlic	=	¼ teaspoon garlic powder
1 teaspoon fresh herbs	=	½ teaspoon dried
1 cup milk	=	½ cup evaporated milk ½ cup water *or* ¼ cup dry whole milk, ⅞ cup water
salt pork	=	bacon